Case Studies in Information and Computer Ethics

Richard A. Spinello

Boston College

 Prentice Hall, Upper Saddle River, New Jersey 07458

Library of Congress Cataloging-in-Publication Data

Spinello, Richard A.
    Case studies in information and computer ethics / Richard A.
Spinello.
        p. cm.
    Includes bibliographical references and index.
    ISBN 0-13-533845-X
      1. Electronic data processing—Moral and ethical aspects—Case
studies. 2. Information technology—Moral and ethical aspects—Case
studies. I. Title.
QA76.9.M65S65   1997
174'.90904—dc20

96-11788
CIP

Acquisition editor: *Angie Stone*
Editorial assistant: *Meg McGuane*
Production editor: *Jean Lapidus*
Copy editor: *Maria Caruso*
Manufacturing buyer: *Nick Sklitsis*
Cover design: *Bruce Kenselaar*

This book was set in 10.5/12.5 Palatino by Compset, Inc.
and was printed and bound by Courier Companies, Inc.
The cover was printed by Phoenix Color Corp.

 © 1997 by Prentice-Hall, Inc.
Simon & Schuster/A Viacom Company
Upper Saddle River, New Jersey 07458

Printed in the United States of America
10 9 8 7 6 5 4 3 2 1

ISBN 0-13-533845-X

PRENTICE-HALL INTERNATIONAL (UK) LIMITED, *London*
PRENTICE-HALL OF AUSTRALIA PTY. LIMITED, *Sydney*
PRENTICE-HALL CANADA INC., *Toronto*
PRENTICE-HALL HISPANOAMERICANA, S.A., *Mexico*
PRENTICE-HALL OF INDIA PRIVATE LIMITED, *New Delhi*
PRENTICE-HALL OF JAPAN, INC., *Tokyo*
SIMON & SCHUSTER ASIA PTE. LTD., *Singapore*
EDITORA PRENTICE-HALL DO BRASIL, LTDA., *Rio de Janeiro*

In Memory of my Uncles,
Gene, Carmen, and John

Contents

Preface

Humanity faces a quantum leap forward. It faces the deepest social upheaval and creative restructuring of all time. Without clearly recognizing it, we are engaged in building a remarkable new civilization from the ground up. This is the meaning of the third wave.[1]

THE BOOK

In these eloquent words futurist Alvin Toffler described the impending information age. Fifteen years later we have ample evidence that his observations were not an exaggeration of technology's impact. The web of information technology that seems to engulf the entire world has certainly transformed our lives and dramatically reshaped the way we conduct business. Its influence has been pervasive and profound. But this rapid diffusion of information technology has also created some notable ethical and social challenges.

These formidable challenges can essentially be divided into two spheres. The first involves the abundance of digital information made available by the unrelenting advances in data storage and processing

[1]Alvin Toffler, *The Third Wave:* (New York: William Morrow and Company, 1980), p. 26.

technologies. The "information revolution" is changing the nature of information from a physical, tangible entity to its digital counterpart that is less fettered by time and space. Networks have expedited the movement of information so that users can be informed more quickly and efficiently. We are also more cognizant that information is a vital commercial asset. Control of information resources is a critical source of competitive opportunity.

A major challenge for executives and other professionals is how to manage this valuable resource in a responsible manner. What are reasonable guidelines for the handling, dissemination, and correlation of information? How do we balance the need to share information with the need to protect its integrity and confidentiality? How do we assess which types of information should be captured and stored, and are there ethical implications of such decisions? And what are the responsibilities of individuals designated as the "custodians" of information resources?

The second sphere of ethical challenges entails those confronted by engineers and computer professionals who are directly responsible for deploying and managing these technological developments. Here we find the traditional topics that are associated with the study of computer ethics: protection of intellectual property, the appropriateness of "reverse engineering," maintenance of adequate computer system security, and the reliability and safety of computer technologies such as software and networks. Thus, while some challenges deal with the management of information, others deal with the management and development of the technologies that create, process, store, and retrieve that information.

This book presents thirty-eight concise case studies in both of these critical areas. For the most part, these cases are based on the actual experiences of managers, engineers, and other professionals who work in the field of computer technology or have some responsibility for managing a company's information resources. Other case studies describe situations that call for an analysis of corporate decisions, policies, and an evaluation of the moral values underlying those policies.

The purpose of these diverse cases is to help students and computer professionals reflect upon the vexing ethical dilemmas and problems that are emerging in the information age. In this fast-paced environment, the rules seem to change quite rapidly and the standards of propriety are difficult to define. The cases are complex and multifaceted, and hence defy facile solutions. But the problems posed here are certainly not insoluble. And as a guide to effective resolution, this book includes an overview of theoretical ethical frameworks. The frameworks include consequentialism, pluralism, and contractarianism. They enable us to analyze moral problems from the viewpoint of consequences, duties, and rights. If used properly, these "avenues" of ethical reasoning can be instrumental in helping us to develop a cogent action plan within the bounds of ethical probity and social acceptability.

The book, then, is divided into four major areas. I am aware that some of the cases could easily have been placed in other sections, but it is necessary to group the cases in some way even if the selection is sometimes somewhat arbitrary. **Part I** consists of two chapters that provide an overview of the ethical issues posed by information technology, along with a description of the ethical theories and normative principles that can serve as a basis for analysis. **Part II** consists of the first grouping of cases that deal with the moral dilemmas of information management. The first chapter in this section includes several case studies on the acquisition or collection of information, while the next chapter focuses on who should have access to various forms of information that have been legitimately captured. The third chapter is comprised of several scenarios that dwell on the custodial responsibility of preventing unauthorized access, maintaining accuracy, and controlling data recombination.

Part III deals with some of the traditional topics and concerns of computer ethics. The initial focus is on software ownership and intellectual property, with cases ranging from apparent acts of piracy on the Internet to the question of whether the "look and feel" of software programs should be protected. The second chapter in this section consists of several case studies dealing with the responsibility of securing computer systems and networks. Among the questions raised in these scenarios are: the difficulty of defining sufficient security from a moral point of view and the need to protect the rights of hackers and others, who are guilty of electronic intrusion. **Part III** concludes with a chapter on the safety, reliability, and viability of computer technology products, especially software. It also concerns the important issue of product liability. The case studies here deal with the problems of vaporware, a company's liability for software failure, and related matters.

In **Part IV**, the final section of the book, our perspective shifts to broader social issues that have public policy implications. One case looks at the expanding role of technology in the gambling industry. Other cases consider some of the contentious social issues provoked by more frequent use of the vast computer network known as the *Internet*. For example, what are the parameters of free speech in cyberspace, and should universal service on an international electronic network be guaranteed by government? Finally, we consider how technology is transforming the workplace, along with the possible social ramifications of the emerging "virtual corporation."

I have also included an appendix with two codes of professional conduct. One is the *ACM Code of Ethics and Professional Conduct* and the other is the *IEEE Code of Ethics.* In addition, there is a selective but thorough bibliography that includes major books and articles in this growing field. It is organized by the topics covered in this book and will facilitate the process of future research on the issues raised in the case studies and the introductory chapters.

THE METHOD

The case study remains a popular instrument of provoking students to grapple with complicated moral problems and quandaries. Cases present such problems in a particular context and as a result, they require students to discern the ethical dimension of a situation among a plethora of intricate, perplexing, and sometimes conflicting information. Further, they compel students to frame the issues carefully and to develop a tenable and morally-defensible action plan. Since these cases are based on real life situations, they prepare students for the ethical dilemmas they will confront in their own professional careers. The expectation is that they will be able to deal with those dilemmas more responsibly and purposefully once they have developed this valuable skill of ethical analysis.

The most significant benefit of using the case study method is that it engages students and requires them to become active participants rather than passive observers. This method is a form of student-centered education that heavily involves students in the learning process. According to Cragg,

> The case system, properly used, initiates students into the ways of independent thought and responsible judgment. It faces them with situations which are not hypothetical but real. It places them in the active role, open to criticism from all sides. It puts the burden of understanding and judgment upon them. It provides them the occasion to deal constructively with their contemporaries and their elders.[2]

The cases in this book have been designed to stimulate dialogue and reflection on a well-defined set of complex issues. They are timely

---

[2]Charles I. Cragg, "Because Wisdom Can't be Told," *Harvard Alumni Bulletin,* October 19, 1940.

and yet embody enduring controversies that will remain with us for many years. They can stand alone or be used with supplementary material such as background essays, articles, and even newsclips available on video. Most of the cases have been tested at various seminars and classes at Boston College and have been chosen because they can function as excellent springboards to productive and lively discussions.

THE AUDIENCE

Interest in the subject matter covered in this book has grown significantly in the last decade. This interest will undoubtedly lead to the development of new courses and workshops in computer ethics and related topics. It is my hope that this case book will be a valuable resource for such courses.

This book can be profitably used in advanced undergraduate and graduate programs in schools of business and engineering. It is most suitable for computer ethics courses and for more innovative ethics courses with a theme of information management. It could also be used in engineering ethics courses, where a major axis of discussion is computer technology. Furthermore, this text could even find a place in some humanities and philosophy courses that treat broader areas such as practical ethics or technology and society. Last, this collection of cases can be an important resource in corporate management education programs. Professional managers need to be introduced to the array of issues presented in these case studies. In any of these contexts this text can be used by itself, or it can serve as a companion piece to a narrative or book of readings on computer ethics.

Ultimately, the goal of this book is to help instructors sensitize students and managers to the vital importance of the careful and responsible use of information technology. It raises many questions, challenges certain assumptions, and even provides a glimpse into the future. But above all, the primary objective is to heighten our ethical awareness in order to help ensure that technology will not be used to create a future inimical to human values or the fundamental principles of justice and fairness.

ACKNOWLEDGMENTS

The completion of a substantial project like this one depends upon the good will, generosity, and gracious assistance of many individuals. I would like to express my profound gratitude to my wife, Susan T.

Brinton, for her help in editing and proofreading this manuscript. More importantly, I appreciate her support and encouragement throughout the various phases of this project. I am also indebted to Fr. William B. Neenan, S.J., Academic Vice President of Boston College, for his tangible and intangible support of this effort. Let me also take this opportunity to thank several individuals at Prentice Hall for expediting the publication of this timely material: Tracie Edwards, Meg McGuane, and Charlyce Jones Owen. And finally I thank my friends and colleagues at Bourneuf House, especially Peg Preston and Carol Hunt-Clerici, for their kind and expert assistance in handling some of the mechanics involved in publishing the manuscript.

The author thanks the following reviewers for their helpful comments and suggestions: C. Dianne Martin, George Washington University; Doris Lidke, Towson State University; and Heinz C. Luegenbiehl, Rose-Hulman Institute of Technology.

Richard A. Spinello
Chestnut Hill, Massachusetts

1

Ethics, Computers, and Information

The computer age presents us with a dual ethical challenge. One set of problems involves the proper deployment of the technologies that process information, including computer hardware, software, and networks. The capabilities provided by these sophisticated technologies provoke many controversial questions such as the following: How do we define intellectual property rights? Does labor and investment engender such rights? How accountable should vendors be for software flaws or unreliable systems? How harmful is "vaporware"? To what lengths and expense should organizations go to minimize security risks?

Thus, we confront moral issues in three main spheres of concern: ownership of intellectual property, the security of networks and computer systems, and the obligation of high tech vendors to provide safe, reliable programs while eschewing false product announcements. Most of these topics have been elaborated upon in traditional books and treatises on computer ethics.

However, there is another closely related set of issues that focus strictly on the management and control of information. As we noted in the Preface, we are clearly in the midst of a fast-paced information revolution. This has obviously come to pass thanks to the substitution of physical information with computer-based information. But the new element in information technology that has truly advanced this "revolution" is the network which has greatly enhanced the mobility and accessibility of information. Peter Keen describes this phenomenon in a business environment as "business networking" which he defines as "the combination of computers, information stores (resources), and telecommunications [that] . . . have been used literally to transform the basis of an industry."[1] Thanks to networking technology, information is no longer an artifact or a thing, "but a process by which people become 'informed.'"[2]

Computers and networking technology "inform" users by processing data and moving the results to them where and when they need it. In other words, information technology transforms data into information by capturing, manipulating, and synthesizing that data and then transmitting it electronically to the appropriate parties. Thus, the raw data, the hardware and software, and the telecommunications are all part of this process of creating information and making users well-informed.

But this new paradigm of information has profound implications. Data can be more efficiently *captured* and aggregated in order to create useful information. Information can be made *accessible* to those inside and outside the organization with remarkable speed and facility. And this information that has become so mobile and dynamic is also more vulnerable, thereby creating the acute need for its *protection*. Hence, the importance of focusing on three key aspects of information management and control: acquisition, access, and stewardship.

Clearly these two general areas of information and computer ethics are distinct but closely related, and hence there is some overlap. For example, the issues of secure computer systems are tightly linked with the issue of information stewardship. Similarly, the issue of access is linked with the theme of intellectual property and, for instance, copyright protection for different information resources. For the most part, however, this case book will treat the ethics of information management separately from the issues traditionally covered under the rubric of "computer science ethics."

Our objective in this introductory chapter is to provide a concise overview of both sets of ethical concerns. Before plunging into the case studies it is instructive to consider the genesis and nature of some of the salient problems and controversies covered in those cases. We begin by first exploring the emerging field of "information ethics."

ETHICS AND INFORMATION MANAGEMENT

Advances in information technology have clearly generated some unique and difficult problems for those charged with managing and controlling information. The increased availability, mobility, and value of information creates a special responsibility to maximize its benefits and to prevent its misuse. We will examine how this responsibility arises in three critical areas: acquisition, access, and stewardship. Any coherent and morally enlightened data policy must take into account what types of information will be gathered and stored, who will have access to that information, how the information will be protected from unauthorized users, and how its accuracy will be maintained.

Acquisition

Managers can now collect all sorts of useful data that years ago would have been virtually impossible or too expensive to obtain. In addition, this information can usually be stored, manipulated, and accessed quite economically. These new information technology capabilites, however, are sometimes the source of moral dilemmas. For example, sophisticated electronic monitoring systems make it possible to track the activities of one's employees in great detail and compile quantifiable data for various purposes. In addition, phone conversations can be monitored and an employee's time away from his or her desk can be measured by these systems. Similarly, most electronic e-mail systems allow for messages to be archived and inspected whenever necessary. But is such surveillance and inspection justified or does it represent a blatant violation of an employee's fundamental right to privacy? Should such information even be collected and, if so, how should it be utilized? Simply because we have the capability to acquire this type of information about employees, it does not mean that such acquisition is ethically justified.

Consider also the complications involved in collecting certain forms of sensitive corporate data. Once data is captured in electronic format it is usually structured and compiled, and in this process assumes meaning and value to those who access it. However, this creation of information is risky since it has value not only to corporate insiders but also to outsiders who may not have the corporation's best interests in mind. These outsiders become privy to this well-structured information either by accident, by theft, or in extreme cases by issuing a subpeona for its release. Davenport describes how this problem surfaced for Otis Elevator: ". . . when Otis Elevator began to compile information on elevator reliability and performance—which would enable sharing among managers, service personnel, and new product designers—the company's internal counsel feared having to produce this information if the company were sued for an elevator-related accident."[3]

The potential dangers of information gathering raise some novel moral questions such as whether it is acceptable to leave data in obscurity and ambiguity in order to avoid the problems anticipated by Otis. Does the opportunity to create information quickly and inexpensively imply an *obligation* to do so when the data in question concerns something like safety-related issues? Should secrecy and data obscurity be replaced by transparency whenever possible?

A similar question is raised by Mary Gentile and John Sviokla who are also concerned about the implications of data capture: "does the ability to 'capture' the data imply a corresponding responsibility to monitor and use that data, or to spot potential patterns which the aggregate data reveals—which would otherwise be invisible to managers—and which suggest possible risks to employees, consumers, and/or others?"[4]

A corporation's data policy, then, must give careful consideration to what types of data should be collected and compiled into useful information. Further, managers formulating this policy should think through how that information might be used by those inside and outside the corporation, bearing in mind that it can be difficult to control the flow of information once it has been created.

Of course, we should not overlook traditional issues in information collection that are not necessarily dependent on advances in information technology. One such issue involves the acquisition of competitive information. Since the early 1980s companies have placed great emphasis on competitive analysis. To some extent this was due to the influence of Michael Porter's teachings on industry analysis which are discussed in two popular books, *Competitive Strategy* and *Competitive Advantage*. Many organizations still struggle with how to gather such potentially sensitive data without violating legal or moral norms. Those norms, however, are sometimes ambiguous, and this creates a gray area where it is difficult to differentiate industrial espionage from competitive analysis.

It is quite evident, therefore, that many controversial ethical issues fall under the area of information collection. The case studies in this section will enable us to consider some of these questions in the context of complex work environments and the pressing demands of corporate life. These questions are closely related to issues of information access and stewardship, but the cases will focus primarily on the moral dimension encountered in decisions concerning data acquisition.

Access

A second dominant issue for those managing information concerns access or sharing. Who will be able to see and use information that has been collected, synthesized, and processed? In other words, which sorts of data will be shared either with those within the corporation or those outside of it? Often determining internal policies regarding information sharing is more complicated and controversial than developing policies for external sharing. Consider, for example, the problem of which departments and individuals within a corporation should be given access to an employee's medical data.

Once these questions are addressed, principles must be developed for the dissemination of information beyond the corporate boundaries. This too can provoke vexing moral concerns. For instance, do companies have a right to sell data they have collected on consumers to outsiders for use as they see fit? Or should permission from those consumers be required before information is disseminated in this fashion?

Access issues point to the difficulty of defining and protecting privacy in the information age. The new trends of "digital disclosure" are often criticized as a grave threat to our personal privacy. Privacy is an important value, regarded by many philosophers as a basic, natural right. While some philosophers have argued that privacy is a fundamental, irreducible right in itself, others contend that the right to privacy is grounded in its status as a necessary condition for other natural rights such as the exercise of our freedom and autonomy. Without the shield of privacy it is difficult to behave in ways that are not inhibited or self-conscious. Thus, there is certainly a close relationship between privacy and respect for persons as autonomous, free, rational beings.[5]

It should be emphasized that informational privacy is at stake in the case studies on access presented in Chapter 4. This term refers to "the utilization, sometimes even exploitation, of information about people for various purposes."[6] But determining what constitutes such "exploitation" can be rather difficult in certain contexts.

For instance, one controversial case in this section deals with government agencies which make their records easily accessible. For instance, as everyone knows the Department of Motor Vehicles (DMV) for each state collects information about drivers when they apply for a driver's license. This information is also updated when drivers renew their licenses. Clearly, this personal data represents a valuable resource for many marketers trying to target their products. Recognizing this, most states sell this data to direct marketers and appear to give little thought as to whether this information should be made available so readily to those outside of the DMV.

Indeed a growing segment of the information economy depends on the secondary use of personal information. Information brokers specialize in buying, recombining, and selling various forms of marketing data that are collected from private and public organizations. In other words, thanks to the increasing capacity of computers, it is possible and feasible to provide easy access to all sorts of personal information, and, for many, this represents a serious erosion of personal privacy. According to one perceptive analysis, "Traditional record-keeping privacy has taken a new face, namely, data about people are used not for the internal business purposes of the organization that collected them, but for the business purposes of whoever is willing to buy the data."[7]

Many organizations, of course, have legitimate needs for information about consumers in order to make informed decisions. Banks and other organizations giving credit to consumers assume that they are fully justified in accessing copious amounts of data about an individual's past credit and employment history. Few would argue with their need for at least some of this sensitive information in order to minimize their credit risks.

Similar concerns about information sharing arise in the workplace where difficult decisions must be made about who gets access to sensitive or confidential employee data. Accessibility to employee medical and fitness data has been an especially troublesome problem because of the rise of wellness programs in many organizations that track this data quite extensively. To what extent should line managers have access to such information and should it play a role in job related decisions?

One key issue that has emerged in the debates over data access concerns who owns the data that has been collected. Do the collectors always have property rights to this data? If retail stores collect data about their shoppers' buying habits do they "own" this information and can they dispose of it as they see fit? This raises another important question about whether or not permission should be obtained for the secondary uses of data. For example, when consumers provide the DMV with personal information, can that information be used for other purposes without the explicit consent of those individuals? Moreover, should the DMV be given the exclusive right to profit from the secondary uses of such data?

All of these questions must be carefully evaluated as companies attempt to develop and defend data policies that determine the parameters and protocol of information sharing. Those policies must attempt to meet the legitimate needs for information while respecting the basic privacy rights of the organization's diverse stakeholders.

Stewardship

The final area of concern is stewardship or custodial responsibility for information. What do we mean by the term "stewardship" and how does it apply to information management? The traditional concept of stewardship implies an obligation to look after property that belongs to another. Thus, a steward is normally charged with taking care of the property that has been entrusted to him. It seems reasonable to assert that one who has responsibility for maintaining a data base of information assumes the obligation of stewardship. If, for instance, one is the data base administrator of the faculty data base at a major university one must assume some "stewardship" responsibility for making sure that this data is timely, accurate, and secure. The gravity of this obligation is obvious. If information under one's control becomes inaccurate and outdated or is accessed by outsiders with malicious intent, serious problems could ensue.

Another stewardship issue involves data recombination which can lead to serious violations of privacy under some circumstances. Information managers therefore must also be circumspect about how their information is combined or "matched" with other data. Is the end result of such matching so revealing that the privacy of the data subjects is seriously compromised? Hence, stewardship responsibility entails the verification of accuracy, the prevention of unauthorized access, and the exercise of some control over data recombination.[8] Let us briefly discuss each of these obligations.

A good starting point is the obligation to verify and preserve data accuracy, which takes on greater significance when "more and more decisions are based on information made available through information technology (IT) capabilities."[9] But how do we determine some reasonable limits for this particular obligation? To what effort and expense should companies go to verify and maintain accuracy, especially when the data in question is highly volatile? For example, should credit bureaus periodically provide consumers with credit reports free of charge in order to get important feedback regarding the accuracy of those reports? How often should records be updated and revised to ensure their accuracy? When grappling with these questions companies must carefully assess the potential negative impact of inaccuracies, since this will help to determine the amount of resources that should be contributed to prevent those errors.

The second obligation implied by stewardship is the implementation of security measures to prevent unauthorized access. Once policies have been developed delineating whom should have legitimate access to information, comprehensive security measures must be deployed in order to keep information from falling into the wrong hands. Some would argue convincingly that a related obligation of those who manage data is to prevent its *misuse* whenever possible. This is especially germane for those who are information brokers or those who disseminate information widely. Do they have an obligation to discriminate between those groups which will use such information conscientiously and those which might use it for questionable or unorthodox purposes? The larger issue is to what extent any company can be held morally liable for the misuse of its product. This problem is most pointedly presented in the case study, "It's Not Your Job to Be a 'Data Cop!'" in Chapter 5.

A final issue regarding stewardship is the exercise of control over the recombination of data. Many technologies such as the relational data base allow users to efficiently correlate data from different sources in order to create new and sometimes revealing information about the data subjects in question. Computer "matching" is a form of data recombination which is a widely used technique among federal agencies in Washington, DC where data from federal data banks are widely shared and compared. For example, according to Rothfeder, "the Internal Revenue Service matches the income Americans report on federal tax forms against lifestyle databanks that detail where people live, what kinds of cars they own, and how many credit cards they carry."[10]

Computer matching or data recombination, then, has the potential to provide an exceptionally thorough and comprehensive profile of the data subject which may unduly compromise that person's personal privacy. But how can such matching and data correlation be dealt with? Should an organization explicitly attempt to control the ways in which their data is recombined with other data? Should it refrain from disseminating information to those who intend to correlate it with other data in ways that seem to threaten consumer privacy? Finally, to what extent are they morally (and perhaps legally) liable for the misuses of this correlated data by other parties and what effort should be expended to prevent that misuse?

We have now briefly examined some of the key ethical implications of collecting and accessing information, and described the primary obligations of those who are custodians of information. All of the issues and questions posed in this overview will emerge in the controversial case studies in Chapters 3, 4, and 5.

As we have observed, it is essential that organizations develop a cogent and responsible data policy to deal with the problems presented here with some fairness and consistency. The salient elements of that policy should cover the following questions: What sort of information should be collected and how should that data be maintained? Who should have access to this data, and should this access be based on certain conditions? Who is responsible for monitoring the accuracy of this data, for determining how and to whom it will be disseminated, and for preventing its misuse? A policy addressing these and related issues recognizes that information is an asset of significant value, while it also manifests respect for the rights and concerns of those who are the subjects of that information. Exhibit 1 illustrates a typical data policy, addressing some of these matters.

Exhibit 1   A Sample Data Policy

Individuals of this organization who are responsible for the following activities have an obligation to treat data as a valuable corporate asset and to respect the rights of any stakeholders affected by the use of that data.

Collectors and Processers of Data

- Implement data quality and security procedures to ensure data integrity:
    -Review systems and methods of data collection for likely sources of errors; implement backup and recovery mechanisms.
    -Review systems for possible security breaches; implement all reasonable efforts to minimize security risks.
- Establish and maintain a technology infrastructure which facilitates the sharing of data across functions and departmental units.
- Monitor and update data on a timely and regular basis.
- Make sure that data bases reflect the current state of the business and that the proper information is available for strategic decision making.
- Understand how and by whom the data will be used.

Database Custodians and those Controlling Access

- Protect data from undesired or unauthorized access.
- Make data available to users within the organization who can demonstrate a legitimate business need for that data.
- Restrict the information available to those outside the company unless they have demonstrated a legitimate business need for that information.
- If there is a disagreement regarding the need for access because the data base custodian believes that data integrity or stakeholder rights are threatened, the Data Policy committee will make the final decision.

Data Users

- Users are fully responsible for the data which they request.
- Ensure that data is correctly used and interpreted.
- Use data *only* for valid business purposes.
- Protect the privacy rights of fellow employees, customers, and all other organization stakeholders. This means that users must prudently weigh the implications for those stakeholders if certain information is made public, redistributed, or recombined in some fashion.

COMPUTER SCIENCE ETHICS

We turn now to some of the traditional issues that fall under the rubric of "computer ethics." These include ownership of intellectual property, the reliability of software and hardware equipment, and the obligation to provide adequate security for computer systems. These are typical problem areas for computer professionals and engineers who work in various segments of the computer industry. In this section of Chapter 1 we will provide a summary of the basic moral questions that arise when dealing with these topics.

Our aim in the case studies on computer ethics is to provoke careful reflection on the nature and scope of moral responsibility of engineers and computer professionals working in this industry. Of course, they can and should turn to the professional ethics codes governing their respective professions for some direction and moral guidance.[11] Nonetheless, there are many difficult dilemmas that will clearly strain our current norms and standards and challenge some of the basic principles articulated in those codes.

Ownership and Intellectual Property

The software industry has become the scene of bitter disputes over property rights that have sometimes become grist for protracted litigation. Moreover, according to Clapes, this litigation is often "thematic . . . dealing with fundamental paradigms."[12] In other words, much of this litigation does not merely involve obscure legal details but significant issues capable of determining the fate of entire companies and even the future direction of the industry. Thus, a good starting place for any discussion on the moral dimension of intellectual property is a brief overview of the legal methods employed by vendors to protect software and other forms of intellectual property.

One such form of protection is the classification of software programs, works in progress, and other commercial ideas as *trade secrets*. Companies usually implement this form of protection by means of nondisclosure agreements which prevent employees from using these ideas, prototypes, software codes, and so on, for their own personal gain or while they are employed at another company. One difficulty with trade secrets is that once a "secret" is in the public domain it is no longer protected and can be used by others with impunity.

A second and increasingly popular method of protecting software programs and related products is to apply for patent protection. Patents are primarily used to protect property rights in machines, inventions, processes, and the like. But since the landmark case of *Diehr v. Diamond* patents have become a legally acceptable way of protecting software programs. Patents normally have a 17-year duration and provide exclusive rights to the patent holder to use and profit from the product or process in question.

The use of patents for software protection has been criticized by many vendors within the industry. They maintain that such exclusive protection is anticompetitive and counterproductive because it inhibits other companies from developing incremental innovations on a protected core technology. They also contend that it stymies the emergence of industry standards. For instance, it is advantageous for the end user if electronic spreadsheet products look and function in a similar fashion; this might not have been possible if one of the early spreadsheets (such as *VisiCalc*) had received patent protection. On the other hand those innovators applying for patent protection claim that such monopoly protection for a limited time frame is a significant stimulus to future research and development. Patents provide an opportunity to reap great financial rewards if the product in question is a success.

The final and most popular means of protecting intellectual property rights in software is the use of the copyright. This became possible in 1980 when Congress amended the Copyright Act. This amendment clarified that federal copyright laws protect both the source code and the object code of a program.[13] It should be pointed out that copyright law protects against the illicit copying of an author's expression of an idea but not the copying of the idea itself. Thus, concepts and ideas along with algorithms, procedures, and processes are not protected by copyright. It is sometimes difficult, however, to distinguish between an idea and its expression. Is the sequence of commands in a user interface part of the expression or the idea? These are thorny questions, and they help account for the confusing legal conflicts that have typified the software industry during the last decade.

Also, contentious disputes have arisen in recent years concerning the scope of copyright protection. Landmark lawsuits such as *Lotus v. Borland* and *Apple v. Microsoft* have surfaced the controversial issue of whether or not copyright protection extends to the "look and feel" of the software. In other words, can software vendors imitate the appearance, structure, and even the commands of a competitor's program or is that sort of appropriation the equivalent of stealing another's ideas?

Intellectual property issues become even more complicated when considered in an international context, since many countries have different conceptions of property rights. In Japan, for instance, the patent and copyright system is based on a philosophy that stresses the diffusion of knowledge and technology to benefit society. The key assumption underlying this philosophy is that "knowledge of any sort is communal and belongs in the public domain where it can benefit many different parties."[14]

Thus, Japan's system only loosely protects the rights of inventors in order to encourage incremental innovations on products or ideas for which patent applications have been filed. Since this approach differs radically from the American system where there is more emphasis on protecting the individual's property rights, the potential for international conflicts is quite high. One such conflict is chronicled in the IBM-Fujitsu case in Chapter 6.

Intellectual property issues are complex and sometimes confusing because of the interplay between the moral and legal issues. In analyzing the case studies on intellectual property it is important to remember that what is legal is not necessarily moral. Therefore, it is instructive to consider briefly the moral justification for intellectual property rights. Before exploring this issue, however, it is essential that we first distinguish between an idea and its expression. There are serious difficulties with the notion that one has property rights in an idea; thus, for example, it is not possible to "copyright" or retain exclusive use over a mathematical formula that one has discovered. As Kuflik observes, "the intellectual property system cannot be satisfactorily grounded in the principle that a person literally owns, as a matter of natural right, the ideas that he is the first to conceive."[15]

But the expression of an idea is a different matter. Thus, one may not have property rights to an algorithm or a formula but may have a property right to a software program in which that algorithm is used for some novel or creative purpose.

The question, then, is how one derives a moral justification for property rights to the expression of an idea rather than the idea itself. One such justification can be found in the writings of Locke, who has maintained that labor and effort engender certain property rights.[16] There does seem to be some merit in the argument that one is entitled to the fruits of one's labor regardless of whether they are real goods or more intangible commodities such as a software program. The application of Locke's theory is not without problems but it does suggest that software developers do have a *prima facie* property right to the expression of their ideas in software programs because of their heavy investments of time, labor, and money in the development of those programs. It is also worth emphasizing that the right of intellectual property has significant social utility, since without respect for this right, there would be less incentive for those who conceive and develop sophisticated technological innovations.

The real issue perhaps is exactly what is included in the "expression" of an idea. Both moralists and jurists disagree on how to answer this question. However, as one attempts to transcend the specific legal issues it becomes clear that several broad philosophies dominate the so-called "software wars." There are the polar extremes of the "strong-protectionist" viewpoint that argues for broad copyright protection and the "weak protectionist" position that advocates narrow protection in order to encourage incremental developments built on earlier innovations. Occupying a middle ground is the position Clapes labels as "traditional protectionist." This view argues for respect for the traditional intellectual property law principles and a balance between the interests of innovators and copiers.[17] The cases in Chapter 6 will prompt readers to formulate their own philosophy about the extent and scope of protection for intellectual property such as software programs.

Security and Computer Crime

The phenomenon of computer crime and security breaches have become all too familiar during the last decade. Viruses, worms, computer espionage, and other forms of mischief have become unfortunate realities on the frontiers of the information revolution. Sometimes these nefarious activities have done significant and costly damage by disrupting operations or by corrupting important data. For instance, the infamous Internet worm incident, perpetuated by a graduate student at Cornell, wreaked havoc on many university and government computers linked together on the Internet computer network. Several major computer systems were shut down for over a day during this crisis while others were temporarily denied access to the network.

Also, many organizations have had to deal with acts of sabotage by their own employees. This has taken the form of theft or of malicious and intentional destruction of key management data, usually as a means of revenge. Of course, another source of difficulties has been the activities of criminals or dishonest competitors. Finally, organizations must still contend with the electronic intrusions of "hackers," who sometimes regard the penetration of presumably "secure" systems and the filching of computer files as a game or a form of recreation.

Lamentably, the migration from mainframe computers to networked personal computers has complicated efforts to secure computer systems. Computers are obviously more vulnerable when they are linked to a network since there is far more opportunity for intrusion. This vulnerability has compelled many corporations to develop more comprehensive approaches to security. For the most part security policies and procedures focus on three main objectives: maintain access control, preserve the integrity of the system and its data, and provide recovery and backup if the system should fail.

But security is not simply a matter of sound business policy. It seems evident that corporations have a *moral obligation* to ensure that their information technology systems are as securely protected as possible. Companies that manifest indifference about security issues or implement sloppy security procedures would clearly be acting in an irresponsible manner. Improper security can lead to unauthorized access which can sometimes cause serious harm to data subjects. For instance, consider the potential adverse consequences if a psychiatric patient's mental health records fall into the wrong hands because of a hospital's leaky LAN (Local Area Network) or other security flaws. Thus, corporate executives must exercise due care and diligence in formulating and executing security policies.

It should be underlined that this responsibility to protect computer systems and the information they handle should be assigned both to the organization and its executives and to the individual programmers who may work on these projects. They too must take seriously the moral imperative to ensure that hardware and software systems are well insulated against the threat of data theft, industrial espionage, and possible sources of corruption such as unauthorized data modification.

In some cases the security breach in question could be considered a minor offense which is not worth much of a fuss. Some would argue, for example, that if hackers merely trespass on another's "electronic property" there is really no harm done. Those who defend the activities of hackers when there is no deliberate destruction of property point out that break-ins sometimes serve a valuable purpose since they uncover security flaws that might otherwise go unnoticed or they help computer wizards sharpen their skills.[18]

What are we to make of such arguments? On the surface they may seem somewhat plausible, but trespassing violates respect for property rights, a highly important value in our society. The distinction between public and private space sometimes becomes blurred in "cyberspace," but just because that distinction may not always be easy to establish, it does not mean that it should be discarded or ignored.

Finally, regardless of the security breach committed, the punishment should fit the crime. On occasion, however, certain government agencies have been overzealous in their pursuit and prosecution of those who have offended the law in this area. Several notorious incidents seem to exemplify this problem, and we will consider one of these incidents in the Neidorf case in Chapter 7.

Liability and Reliability

As computer technology becomes more powerful and more widely used for mission critical applications, the consequences of failure become more grave and potentially calamitous. Millions of individuals and organizations count on their computers to manage inventory, help fly airplanes, process sophisticated financial transactions, and so forth. Hardware reliability is less of a problem since the risks of failure can be reduced by redundancy. In other words, if the primary system fails, applications or programs can be switched to a backup system. But software reliability is a more difficult challenge. Most complex software products such as computer operating systems have millions of lines of code where mistakes can lurk for many months or even years before they manifest themselves in some way and perhaps lead to a catastrophe. Thus, software "bugs" or errors can be quite disruptive and costly. For example, in February 1994 an obscure bug in a software program caused Chemical Bank in New York to double-debit customers who made automatic teller withdrawals. And in March 1995 Intuit Inc. announced that its popular TurboTax software program had serious bugs that could botch a user's tax returns. These problems caused considerable consternation and aggravation for those users who had already filed returns using this buggy software. Some are concerned that similar software errors could cause even more devastating problems such as an erroneous medical diagnosis or perhaps even a plane crash.

These inevitable problems with software programs generate numerous questions about the moral and legal liability for the vendors who produce and market these programs. Should these companies be held liable for *all* of the defects that lurk in their programs even if those programs were thoroughly and conscientiously tested? Or should there be liability only in those situations where there is carelessness or negligence?

Further, in our networked environment the issue of liability is not confined to vendors which provide software or hardware products. There are also liability questions for on-line service providers like CompuServe or Prodigy when their subscribers libel someone on a bulletin board or infringe a copyright. These companies have tried to remain above the fray of costly liability disputes but so far their efforts have been in vain.

In order to address some of these issues we must make some important distinctions between accountability, blame, and responsibility. According to Aristotle (384–322 B.C.), we are responsible for voluntary actions but not for involuntary ones; actions are involuntary "when they are performed (1) under compulsion, (2) as the result of ignorance."[19] Aristotle makes a crucial distinction between excusable and inexcusable ignorance. Ignorance is excusable when through no fault of one's own, one is ignorant of the circumstances or consequences of an action. On the other hand, ignorance is not a valid excuse if that ignorance is the result of carelessness or neglect, or if it is deliberately willed.

Hence, a person is considered "responsible" when his or her actions caused the harm; at the same time the person's actions must have been voluntary, that is, intentional and not the result of excusable ignorance. According to Nissenbaum, the related concept of blame is an extension of responsibility, since blame is not limited to situations in which our actions were intentional or deliberate. She writes that "if a person fails to take precautions of which he is capable, and that any reasonable person with normal capacities would have taken in those circumstances, then he is not excused from blame merely because he did not intend the outcome."[20] Responsibility and blameworthiness are normally subsumed in the "intuitive notion" of accountability, for when someone is accountable for an injury or misdeed "he or she is liable to punishment or is liable to compensate a victim."[21] One who is accountable for an action then is usually responsible for its cause, deserves blame, and is liable for some sort of punishment. But there are exceptions to this such as the standard of strict liability which holds individuals or companies accountable (and liable) even if they are not at fault.

Another relevant distinction must be made between moral responsibility or accountability and one's *legal* liability. It is instructive to briefly consider the issue of legal liability, since it will emerge in several case studies. The two most pertinent product liability categories for our purposes are strict liability in tort and negligence. According to the strict liability standard a vendor is legally responsible for any injury caused by its product regardless of whether or not it was at fault. This exacting standard does not prevail if the damages are purely economic. The second liability category is negligence. To avoid being guilty of negligence vendors must demonstrate reasonable conduct and prudence in the design, development, and testing of their products. Thus, a software company that rushed its product to market without adequate quality assurance testing could be found guilty of negligence and subject to serious legal sanctions.

These concepts are quite useful but they still leave us with many questions about fairness and equity. For instance, what if a company dutifully fulfills its legal obligations and has been diligent in every phase of its product development? Nevertheless a user encounters a defect that disrupts his or her business and results in financial losses of considerable magnitude. To what extent should the vendor be held responsible for such unforeseeable problems? Is there a moral imperative to make restitution to the company that suffered the losses? There seems to be considerable ambiguity in these situations which is well illustrated in the NCR case that is included in Chapter 8.

An issue closely related to product liability concerns the viability or reliability of new computer technology products such as applications software. In recent years the software industry has been plagued by vendors selling new products before they are ready for the marketplace. Others have engaged in the questionable practice of "preannouncing" new products or announcing unrealistic release dates. Some prominent companies have announced the availability of new products even though they are a long period of time away from the actual release date when it is difficult to estimate a completion time. Such mythical products have become known throughout the industry as "vaporware." We also include in this category of "vaporware" those products which are brought to the market prematurely often without adequate testing or preparation.

Some have defended vaporware as inconsequential and even as a means of survival in the competitive software industry. However, it can often have adverse consequences for a company's stakeholders. It has been alleged, for example, that Microsoft has used the tactic of vaporware to enhance its monopoly position in the software industry. If vaporware is used deliberately to exclude rivals from the marketplace, it is probably a violation of antitrust laws. Furthermore, according to Stern, "deliberately false vaporware announcements . . . harm the public and also discourage potential market entrants from creating new software."[22]

One could certainly argue, then, that vendors have a minimal moral obligation to eschew any forms of deliberate deception or bluffing when making product announcements. Moreover, companies should be especially careful to differentiate between product announcements and general statements of product direction. Product announcements including release dates should be made later in the product development cycle in order to increase the probability that the product will be released on or close to schedule.

Several case studies in Chapter 8 will examine how managers should deal with these troublesome questions about vaporware and new product announcements in situations that are ethically ambiguous. Other case studies will focus attention on the important issue of one's ethical and legal liability for computer technology products that malfunction. And the Prodigy case deals with the problematic question of whether or not on-line service providers should be held liable for the content of messages posted on their bulletin boards. After considering the intricacies of these cases and developing an appropriate action plan, it would also be worthwhile to ponder their corporate and public policy implications.

In his essay, "What Is Computer Ethics," Moor writes that "computer ethics is not a fixed set of rules which one shellacs and hangs on the wall"; instead, "it requires us to think anew about the nature of computer technology and our values."[23] All of the cases in Part 3 dealing with intellectual property, computer security, safety, and reliability, are designed to stimulate such thinking about how to use technology in a way that maximizes efficiency but also manifests respect for the rights and needs of others. The cases also reveal how the expanded use of computer technology has amplified and complicated the responsibilities of those who work in this challenging profession.

COMPUTER TECHNOLOGY AND SOCIETY

We turn finally to a realm of broader issues that focus on the extraordinary impact of these new technologies on society and culture. Beyond question, the information revolution and the growing reliance on cyberspace communications are bringing about profound and enduring social changes. The case studies in Part IV attempt to examine and assess the impact of these profound changes.

For the most part these cases consider the Internet's encroachment on our personal and professional lives. The growing reliance on cyberspace has created wonderful opportunities to expand the scope of global communications and to create virtual communities all across the network. However, as we shift communications to international networks such as the Internet, complex questions appear to emerge: How do we control this borderless global technology? What about the possible need for censorship of pornographic material that has become so widely available on the 'Net? How can privacy and intellectual property rights be protected in cyberspace? In other words, how does the world community prevent the threat of moral anarchy on the global web of computer networks which we have assembled? While many users are still network libertarians, others perceive the need for strong regulations and controls. The case entitled "Social Questions and the Internet" will be devoted to these issues.

We will also examine in Part IV a less publicized problem, but one that is still disturbing and merits thoughtful consideration: the negative social impact of high-tech gambling. To what extent do technology-based gambling products such as video poker machines and cyberspace casinos increase the level of gambling and its attendant social problems? This phenomenon also raises questions for IT professionals who are responsible for designing and building these sophisticated systems: Should they be held accountable for the ill effects of their products? In general public policy makers and others must consider whether the perils and costs of high tech gambling are worth the benefits.

The final topic of discussion in Part IV concerns the exceptional impact of technology on the workplace. Information technology is revolutionizing the work environment, but this is not happening without some social costs. The changing nature of information has undoubtedly made many types of work less burdensome. Moreover, changing workflow patterns have helped to dismantle hierarchical structures in favor of organizations that are flatter and more responsive to market demands.

On the other hand, the productivity gains have resulted in job cutbacks and downsizing that inevitably leads to some social upheaval. Also, some contend that IT is directly responsible for diminishing the quality of work life. Office work, for example, has become more mechanized and automated. Zuboff has eloquently described the phenomenon of "deskilling" and its negative impact on many work environments. Deskilling is the result of increasing amounts of workplace automation which Zuboff defines as "applying technology in ways that increase self-acting and self-regulating capacities of machine systems, thus minimizing human intervention."[24] Also, technology has led to the proliferation of many low skill jobs such as telemarketers whose situations are sometimes made worse due to the predominance of electronic monitoring devices used to tightly control the work environment. In this new and changing workplace the challenge for managers seems clear: to optimize the benefits of technology while ensuring that the work environment does not become less humane or less responsive to the legitimate needs of its employees.

NOTES

1. Peter Keen, "Information Technology and the Management Difference: A Fusion Map," *IBM Systems Journal,* vol. 32, no. 1, 1993, p. 20.
2. Ibid., p. 21.
3. Thomas H. Davenport, "Saving IT's Soul: Human-Centered Information Management," *Harvard Business Review* (March-April) 1994, p. 125. See also the case study by Donna Stoddard, "OTISLINE (A)" in James Cash et al., *Corporate Information Systems Management: Text and Cases,* 3rd ed. Homewood, IL: Irwin, 1992, pp. 205–217.
4. Mary Gentile and John Sviokla, "Information Technology in Organizations: Emerging Issues in Ethics and Policy," Cambridge, MA: Harvard Business School Publications, 1991, p. 3.
5. For more discussion on this notion see S.I. Benn, "Privacy, Freedom, and Respect for Persons," in *Philosophical Dimensions of Privacy: An Anthology,* ed. Ferdinand Schoeman. New York: Cambridge University Press, 1984.
6. Willis H. Ware, "The New Faces of Privacy," *The Information Society,* vol. 9, 1993, p. 195.
7. Ibid., p. 208.
8. See the brief discussion of this in James Cash et al., *Building the Information Age Organization.* Burr Ridge, IL: Irwin, 1994, p. 248.
9. Gentile and Sviokla, p. 8.
10. Jeffrey Rothfeder, *Privacy for Sale.* New York: Simon & Schuster, 1992, p. 142.
11. These codes have been reproduced in the Appendix.
12. Anthony Lawrence Clapes, *Softwars.* Westport, CN: Quorum Books, 1993, p. x.
13. Source code represents the lines of computer code written in a high level language such as COBOL, PL-1, PASCAL, etc.; the object code is the machine readable binary code created when the source code is compiled.
14. Richard A. Spinello, *Ethical Aspects of Information Technology.* Englewood Cliffs, NJ: Prentice Hall, 1995, p. 162.
15. Arthur Kuflik, "Moral Foundations of Intellectual Property Rights," in Deborah Johnson and Helen Nissenbaum (eds.). *Computer Ethics and Social Values.* Englewood Cliffs, NJ: Prentice Hall, 1995, p. 169.
16. See Chapter 5 of John Locke, *Second Treatise of Civil Government.* New York: Bobbs-Merrill, 1964.
17. Clapes, p. 19.
18. For more background on this topic consult Eugene Spafford, "Are Computer Hacker Break-ins Ethical?" *Journal of Systems Software,* January 1992, p. 45.
19. Aristotle, *Nicomachean Ethics* trans. J.A.K. Thomson. New York: Penguin Books, 1955, p. 77.
20. Helen Nissenbaum, "Computing and Accountability," *Communications of the ACM,* January 1994, p. 74.
21. Ibid.
22. Richard Stern, "Microsoft and Vaporware," *IEEE Micro,* April 1995, p. 85.

23. James Moor, "What Is Computer Ethics," found in Johnson and Nissenbaum, *Computer Ethics and Social Values*, p. 9.

24. Soshana Zuboff, "Informate the Enterprise: An Agenda for the Twenty-First Century," in Cash et al., *Building the Information Age Organization*, p. 227.

2
Frameworks for Ethical Analysis[1]

WHY BE MORAL?

Before discussing the ethical frameworks that can guide our analysis of the cases that lie ahead, it would be instructive to consider how we might answer the question, "Why be moral?" Why should engineers, computer professionals, and managers be concerned with morality and doing the right thing? Why should they take into account the interests of others or aspire to ideals such as justice, honesty, and generosity?

Some would say that it is difficult enough to be a successful professional and to make sound management decisions without muddying the waters by worrying about morality. Also, if the prospects of being caught are slim or nonexistent, then the temptations to flout the norms of morality are even greater. Others might note that morality can actually interfere with a prosperous career since we must compete against many professionals who are not always so moral. Recall Machiavelli's admonition in *The Prince* that "a man who wishes to profess goodness at all times must fall to ruin among so many who are not good."[2]

Why, then, should one adopt the moral point of view? What can be gained by following one's moral duty or performing acts of self-sacrifice? The philosopher Immanual Kant raises this important question in his famous essay, *Grounding for the Metaphysics of Morals,* but he does not really answer it directly. Throughout this work, however, he expounds on the simple notion that if individual immoral acts such as lying or promise breaking were universalized, the world would be a terrible place. For Kant, the moral agent must constantly ask himself questions such as "What if everybody did what I did? What sort of world would it be?" Therefore, in Kant's view, the moral law commands us to perform actions which can be universalized without contradiction.

A similar argument is advanced in Fuller's seminal work, *The Morality of Law.* He makes a distinction between the morality of duty and the morality of aspirations. He observes that the morality of duty espouses the "basic rules without which an ordered society is impossible, or without which an ordered society directed toward certain specific goals must fail in its mark."[3] Hence, unless we abide by the basic laws or duties of morality we will fail to live up to the minimal requirements of social living. To a great extent our well-being depends on the well being of society and its well-being depends on our willingness to act morally and responsibly. Clearly, then, to a large extent our moral behavior is in our own best interest. As Hobbes has written in Chapter 13 of the *Leviathan,* life without some sort of order and morality would be "solitary, poor, nasty, brutish, and short."[4]

Philosophers have argued for centuries that our human nature virtually compels us to be moral, since we cannot realize our potential as human beings unless we act morally. In other words, morality is essential for "human flourishing." Also, since we cannot achieve genuine human flourishing in isolation but only in community, we come back to the idea that since acting morally benefits the community it will also benefit us. According to Father Loughran, "Since man is and flourishes as 'person-in-community,' then whatever promotes community promotes personal life; and whatever promotes personal life promotes community."[5]

Beyond any doubt, engineers and managers bring credit to their profession and strengthen the bonds of their respective communities when they behave according to the highest moral standards. Their "flourishing" as individuals and as professionals depends on the mutual cooperation and companionship that can only occur within a harmonious community setting. Hence, the critical need to take morality seriously and to analyze ethical dilemmas with the same care that is devoted to technical or other managerial problems.

LAW AND MORALITY

What about relying on the law as a practical guide for discerning the "right" course of action? Does this approach have any pitfalls? Law and morality do have in common certain key principles and obligations. Often, as in areas such as intellectual property or product liability, law and morality can become seriously entangled. Indeed, the interplay of legal and ethical issues in intellectual property cases makes them extremely complex. However, despite this interrelationship, it is too simplistic to reduce morality to legality or to embrace the suggestion that following the law exhausts an executive's moral responsibility. Individuals and corporations cannot assume that just because the law permits a certain course of action that this action is morally acceptable. History is replete with many examples of so-called "laws" that have been blatantly immoral. We need look no farther than the hideously discriminatory laws of Nazi Germany or America's own slavery laws to illustrate this point.

Of course, as we have intimated, the law does often embody moral principles along with standards of fairness and procedural justice that deserve our respect and allegiance. However, since this is not always the case, there is a need to evaluate issues from a legal as well as a moral perspective. For example, because the Courts may allow a software vendor to "reverse engineer" another company's product, it doesn't necessarily follow that this action is not tantamount to the theft of intellectual property. Or if the law allows for electronic surveillance or monitoring employee e-mail one cannot assume that those activities are within the bounds of ethical propriety. One must consider these forms of behavior from a distinctly moral point of view. This means asking questions such as the following: Whose rights have been violated? Whom could the action injure? Does the option chosen respect basic human goods?

Clearly, therefore, law and morality do not always overlap or easily substitute for one another. Legal constraints and judicial decisions, no matter how nuanced, do not necessarily provide sufficient guidelines for addressing the complicated ethical issues in information technology and computer science that are the focus of this text.

Another problem with exclusive reliance on the law as a guideline or surrogate for morality is that the law is essentially reactive. Laws and regulations are rarely proactive, anticipating problems or possible inequities; rather, they react to problems that have surfaced and usually in a manner that is painstakingly slow. For example, in the view of many privacy advocates, the legal system has been too slow to react to a steady erosion of privacy made possible because of rapid technological advancements. But, if companies resolve to be morally responsible about issues such as respect for privacy rights they will not wait for new laws or regulations. Rather, they will exercise their moral obligation and regulate their corporate activities accordingly.

Thus, although it is certainly important to comprehend the legal dimension of some of the problems that we will be considering, legal issues should not be confused with moral ones. As we shall see, moral issues focus on rights and duties, whether harm has occurred, and so forth. Our main purpose here is to help individuals think through the "right" thing to do, and this may sometimes go beyond the parameters of the law, especially when the law is ill-defined or has not caught up with the rapid pace of technological change.

INDIVIDUAL AND CORPORATE RESPONSIBILITY

In addition to the distinction between law and morality, we must also appreciate the important distinction between individual and corporate responsibility. An underlying assumption of our analysis throughout this volume is that individuals are responsible for their actions. To some extent, these responsibilities are defined and shaped by one's personal value system. In effect, we are all *moral agents* who have various moral responsibilities in our different roles as citizens, neighbors, parents, professionals, and so forth. Obviously, when someone is hired into a corporation that person does not abandon his or her moral duties, commitments, and aspirations. However, there are sometimes conflicts between an individual's personal moral values and organizational values. For instance, one may value honesty but find oneself in an organization where lying and deception are taken for granted as a means of doing business. These practices will surely conflict with that manager's personal moral conviction thereby creating a difficult dilemma: Should he or she be loyal to the organization or to his or her own values? Regardless of how one resolves this problem, an individual's responsibility for his or her actions can never be shrugged off or denied. As Llewellyn reminds us, "Choice is your own. You answer for your choice. There are no rules to shoulder *your* responsibility."[6]

To further complicate matters, corporate executives, as executives, assume a different set of responsibilities, since they have a fiduciary obligation to act in the best interests of the shareholders. This raises the difficult question as to whether this fiduciary responsibility in any way limits or constrains one's *moral* responsibility. Executives also have obligations to the corporation's other constituencies such as labor unions, customers, suppliers, government agencies, and so forth. These obligations can conflict with the fiduciary obligation to stockholders or possibly with a manager's personal moral convictions. In other words, corporate managers as organization leaders may experience many different types of conflicts: those between their obligations to shareholders and their obligations to other constituencies; and those between their organizational duties and personal value system.

Finally, we can assume that the corporation itself is a moral entity in its own right. The corporation is analogous to a person, and hence it too can be considered a moral agent with various rights and obligations. Thus, the corporation or organization must be held responsible for its corporate acts. Although this view attributing responsibility to the corporation is not unanimously embraced by contemporary philosophers, it is well grounded in the philosophical and legal tradition.[7] Moreover, it does seem plausible to maintain that a corporation with a culture or climate that fosters moral behavior either informally or formally through the use of an ethical code is more responsible than one that ignores moral issues or even encourages reprehensible behavior in the name of higher profits or other corporate objectives. Of course, even if corporations are held accountable for immoral activities, this does not mitigate the responsibility of executives or others in the company. Thus, for example, under certain conditions we might hold both individuals within the corporation and the corporation itself liable for the theft of intellectual property especially if the corporate culture was one that implicitly (or even explicitly) promoted and tolerated such behavior.

In the cases that follow in the various chapters, the primary focus will sometimes be on corporate responsibility. Such cases will consider whether or not the corporation has acted responsibly, that is, has it acted with respect for the rights and legitimate interests of others? Has it taken seriously its ethical duties as well as its economic ones?[8] *Chicago* and *Data Accuracy and the Credit Bureau Industry* are examples of case studies that focus primarily on corporate behavior and corporate responsibility. In other cases, the emphasis is more on the individual's personal values. For example, the case entitled *Whose Program Is This?* deals explicitly with an issue of personal integrity and the ambiguity of intellectual property ownership.

BASIC ETHICAL THEORIES

Ethical theories and principles that will serve as the ultimate guidelines for our analysis will be our next consideration. Ethical theories present those principles which enable us to reach the normative judgments that will guide our actions and help us to differentiate right from wrong conduct. These theories explain and define what it means to act morally and thereby reveal to us the moral imperative that we must assume if we aspire to be responsible and upright individuals. Thus, if our decisions or choices are guided by a particular theory, it can be plausibly demonstrated that the moral principles of the theory demanded that we make this decision. As we shall see, these theories are by no means flawless nor are they able to function as formulas that give us simple answers to complex moral dilemmas. Rather, they are "avenues" or approaches to such problems that facilitate analysis and reflection on the issues at hand.

For the most part we will be considering modern ethical theories, and these can be divided into two broad categories: teleological and deontological, the ethics of ends and the ethics of duty. The term *teleological* is derived from the Greek word *telos*, which means end or goal. Teleological theories give priority to the good over the right and evaluate actions by the goal or consequences that they attain. In other words, the right is adjectival to the good and dependent upon it. Thus, right actions are those that produce the most good or optimize the consequences of one's choices, whereas wrong actions are those that do not contribute to the good. We will consider one example of a teleological approach to ethics, namely utilitarianism. Utilitarianism is a form of consequentialism, a theory predicated on the assumption that consequences determine the rightness or wrongness of moral actions.

Deontological theories, on the other hand, argue for the priority of the right over the good or the independence of the right from the good. *Deontological* is also derived from a Greek word *deon*, which means obligation. According to a deontological framework, actions are intrinsically right or wrong regardless of the consequences which they produce. The "right" or ethically proper action might be deduced from a duty or a basic human right but it is never contingent on the outcome or the consequences of an action. Deontological theories include both duty-based and rights-based approaches to ethical reasoning. These are sometimes referred to as pluralism and contractarianism, respectively. We will discuss both of these theories after our treatment of utilitarianism.

UTILITARIANISM

A. The Theory

The theory of utilitarianism is a teleological theory and a widely used form of consequentialism. Classic utilitarianism was developed by two British philosophers, Jeremy Bentham [1748–1832] and John Stuart Mill [1806–1873]. According to this theory, the good or the end (*telos*) is happiness or more specifically "the greatest happiness for the greatest number." This good can also be described as "utility," and this principle of utility is the foundation of morality and the ultimate criterion of right and wrong. According to Bentham,

> By the principle of utility is meant the principle which approves or disapproves of every action whatsoever, according to the tendency which it appears to have to augment or diminish the happiness of the party whose interest is in question, or what is the same thing, in other words, to promote or oppose that happiness.[9]

Thus, actions are right in proportion to their tendency to bring about happiness and wrong to the extent that they bring about pain or less happiness than another alternative.

It should be emphasized that an action is right not if it produces the most happiness for the person performing that action but for *all* parties affected by the action. In summary, then, utilitarianism is the moral doctrine that an action is morally right if it produces the greatest happiness for the greatest number of people affected by it. Like all teleological theories, utilitarianism is committed to the maximization of the good, that is, happiness or utility, or, to put in more relevant language, it is committed to the optimization of consequences.

Utilitarianism assumes that we can somehow measure the benefits and harms produced by an action and thereby determine a sum of those benefits and harms. According to Velasquez, "the principle assumes that all benefits and costs of an action can be measured on a common numerical scale and then added or subtracted from each other."[10]

In practice, therefore, utilitarianism requires one to develop and execute a sort of moral calculus. This is usually in the form of a cost-benefit analysis which can be utilized in situations where there are several possible alternatives or courses of action. Once one has determined all of the possible alternatives, each alternative is evaluated in terms of its costs and benefits (both direct and indirect). Based on this analysis, one chooses the alternative that produces the greatest net expectable utility, that is, the one with the greatest net benefits (or the lowest net costs) for the widest community affected by one's actions.

Obviously, a key notion in the formulation of the moral principle of utility is happiness. But, how do utilitarian philosophers understand and define happiness? Bentham simply equates happiness with pleasure; this implies that the objective of ethical analysis is to maximize pleasure in the world. Mill agrees with Bentham to a certain extent but argues for a hierarchy of pleasures. For example, intellectual pleasures are superior to sensual pleasures. Other philosophers, known as pluralistic utilitarians, have maintained that happiness involves many intrinsic values such as friendship, knowledge, courage, health, and so forth.

But despite this ambiguity and disagreement about what constitutes happiness, the core idea of utilitarianism that only consequences matter has considerable merit. Even philosophers who categorically reject utilitarianism and embrace other frameworks would admit that a basic requirement of ethical reasoning is attention to the probable consequences of one's decision. The consequences of one's action, whether they promote happiness or cause misery, must be admitted as extremely important in formulating moral decisions. Also, utilitarianism is appealing to many as a natural, common sense approach to morality. Many managers and professionals make decisions focusing on consequences and considering the costs and benefits of various alternatives. When these managers assert that they have a moral obligation to do something they usually justify that obligation in terms of the net benefit an action will have. Further, another key advantage of utilitarianism is that it requires one to consider as objectively as possible the interests of all parties affected by one's action. Hence the superiority of this theory over ethical egoism which does not take into account the interests of others.

As an example of the use of utilitarian reasoning in business decisions consider Karl Kotchian, the former president of Lockheed, who was accused in the early 1970s of paying $12 million in bribes to Japanese officials in order to persuade them to buy Lockheed's TriStar plane. Kotchian advanced two arguments to defend these illicit payments: (1) they did not violate any American laws; (2) in the long run they were quite beneficial to many constituencies in the United States, since by securing the purchase of these planes they all reaped big rewards. Stockholders certainly benefited through enhanced profits. At the same time, Lockheed's suppliers, its employees and their communities, and to some degree the entire U.S. economy benefited from this action. Moreover, the Japanese received an excellent airplane at a reasonable price. Of course, there were some costs to Lockheed's competitors and perhaps to the general level of trust in society, but one could reasonably argue that these were most likely outweighed by the tangible benefits received by Lockheed's diverse stakeholders.[11]

The Lockheed example illustrates a key aspect of utilitarianism: What matters first and foremost are the consequences; how these consequences are achieved is only a secondary matter. This points to one of the most serious deficiencies with utilitarianism. It strongly implies that there are no intrinsically evil acts. To be sure, utilitarians would maintain that actions such as deceit, murder, theft, and so on, are usually morally wrong because of the harmful consequences that they bring about. But at the same time, these actions can be ethically justified if it can be decisively proven that they produce the greatest good or maximize net expectable utility. Presumably, then, even human or moral rights are not absolute, since a person's or group's rights could be taken away for the sake of maximizing utility. However, are there not rights that transcend utilitarian calculations such as the rights to life and liberty? If we could somehow maximize happiness for a society by enslaving a small segment of that society would that action really be morally justified?

Another difficulty with consequentialism or utilitarianism concerns the question of how we define the "good" or "happiness." There seems to be no univocal definition of this sometimes elusive commodity. Rather, conceptions of the good and happiness are multiple and heterogeneous. A failure to agree on the meaning of happiness, the goal or maximand of all actions, poses real problems for properly evaluating those actions.

In addition, the utilitarian approach assumes that the goods involved in each alternative are commensurable. In other words, they can be measured and evaluated according to some common standard. But very often this is simply not the case, since the goods compared will at times be incommensurable. For example, how do we compare these two options: an automobile manufacturer can choose to install safer back seat belts in one of its most popular models at a cost of $87 million *or* it can refuse to do the installation, endure some bad publicity, but save $87 million. If the seat belts are installed it is estimated that they would probably save about 10 lives a year. Should the company install the safer seat belts? If we attempt a cost-benefit analysis to answer this question, how can we compare lives saved with dollars and cents? Aren't these goods completely incommensurable? Or we might consider two goods such as justice and theoretical truth. If these goods are at stake in a moral decision how does the consequentialist choose between them? Thus, according to the philosopher, Grisez, if a consequentialist admits that two goods are "fundamental and incommensurable, then the consequentialist also admits that the 'greatest net good' is meaningless whenever one must choose between promoting and protecting or impeding and damaging these two goods in some participations."[12]

The final difficulty with this popular theory is a practical and procedural one. Can managers and professionals objectively work through the sort of moral calculus demanded by consequentialism? Can these individuals avoid self-serving assumptions and various prejudices in the process of moral reasoning? Unfortunately, all too often consequentialist reasoning that does not overcome those assumptions ends up by yielding mere rationalizations of unethical or selfish behavior. The task of objectively considering carefully *all* the diffuse consequences of an action and estimating the costs and benefits can at times be overwhelming and ultimately self-defeating.

B. Utilitarianism and Information Technology

As we have observed, utilitarian analysis entails the identification of the costs and benefits of each decision alternative along with selection of the alternative that maximizes utility or benefit for all parties affected by the decision. We can present several examples of how this framework can be especially useful in resolving ethical problems that arise for IT professionals and other managers. Moreover, these illustrations should suggest many other possibilities for the application of utilitarianism.

For many employees a downside to the information revolution is the threat to workplace privacy posed by new IT capabilities such as electronic monitoring. Those corporations that seek to justify the use of this controversial technology could argue that such monitoring maximizes utility. Although there may be some costs for employees such as some inconvenience or loss of mobility, these costs are far outweighed by several appreciable benefits including increased productivity and greater efficiency. This tangible result will benefit consumers who will pay lower prices and shareholders who will enjoy a greater return on their investment. Higher productivity and efficiency is also positive for the whole economy since the monetary savings which they yield can be used for other investments. It could also be argued that the employer will benefit not only through increased productivity but also by having more thorough and objective data for evaluating an employee's performance. This could ultimately lead to fairer employee appraisals which in turn will significantly benefit the employees themselves. Thus, from a utilitarian perspective, a strong case can be made to legitimize the practice of electronic monitoring. This is not to imply that these arguments are necessarily decisive or that there are not strong utilitarian reasons for not employing this procedure, but it does illustrate how this theory can enable one to make a convincing ethical case for the use of monitoring.

We might also consider how the utility principle could be applied to the problem of defining the scope of intellectual property rights. As we will discern in several of the cases on intellectual property in Chapter 6, some countries have much looser protection of property rights than the United States. The Japanese, for example, have patent laws that permit the "laying open" of patents; this practice encourages others to use this information as a basis for further innovations or commercial applications. Once again a tenable rationale for this approach can be developed by invoking utilitarianism: By loosely protecting intellectual property society benefits through the more rapid diffusion of technology. Thus, a scheme of weak protections will inevitably lead to beneficial social consequences. There are utilitarian arguments on the other side of this issue, since stronger protection can be seen as an important incentive to stimulate innovations. Regardless of where one stands on this issue, the point is clear: The utilitarian perspective can play a major role in developing cogent ethical arguments to support one's position.

DUTY-BASED ETHICAL THEORY (PLURALISM)

We turn our attention now to deontological ethical theories. We will first consider pluralism or duty-based approaches as expressed in the philosophies of Immanuel Kant (1724–1804) and W. D. Ross (1877–1940).

A. Immanuel Kant

Kant's ethical theory is indeed a model of the deontological approach to morality which stresses fidelity to principle and duty. Kant's ethical philosophy, known for its severity and inflexibility, focuses on duty divorced from any concerns about happiness or pleasure. This philosophy is articulated and developed in Kant's second critique, *The Critique of Practical Reason,* and in a much shorter and more concise work, *Grounding for the Metaphysics of Morals.*

Kant's moral philosophy is firmly opposed to utilitarianism and modern natural rights theories first developed by Hobbes and Locke. In the Preface to *The Critique of Practical Reason* Kant indicates his intention to construct a "pure moral philosophy, perfectly cleared of everything which is only empirical, and which belongs to anthropology."[13] This pure moral philosophy is grounded not in the knowledge of our human nature but in a common idea of duty. This common idea of duty, including imperatives such as "One should not tell a lie," applies not only to all human beings but to all *rational* beings including God Himself. Thus, if duty is applicable to all rational beings and even to God, it cannot be based on human nature. Morality, then, for Kant consists of obligations that are binding on any being who is rational.

However, what is this common idea of duty? To begin with, duty embodies the idea that one should do the right thing in the right spirit. In other words, according to Kant, "an action done from duty has moral worth, not in the purpose that is attained by it, but in the maxim according to which the action is determined."[14] Thus, an action's moral worth is not found in what it tries to accomplish but in the agent's intention and the summoning of one's energies to carry out that intention. Results, purpose, and consequences cannot be taken into account to establish the validity of the moral law or to make exceptions to that law. This is obviously in direct contrast to utilitarianism. For Kant, then, the moral individual must perform actions for the sake of duty *regardless of the consequences.*

What is the ground or basis for this duty? In Kant's systematic philosophy our moral duty is simple: to follow the moral law, which like the laws of science or physics must be rational. Also, the same as all rational laws, the moral law must be universal, since universality represents the common character of rationality and law. This universal moral law is expressed as the categorical imperative: "I should never act except in such a way that I can also will that my maxim should become a universal law."[15] The imperative is "categorical" because it does not allow for any exceptions.

A "maxim" as referred to in Kant's categorical imperative is simply a subjective principle or rule underlying a pattern of actions. If, for example, I usually break my promises, then I act according to the private maxim or rule that promise breaking is morally acceptable when it is in my best interests to do so. But can one take this individual maxim and transform it into a universal moral law? As a universal law this particular maxim would be expressed as follows: "It is permissible for everyone to break promises when it is in their best interests to do so." Such a law, however, is invalid since it contains a logical contradiction. Universal promise breaking is logically impossible (like a square circle), since if everyone broke promises, the entire institution of promising would collapse; there would be no such thing as a "promise" because in such a climate anyone making a promise would lack credibility. Thus, this maxim would destroy itself as soon as it was transformed into a universal law.

Kant's categorical imperative, then, is his ultimate ethical principle. In the simplest terms, it is a test of whether an action is right or wrong. Can the action in question pass the test of universalization? If not, the action is immoral and one has a duty to avoid it. The categorical imperative is a "moral compass" that gives us a convenient and tenable way of knowing when we are acting morally.

Although there is only one categorical imperative or moral law, it can be expressed in several different ways. In some regards Kant's second formulation of this imperative makes his position even clearer: "Act in such a way that you treat humanity, whether in your own person or in the person of another, always at the same time as an end and never simply as a means."[16] In other words, the principle of humanity as an end-in-itself serves as a limiting condition of every person's freedom of action. We cannot exploit other human beings and treat them exclusively as a means to our ends or purposes. Quite simply, one's projects or objectives cannot supercede the worth of other human beings. For Kant, this principle can be also summed up in the word *respect*—the moral law can be reduced to the absolute principle of respect for other human beings who deserve respect because of their rationality and freedom, the hallmark of personhood for Kant.

Clearly, Kant's ethical theory has many virtues. It is also controversial and fraught with serious problems because of its inflexibility and rigid absolutism. Specifically, do we really have absolute duties to keep promises or tell the truth? What if by lying to a criminal or a madman I can save the life of an innocent person? Am I still obliged to tell the truth under such circumstances? Kant would appear to say that the duty to tell the truth always prevails since lying cannot be universalized. But this seems to violate moral common sense, since we all recognize conditions when lying or deception is appropriate behavior. Consider the overwrought but helpful example of telling a lie to save someone from a ruthless murderer. In this case there is a conflict of universal laws: the law to tell the truth and the law to save a life in jeopardy. We must, of course, admit an exception to one of these laws. As Ewing points out,

> in cases where two laws conflict it is hard to see how we can rationally decide between them except by considering the goodness or badness of the consequences. However important it is to tell the truth and however evil to lie, there are surely cases where much greater evils can still be averted by a lie, and is lying wrong then?[17]

Thus, it is difficult to avoid an appeal to consequences when two laws conflict, and this is a grave problem for Kant.

Also, it is worth pointing out that some philosophers such as Hegel have criticized Kant's categorical imperative because it is only a formal principle and, as such, it is empty and deficient. For Hegel, the moral law presented by Kant requires an empirical content, some genuine substance, and there is no content that can fit with its formal universality. Also, in some cases the universalization of a maxim such as "One should help the poor" is contradictory, since it would result in the suppression of poverty. Thus, Hegel argues that for duty to be respected, duty must preserve its opposite—the duty to help the poor, for example, requires the perpetuation of poverty. On this basis Hegel, then, rejects Kant's conception of duty and his formal approach to ethics.[18]

However, in some respects this criticism, which has been repeated by other philosophers, is somewhat unfair to Kant. There *is* a content to Kantian moral philosophy that is implicit in the categorical imperative. Recall that the second formulation of this imperative commands us to treat humanity as an end and never simply as a means. Thus, the dignity of the other as an end is the unconditioned principle and "content" of Kant's moral philosophy. It is true, of course, that the categorical imperative is a very general moral principle, but this is precisely what Kant intended. It is a compass or guide that provides us with a test for determining our concrete ethical duties. Indeed, it becomes clear that this emphasis on respect for persons endows Kant's ethics with a certain vitality. For Kant, the ethical life is never realized or achieved; rather, we are always striving to close the distance between our real moral situations and the ideal of the categorical imperative. There is never an achievement of morality, and, to be sure, the history of humanity bears this out.

B. W. D. Ross

The British philosopher W. D. Ross developed a duty-based ethical theory in his book *The Right and the Good* which can be viewed as an extension of Kant's focus on a single, absolute duty. Ross claims that through reflection on our ordinary moral beliefs we can intuit *the* rules of morality. These moral rules or duties are ultimate and irreducible; hence, they are the first principles of moral reasoning. Ross, however, in contrast to Kant, refuses to accept these duties as absolute or prevailing without exception. Rather, he argues that they are *prima facie* duties which means that they are moral imperatives that should apply most of the time under normal circumstances. But they are not categorical imperatives which hold regardless of the situation.

In simplest terms, a *prima facie* obligation is a conditional one that can be superceded by a more important, higher obligation, usually under very exceptional circumstances. Thus, we do have a *prima facie* duty to be honest and truthful. However, if a murderer comes to the door of your home looking for his wife whom you have hid in the basement, your obligation to tell the truth becomes subordinate to your obligation to protect human life. Quite simply, a moral principle can be sacrificed, but only for another moral principle, not just for arbitrary, pragmatic reasons. Although these *prima facie* duties must not be dismissed lightly or cavalierly, each of them has exceptions and in extraordinary circumstances can be overriden.

According to Ross, there are seven basic moral duties that are binding on moral agents. These duties are as follows:

1. One ought to keep promises and tell the truth (*fidelity*)
2. One ought to right the wrongs that one has inflicted on others (*reparation*)
3. One ought to distribute goods justly (*justice*)
4. One ought to improve the lot of others with respect to virtue, intelligence, and happiness (*beneficence*)
5. One ought to improve oneself with respect to virtue and intelligence (*self-improvement*)
6. One ought to exhibit gratitude when appropriate (*gratitude*)
7. One ought to avoid injury to others (*noninjury*)

Ross does not maintain that this list of duties is complete or exhaustive, but he does believe that these duties are indisputable and self-evident. They are manifest to the mind through simple intuition. As he writes in *The Right and the Good:*

> I am assuming the correctness of some of our convictions as to *prima facie* duties, or more strictly, am claiming that we *know* them to be true. To me it seems self-evident as anything could be, that to make a promise, for instance, is to create a moral claim on us in someone else. Many readers will say that they do *not* know this to be true. If so, I certainly cannot prove it to them: I can only ask them to reflect again, in the hope that they will ultimately agree that they know it.[19]

As Ross indicates here, he makes no effort to provide substantial reasons or arguments which will convince us to accept these duties. If one doesn't see them he or she must be simply obtuse or morally blind!

There is one final issue regarding these *prima facie* duties which points to a deficiency in Ross's approach to morality: How do we handle cases where duties conflict? If two such duties are in conflict, Ross recommends that this basic principle should be followed: "That act is one's duty which is in accord with the more stringent *prima facie* obligation." If the situation is even more complex and there are more than two duties in conflict, then we must abide by a different guideline: "That act is one's duty which has the greatest balance of *prima facie* rightness over *prima facie* wrongness."[20]

Both of these principles, however, are somewhat vague and do not really facilitate resolving difficult conflicts between basic duties. They seem to raise more questions rather than help us reach answers. What is meant by Ross's use of the word "stringent"? What makes one obligation more compelling or stringent than another? Ross is silent on this issue, and this represents a serious flaw in his ethical philosophy. Similarly, Ross's second principle is riddled with ambiguity. He states that when various duties conflict, we should choose the duty that produces or yields the greatest proportion of "rightness." But this too begs the question and doesn't really offer us much assistance in deliberating over the question of which duty takes precedence.

Despite these shortcomings, however, Ross's theory is certainly not without merit. A focus on one's duty in a particular situation is an excellent starting point for determining the right course of action or resolving an ethical dilemma. Moreover, Ross's approach, unlike that of Kant, provides for some flexibility, which to a certain extent better permits its application to complex moral problems. Finally, several other ethical theories such as natural law also highlight duties or obligations similar to Ross, but these duties are derived differently.

UNIVERSAL ACCEPTABILITY

A variation of Kant's morality which is worth a brief treatment in this section on the duty-based approach to ethics is the notion of universal acceptability. This is another way of interpreting and formulating the categorical imperative. It considers the act or the moral judgment which someone has made from the perspective of other disinterested parties. The criterion for differentiating between right and wrong, then, becomes the following: Do all rational beings accept this action or decision regardless of whether they are the perpetrators or the victims? In other words, would the victim and other neutral parties consider my actions moral and above board? This sort of thinking forces us to step out of our egoistic framework and consider our actions from the perspective of the other, especially the potential victim. This approach is certainly consistent with Kant's ethics and what has been traditionally known as the "Golden Rule": Do unto others as you would have them do unto you.

Thus, the key to this ethical viewpoint is to pose the simple question: Is my action *universally acceptable* even to those who are directly affected by it? Another approach is to consider whether one's actions can pass a "publicity test." Would others accept what I have done if it were to become public knowledge? In her essay "Ethics Without the Sermon" Nash phrases the question this way: "Could you disclose without qualm your decision or action to your boss, your CEO, the board of directors, your family, or society as a whole?"[21] If we would feel diffident about such disclosure because we thought that this "public" could not accept our actions, then there is probably something seriously wrong.

D. Pluralism in the Context of Information Technology

We now consider the relevance and practical value of pluralism or an orientation to ethics based on duty. How do we apply such an ethic to resolving moral issues that arise in information technology? To begin with, Ross's list of *prima facie* duties serves to remind both corporations and IT professionals of some specific secondary obligations that can be derived from his general *prima facie* duties. These include the following: avoid using computers to harm others, respect intellectual property rights, be honest about product capabilities and availability, and so forth. In addition to these and other moral obligations there are those duties that managers assume by virtue of their role as economic agents. These include fiduciary obligations to shareholders to maximize the firm's profit and return on shareholder's equity.

Managers, therefore, must take into account all of these various obligations when they make decisions, and this can sometimes create some difficult challenges. In several cases, for example, we will see how information technology vendors often possess considerable leverage over their clients who depend heavily on technology products to run their business. These vendors must sometimes make difficult decisions regarding the extent and scope of quality control testing especially when they are behind schedule for a particular product release. Key corporate objectives such as profitability and increased revenues can then conflict with the customer's need for a reliable and safe product. The pluralist mode of reasoning would direct such companies to balance their duty to seek profits and maximize returns for shareholders with ethical duties such as honesty and the avoidance of any ostensible harm to their customers.

In regard to product announcements, vendors must seriously consider the ethical duty to be honest and to avoid fraudulent, deceptive, or misleading claims. This is a fundamental ethical imperative which cannot be easily dismissed for the sake of economic considerations or financial expediency. Of course, *how* a manager balances this obligation with his or her other duties is a formidable challenge. Moreover, from a Kantian perspective one cannot justify misrepresentation about products since, as with lying, the maxim on which such misrepresentation is based could never become a valid universal moral law.

RIGHTS-BASED ETHICS (CONTRACTARIANISM)

A. Theoretical Overview

A third distinct approach to ethics focuses on individual rights and respect for those rights. This rights-based avenue of ethical thinking is another example of a deontological approach to ethics with its focus on moral principle instead of consequences. A right can be most simply defined as an *entitlement* to something. Thus, thanks to the First Amendment of the Constitution, all Americans are entitled to freedom of speech. This right is derived from and guaranteed by our legal system so it is a "legal right." There are also moral or human rights which are entitlements that all human beings should have by virtue of being human. Such rights are universal since they are grounded in our common human nature. Hence, unlike legal rights they are not confined to a particular legal jurisdiction. In addition, these human rights are equal rights; everyone, for example, equally shares in the rights to life and liberty regardless of their nationality or status in society.

Philosophers make an important distinction between positive and negative rights. Negative rights imply freedom from outside interference in certain activities. Examples of negative rights include freedom of expression, the right to liberty, and the right to privacy. Thus, if one has a right to privacy in the workplace, an employer cannot interfere with one's private affairs. Obviously, the corollary of these rights are duties such as the duty to respect the privacy rights of others. A positive right, on the other hand, implies a requirement that the holder of this right be provided "with whatever he or she needs to freely pursue his or her interests."[22] The rights to health care and education are examples of positive rights. If someone had a right to medical care there would be a correlative duty on the part of some agent (probably the government) to provide that care in some fashion. In American society there has been far more emphasis on negative rights than on positive rights.

The rights-based viewpoint is synonymous with *contractarianism,* which has its roots in the social philosophy of philosophers such as Hobbes, Locke, and Rousseau. According to these philosophers, morality is grounded in the so-called social contract. This contract is necessitated because of the prepolitical state of nature which preceded civil society and in which there was absolute freedom accompanied by anarchy, war, and strife. In order to overcome these intolerable conditions, a civil government is established and all individuals enter into a tacit, implicit contract with that government to respect the other's desires for life and liberty. In return, civil society agrees to respect and protect the basic rights of its citizens, specifically, the rights of life, liberty, property, and so forth. Society owes each individual protection of these rights in exchange for their obedience to the law. These are contractual rights which are usually synonymous with the legal rights guaranteed by the Constitution.

Several contractarians such as Locke have argued for the social contract but also support the notion that our rights are fundamental and not dependent on this contract. Locke maintained that the rights of life, liberty, and property are natural, God-given rights that can never be abrogated by the state. What Hobbes and Locke and other social contract philosophers have in common is their strong emphasis on *rights* as the fundament of morality. According to this perspective, moral reasoning should be governed by respect for individual rights and a philosophy of fairness. As Goodpaster observes, "fairness is explained as a condition that prevails when all individuals are accorded equal respect as participants in social arrangements."[23] In short, then, contractarianism focuses on the need to respect an individual's legal, moral, and contractual rights as the basis of justice and fairness.

For our purposes a rights-based analysis of moral problems should consider whether a particular course of action violates any of an individual's human or legal rights such as the right to privacy, the right to own property, or the right to free speech. As we shall see in subsequent chapters, the primary challenge confronting this sort of analysis emanates from the difficulty of establishing the parameters of these rights and determining whether or not rights such as freedom of expression are absolute.

It should be evident that like pluralism this approach to morality is markedly different from utilitarianism which regards rights or entitlements as subservient to the general welfare. For utilitarians rights can be circumscribed or even taken away if by doing so one can maximize the common good. But those who embrace contractarianism would categorically reject this claim.

Finally, one can surely observe that an ethical theory based on rights has certain shortcomings. In American society there is a tendency to argue for a proliferation of various rights without an accompanying discussion of the limits that must be imposed on those rights. For example, what are the limits of the right to free expression? Also, this avenue of ethical reflection can lead to introversion and a focus on *my* rights instead of the correlative duties imposed by another's rights. In addition, philosophers provide little guidance for reconciling conflicting rights, and this can make the practical application of this theory somewhat difficult. These shortcomings however, by no means undermine this avenue of ethical reasoning which has many important features including its special focus on basic human values such as equality and freedom.

B. Rawls's Theory of Justice

John Rawls is a contemporary social contract philosopher whose theory of justice focuses on justice as fairness. He follows in the tradition of Hobbes and Locke and represents a contemporary approach to a deontological moral framework that emphasizes rights as the basis of morality. Rawls's ethic is a true deontological theory which gives priority to the right over the good. The right actions are those that are consistent with his principles of justice which emphasize an individual's basic rights or liberties.

Rawls's theory of *justice as fairness* establishes conditions that must be established in order to reach an agreement acceptable to all parties. According to Rawls, the principles of justice are those which equal, rational, self-interested individuals would choose as the terms of a social contract for themselves and their descendants. Rawls postulates a fundamental, prepolitical "original position" where this choice would be made. This corresponds to the state of nature in the traditional theory of social contract. It is a hypothetical construct which enables one to formulate morally acceptable principles of justice which would command universal assent. It is assumed that all parties act under the "veil of ignorance," which will prohibit the knowledge of any contingencies which one could conceivably use to exploit others. Thus, one is not cognizant of one's natural abilities, social status, interests, intelligence, and conception of the good life. One is cognizant of certain general facts such as elements of social and economic theory. Consequently, this control of information will make it impossible to design principles to suit one's own circumstances, and will assure pure procedural justice since the results will be free from any arbitrary influences.

Although parties in the original position do not know their conception of the good nor any specific needs and desires, they do realize that they desire as much as possible of primary social goods. Among these goods are rights, opportunities, powers, income, wealth, and self-respect. These are goods necessary for one's self-fulfillment and the advancement of one's interests, goals, and the overall plan of life.

With this in mind, Rawls argues that those in the original position are virtually compelled to be fair to everyone so that they can be fair to themselves. Given their aversion to risk and the chance that they could be among the disadvantaged of society, Rawls assumes that their rational course of action would be to adopt the perspective of the potentially most disadvantaged group in society. It would be to their advantage to maximize this position in case they themselves were included in this group. This would be the safest and most enlightened strategy under these conditions of ignorance.

This kind of reasoning leads to the choice of the following principles:

FIRST PRINCIPLE

Each person is to have an equal right to the most extensive total system of equal basic liberties compatible with a similar system of equal liberty for all.

SECOND PRINCIPLE

Social and economic inequalities are to be arranged so that they are both: (1) to the greatest benefit of the least advantaged, consistent with the just savings principle, and (2) attached to offices and positions open to all under conditions of fair equality of opportunity.[24]

The principles are arranged in "lexical order," which means that the second cannot be satisfied at the expense of the first.

In the first principle Rawls is arguing that those in the original position would certainly demand an extensive system of liberties, which is essential if one is to pursue different goals, develop one's personality, and fulfill one's life plan. Included in this list of liberties is the right to vote, freedom of speech, liberty of conscience, and "freedom of the person along with the right to hold personal property."[25] Also, according to Rawls, "These liberties are all required to be equal by the first principle, since citizens of a just society are to have the same basic rights."[26] This important statement merely means that these political liberties must equally apply to everyone. Thus, for example, it is required that the laws or rules for the acquisition and transfer of property will equally apply to all citizens. Each person has an equal right to acquire, own, and dispose of property. However, the statement does *not* mean that everyone must own the same amount of property.

While the first principle guarantees a system of equal liberty, the second deals with the distribution of social goods. According to Rawls, those in the original position would definitely not opt for an egalitarian society wherein all goods are distributed equally. Rather, they would choose the second principle of justice known as the *difference principle.* This means that disparities in the distribution of wealth and other social goods would be tolerated *only* if they could be shown to benefit the "least advantaged," the lowest on the social scale. Thus, a just society is not necessarily an egalitarian one where all goods are distributed equally, but one in which inequalities must work to everyone's advantage, especially the most disadvantaged.

It is evident that Rawls is indebted to the contractarian tradition since he relies heavily on the notion of individuals agreeing to a contract outside of an organized social system. Moreover, this contract is the ground of their rights, duties, liberties, and the condition for the distribution of society's goods. Rawls's theory, like the theory of Locke and other predecessors, emphasizes fundamental rights or liberties which can never be suspended for any utilitarian considerations.

Rawls's ethic and the viewpoint of a rights-based approach to morality has many difficulties. One difficulty with Rawls is that the implementation of the difference principle could prove to be an almost impossible task. To begin with, there is a serious problem in the identification of the "least advantaged" who must be somehow aided by inequalities in society. Are they simply those with the lowest income? Couldn't one make the case with equal persuasion that the least advantaged are prosperous blacks or Hispanics who cannot live where they want or well-paid but overtaxed, undervalued, and "alienated" assembly line workers? In short, many different groups in society could qualify in one way or the other for their being the "least advantaged" and this could pose problems for translating Rawls's difference principle into concrete terms.

C. Rights, Justice, and Information Technology

The issue of rights seems especially pertinent for computer professionals because of the grave threat which technology *could* pose to some commonly accepted rights. This threat is probably most pronounced in the area of informational privacy. As a result, it seems essential to formulate the scope of an individual's "information rights," that is, the rights that individuals should possess regarding their personal information that is scattered about in various data bases. It can be plausibly argued that at a minimum every person deserves a right to the privacy, accuracy, and security of such information.

Let us briefly elaborate on these rights. To begin with, this information should be regarded as confidential; it should not be distributed to other interested parties without the data subject's permission. Individuals have a basic right to privacy since privacy is essential for the protection of their freedom and autonomy. One could maintain, therefore, that this fundamental right to privacy should serve as a constraint on certain data collection and dissemination activities.

Second, individuals have a right to the accuracy of their personal information. In other words, this information should be kept up-to-date, germane, and verified. Thus, banks, credit bureaus, hospitals, and others have an obligation to the data subject to ensure that its information is as accurate and error-free as possible, since the distribution of inaccurate information could be quite damaging. Individuals should also have a right to the security of their personal information. This means that data collectors and handlers have an obligation to protect computer systems from breaches of confidentiality. In summary, therefore, the data subject has the right to have its data maintained in a way that keeps it confidential, accurate, and secure.

However, these information rights for an individual must be juxtaposed against a corporation's "information property rights." Organizations claim with some legitimacy that their information resources are their property and that they have a right to dispose of their "property" as they see fit. But how do we establish which set of rights takes precedence? The problem is that certain rights are like Ross's duties—they too are *prima facie* or conditional claims that can conflict with other rights and interests.

Finally, Rawls's rights-based theory dwells on the important issue of justice which is certainly applicable to many problems that arise in the sphere of information technology. Equal or universal access to the emerging information "highway," for example, is an important justice issue which will be discussed in Chapter 9. A strict application of Rawls's theory would seem to require that significant inequities or disparities in service could not be tolerated unless they somehow benefited the least advantaged. Justice as fairness seems to demand universal access of all persons regardless of income, background, or location. Moreover as technology becomes increasingly important for one's economic and social well-being this justice issue will become even more significant.

A GENERAL FRAMEWORK FOR ETHICAL ANALYSIS

We have presented here three different ethical frameworks and noted the general polarity between teleological and deontological approaches to morality. The former is a pragmatic morality of ends while the latter stresses fidelity to principle in the form of rights or duties. Despite these differences, each approach represents a unique perspective from which one can assess and deliberate over moral issues. All of these theories seek to elevate the level of moral discourse from preoccupation with "feelings" or gut reaction to a reasoned and thoughtful consideration of the right course of action. Reliance on these theoretical frameworks therefore will surely improve the clarity and substance of ethical decision making. As we have illustrated, each of these theories has certain flaws, but this does not detract from its role as an avenue for assessing moral dilemmas.

As we attempt to apply one or more of these approaches to the various case studies a good starting point would be the following questions which enable us to put these different theories into action.

- *Consequentialism* or *goal-based analysis:* Managers must consider which action generates the best overall consequences for all parties involved. This often entails a cost/benefit analysis aimed at identifying the action that will maximize benefit for all the stakeholders of the organization.
- *Duty-based ethics:* If a manager follows this avenue of ethical reflection he or she should consider the following questions: Can I universalize the course of action I am considering? Does this course of action violate any

basic ethical duties? Are there alternatives which better conform to these duties? If each alternative seems to violate one duty or another, which is the stronger duty?

- *Rights-based ethics:* Managers must carefully consider the rights of affected parties—which action or policy best upholds the human rights of the individuals involved? Do any alternatives under consideration violate their fundamental human rights (i.e., liberty, privacy, etc.) or one's institutional or legal rights (e.g., rights derived from a contract or other institutional arrangement)?

Finally, how do we incorporate these ethical questions into a thoughtful analysis of the cases in this text? Perhaps the best way to proceed is to outline a general approach to these case studies along the lines of the structure in Table 2.1. There are, of course, other questions which can be raised and many different methods of analyzing case studies. This broad framework, however, represents a reasonable starting point which can certainly be embellished and supplemented by the student depending upon his or her interests and perspectives.

Table 2.1   Steps for Ethical Analysis

1. Identify and formulate the *basic ethical issues* in each case. Also consider the *legal issues* (if any) and whether or not there seems to be a conflict between law and morality.
2. What are your first impressions or reactions to these issues—in other words, what does your *moral intuition* say about the action or policy under consideration: Is it right or wrong?
3. Consult the appropriate formal guidelines. This includes relevant corporate ethics codes or professional codes of conduct such as the ACM code (see Appendix).
4. Analyze the issues from the viewpoint of one or more of the *ethical theories* (consequentialism, pluralism, contractarianism).
5. Do the ethical theories point to one decision or course of action or do they bring you to different conclusions? If so, which principle or avenue of reasoning should take precedence?
6. What is your *normative conclusion* about the case (what should be the organization's or individual's course of action?).
7. Finally, what are the *public policy implications* of this case and your normative conclusion? Should the recommended behavior be prescribed through legislation or regulations?

STAKEHOLDER ANALYSIS

One final word about theory. In discussing the various ethical themes we often referred obliquely to the "parties involved." We should be more precise about those affected by a manager's actions and decisions. They are often referred to as "stakeholders." A stakeholder is defined as any group or individual who can affect or is affected by the achievement of the organization's objectives. Some examples of a corporation's stakeholders include its employees, stockholders, customers, suppliers, communities, relevant government agencies, society at large, and even its competitors.[27]

Much has been written about the ethical relationship between management and stakeholders. A full treatment of this topic, however, is beyond the scope of this work. Suffice it to say that stakeholders are more than mere instrumental forces that can help or hinder a corporation from reaching its objectives. Rather, the moral point of view would strongly suggest that each stakeholder group deserves respect in its own right; the corporation and its managers, in other words, have certain moral obligations to their diverse stakeholders that can be defined by the ethical theories outlined in the previous section.

Stakeholder analysis can probably best be accomplished when it is done in conjunction with one or more of these theories. Such analysis entails first indentifying the key stakeholders, those who have a real interest or "stake" in the decision at hand. One must also consider the goals of each stakeholder group along with their preferred outcome and their leverage for affecting that outcome. Finally, managers must consider a moral position or posture toward these stakeholders. If they follow consequentialism, they can decide to *maximize stakeholder equity*, that is, choose the alternative that optimizes consequences for all the affected stakeholders. On the other hand, a pluralist or duty-based approach would require managers to consider their duties to stakeholders and, if there are conflicts, to identify the stakeholder groups (such as stockholders) to whom the manager has the highest obligation. In these and other ways stakeholder analysis can be integrated with ethical analysis to reach some defensible and coherent resolution to intricate moral quandaries. Including this level of analysis has the advantage of alerting managers to the interests and concerns of the many groups affected by their decisions and actions.

PROFESSIONALISM AND CODES OF CONDUCT

A. The Professions

Before concluding this background chapter we must say a few words about professionalism and the codes of conduct that govern computer scientists, engineers, and information technology professionals. As we discussed, one step in the process of ethical analysis should be consultation of these codes for guidance and insight (see Table 2.1).

To begin with, what exactly do we mean by the term "professional" and are engineers and computer technicians really members of a profession? Also, does professional behavior imply adherence to certain moral standards? There is no univocal definition of the term *professional*, but we can delineate certain common characteristics of someone who belongs to a profession. One feature that is common to all professions is the requirement of extensive intellectual training in order to master a complex body of knowledge. Thus, lawyers, doctors, and engineers must undergo many years of formal training in order to develop the intellectual skills necessary to practice their chosen professions. During this period they acquire theoretical principles that can be applied to the solution of human and social problems.

Another characteristic of professionals is their contribution to society through the services that they provide. Society relies heavily on professionals for its well-being and stability. In addition, in most circumstances professionals have monopoly control over the provision of those services. This is accomplished by establishing rigid admission criteria to the profession. For example, in order to practice law aspiring attorneys must pass a rigorous state bar exam.

Another common feature of professionalism is autonomy. Professionals, in other words, can exercise their autonomous judgment in their work because of their expertise. There are, of course, restrictions on that autonomy but the judgments and decisions of professionals are usually highly respected and sought after.

Finally, it is important to observe that most professions are regulated by a set of behavioral standards that are embodied in a code of conduct. For instance, lawyers are tightly regulated by the American Bar Association's Model Rules of Professional Conduct. If a lawyer violates one of the statutes in this code the penalty is often disbarment. The professions regulate themselves in this way in order to ensure that their members do not abuse their privileges and power. Without such codes that are strictly enforced, the professions would be hard pressed to ensure the proper conduct of their members.

We can now summarize the common characteristics of most typical professions—intellectual training to master a complex corpus of knowledge, service to society, monopoly power, and governance by a code of conduct. All of these features seem to apply to the mainline, traditional professions such as law and medicine. However, they do not all apply to more marginal and contemporary professions such as consulting and engineering. Consultants, for instance, are not governed by a universal ethical code; moreover, there are no licensing requirements or "barriers to entry" in this profession. Therefore, anyone can call himself a consultant and initiate a practice. Also, although engineers are certainly considered to be professionals, it is evident "that they are deficient in professional autonomy . . . [and] do not hold a monopoly on the provision of professional services."[28] Similarly, computer scientists, programmers, and information technology specialists also lack autonomy and do not exercise any monopoly power over their services. However, they do meet some of the other criteria such as mastery of a difficult and abstruse body of knowledge. Also, they perform an important social function by supporting social institutions and other professions. According to Deborah Johnson, although "computing does not fit the classic paradigm . . . computer professionals are much closer to the paradigm of special professionals than, say, stockbrokers or carpenters or mail carriers."[29]

B. Codes of Conduct

Now that we have clarified the nature of a profession and concluded that engineers and computer scientists belong to developing professions, we can examine the codes of conduct that do govern these "professions." In the Appendix to this book we have reprinted the relevant codes that pertain to engineers and software professionals. Before explicitly considering those codes, however, we should consider the benefits and disadvantages of relying on any ethical code of conduct.

The advantages of using such codes should be evident enough. To begin with, codes can help to create an environment that is conducive to moral rectitude. A professional code is a stimulus to abide by certain norms regardless of the context. Codes give support to professionals with high ideals who are motivated to do the right thing even in the midst of an unsupportive environment. In addition, codes can be beneficial in orienting new workers to a profession's values. Thus, codes serve as moral compass for professionals who find themselves in a quandary; although a code will not solve complex moral problems it can serve as a good starting place for such resolutions. Finally, the process of formulating and revising codes of ethics can be a valuable exercise for a profession, since it requires members of that profession to reflect seriously on important moral considerations that might otherwise be neglected.

Of course relying on codes of conduct to regulate a profession has certain limitations. It is difficult to implement codes so that professionals take them seriously. It is also difficult to enforce the various elements of the code—decisions must be made about who will oversee the code, appropriate penalties that fit the infraction, and the vital question of due process for those who have allegedly violated some tenet of the code.

Moreover, aside from these implementation questions, it is also worth noting the difficulties of formulating codes that avoid meaningless generalities but are not so specific that they lack the necessary flexibility.[30]

Codes then do have certain inherent limitations but these seem overshadowed by the benefits they provide such as a clear, albeit general, sense of moral direction. The most relevant code for our purposes is the ACM Code of Professional Conduct which is reproduced in the Appendix. The Association for Computing Machinery (ACM) is a large and influential organization of computer professionals which adopted these norms in 1973. This code was revised and updated in 1992. One finds here an emphasis on basic moral values such as truthfulness and fidelity. At a minimum this code serves as a reminder that these values should not be casually overlooked for purely pragmatic or economic considerations.

The second code which appears in the Appendix is the Institute of Electronic and Electrical Engineers (IEEE) Code of Ethics. This code, too, offers general ideals but contains few specifics regarding how one should behave under certain circumstances. For instance, neither this code nor the National Society for Professional Engineers Code of Ethics deals with the question of whistleblowing which is a major concern for many engineers. These codes, therefore, serve a useful purpose but they are no substitute for the conscientious reflection and careful deliberation that can be facilitated by relying on the ethical frameworks and principles explicated in this chapter.

NOTES

1. This is a revised and modified version of "Frameworks for Ethical Analysis," Chapter 2 of *Ethical Aspects of Information Technology*. *(Prentice Hall)*
2. Machiavelli, *The Prince*, trans. by Mark Musa. New York: St. Martin's Press, 1964. Chap. XV, p. 127.
3. Lon Fuller, *The Morality of Law*. New Haven, CT: Yale University Press, 1964, pp. 5–6.
4. Hobbes, *Leviathan*, ed. Michael Oakeshott. London: Collier-MacMillan, LTD., 1969, p. 100.
5. James Loughran, S.J., "Reasons for Being Just," *The Value of Justice: Essays on the Theory and Practice of Social Virtue*. New York: Fordham University Press, 1979, p. 55.
6. Karl Llewellyn, *The Bramble Bush: On Our Law and Its Study*. New York: Oceana Publications, 1981, p. 17.
7. See, for example, the writings of Kenneth Goodpaster such as "The Concept of Corporate Responsibility" in *Just Business: New Introductory Essays in Business*

Ethics, ed. Tom Regan. New York: Random House, 1984, pp. 292–322. For a discussion of the legal perspective on this issue consult Christopher D. Stone, *Where the Law Ends*. New York: Harper & Row, Inc., 1975, pp. 58–69.

8. For a more thorough discussion on the nature of corporate responsibility see Kenneth Goodpaster and John B. Matthews, "Can a Corporation Have a Conscience," *Harvard Business Review*, (January-February) 1982, pp. 132–141.

9. Jeremy Bentham, *An Introduction to the Principles of Morals and Legislation*. London, 1789, Chap. 1, sec. 2 in *Ethical Theories*, ed. A.I. Meldon. Englewood Cliffs, NJ: Prentice Hall, 1967, p. 369.

10. Manuel Velasquez, *Business Ethics: Concepts and Cases*, 3rd Ed. Englewood Cliffs, NJ: Prentice Hall, 1992, p. 61.

11. See the discussion of Lockheed in John R. Boatright, *Ethics and the Conduct of Business*. Englewood Cliffs, NJ: Prentice Hall, 1993, pp. 42–43.

12. Germain Grisez, "Against Consequentialism," *The American Journal of Jurisprudence*, 23 (1978), p. 39.

13. Immanuel Kant, *The Critique of Practical Reason*. London: Longmans Green and Co, 1909, p. 3.

14. Immanuel Kant, *Grounding for the Metaphysics of Morals*. Indianapolis: Hackett Publishing Company, 1981, pp. 12–13.

15. Ibid., p. 14.

16. Ibid., p. 36.

17. A. C. Ewing, *Ethics*. New York: Free Press, 1965, p. 58.

18. G. W. F. Hegel's criticism of Kant is expressed in works such as *Natural Law* trans. T. M. Knox. Pennsylvania: University of Pennsylvania Press, 1975.

19. W. D. Ross, *The Right and the Good*, quoted in R. Fox and J. CeMarco, *Moral Reasoning*. Fort Worth, TX: Holt Rinehart, 1990, p. 142.

20. Ibid., p. 144.

21. Laura Nash, "Ethics Without the Sermon," in Kenneth Andrews, *Ethics in Practice*. Cambridge: Harvard University Press, 1987, p. 252.

22. Velasquez, p. 76.

23. Kenneth Goodpaster, "Some Avenues for Ethical Analysis in General Management," in Kenneth Goodpaster, John Matthews, and Laura Nash, *Policies and Persons*, 1st Ed. New York: McGraw-Hill, 1985, p. 497.

24. John Rawls, *A Theory of Justice*. Cambridge: Harvard University Press, 1971, p. 302.

25. Ibid., p. 61.

26. Ibid.

27. For more discussion on this, see R. Edward Freeman, *Strategic Management: A Stakeholder Approach*. Boston: Pittman Publishing Inc., 1984, pp. 31–49.

28. Charles Harris, Michael Pritchard, and Michael Rabins, *Engineering Ethics: Concepts and Cases*. Belmont, CA: Wadsworth Publishing Company, 1995, p. 28.

29. Deborah G. Johnson, *Computer Ethics*, 2nd Ed. Englewood Cliffs, NJ: Prentice Hall, 1994, p. 42.

30. For more discussion on this, see Earl A. Molander, "A Paradigm for Design, Promulgation and Enforcement of Ethical Codes," *Journal of Business Ethics*, 6 (1987), 620–622.

3

The Acquisition of Information

INTRODUCTION

This chapter deals primarily with the ethical dimension of data collection or acquisition. The growth of digital information has made us more cognizant of data collection activities along with the centrality of information in every organization. Acquisition of the right information in a timely fashion is often a key determinant of an organization's success.

Various computer capabilities including powerful storage media, scanning devices, more advanced hardware processors, and sophisticated software packages facilitate extremely rapid and efficient collection of disparate data. Furthermore, thanks to these technologies, the costs of electronically capturing and archiving data have been steadily decreasing. As a result, many organizations now rely on cost effective methods such as "data warehousing" to preserve large amounts of data for future reference.

However, what forms of data *should* be collected? What types of customer and employee data should be gathered and utilized by an organization? For instance, is it legitimate to closely monitor employees in order to acquire extensive quantitative feedback about their performance? Just because a company has the technological capability to collect vast amounts of data about its employees that does not necessarily mean that it has the right or the prerogative to do so.

Each of the cases in this chapter will present a different and controversial dimension of data collection activities. Although the primary focus is on how data collection has been expedited by information technology, the first case, *Competitive Analysis at PM Software, Inc.,* presents a traditional problem that is not really related to the emergence of new technologies. This case focuses on the propriety of certain methods used to assimilate sensitive competitive information. It challenges us to determine how one draws the line between data collection for competitive analysis and corporate espionage.

The second case in this series, *Fare Game or Foul Play?* describes a major dispute between Northwest Airlines and American Airlines over a related issue, the alleged pilfering of trade secrets. It too raises a crucial and complicated moral question: To what extent can corporations use information from employees who have been hired away from competitors? Has Northwest been too aggressive in collecting and exploiting such information? Trade secrecy laws do protect proprietary information from misappropriation, but they actually protect against using improper means (such as fraud) to obtain that information. According to Samuelson, "Trade secret law has generally not regarded the secret itself as 'property' of its holder, but only as an interest that should be protected from unfair methods of competition."[1]

Both of these cases, then, involve the difficult question of how to define the limits and ethical parameters of gathering valuable information from or about one's competitors especially in light of unclear laws and the ambiguities of ownership.

From these case studies we turn to a different set of issues regarding corporate policies on the collection of employee information. Questions must be addressed regarding the type of information to be gathered and the methods used in the process. The first of the two cases considering this issue is *E-Mail Policy at Johnson & Dresser.* It concerns the increasingly popular but questionable practice of archiving electronic messages for future inspections. An Information Systems manager must decide on a policy that is morally and economically feasible. The second case, *The Topper Travel Agency,* looks at the broader issue of electronic monitoring in the workplace and the use of technology to collect and to measure various employee data. Does the use of this technology violate an employee's right to privacy or create an oppressive environment as some labor unions have alleged? How can the right to privacy and a decent working environment be properly balanced against a corporation's obligation to maximize profits for its shareholders?

The final case, *The Franklin Trucking Corporation,* anticipates the main thematic content of Chapter 4, access to information. In the Franklin case, issues of information acquisition and access seem to be especially intertwined as managers of a transportation company must decide what kinds of reliability and safety information to maintain about its trucking fleet. Also, if such information is collected and aggregated, how does the company control access to this data and prevent any negative repercussions of its decision?

Case 3.1 Competitive Analysis at PM Software, Inc.

Maureen Preston felt particularly anxious as she took her seat on the 8:20 AM ferry to downtown Seattle. It was Thursday and she was traveling to her new employer, one of the city's premier software companies. She had only been working here for 2 weeks and yet it already seemed like 2 years. As she stared at the placid waters and sipped her coffee, she wondered how things could go so wrong so quickly.

COMPANY BACKGROUND

Preston worked for PM Software, Inc., a major producer of project management software systems primarily for IBM mainframes along with DEC and Hewlett-Packard minicomputers. The company also marketed a scaled-down version of its product for the IBM PC and IBM compatible machines. PM Software was a 20-year-old, privately held company with its software packages installed at thousands of sites worldwide. Its revenues in 1995 exceeded $40 million and its net profits were about 6.5 percent of sales, slightly below average for this industry. Its main office was in Seattle, but it had branches in many U.S. cities and subsidiaries in the United Kingdom, Singapore, and Australia.

Project management software systems comprised an unglamorous but steady segment of the lucrative software industry. These systems enabled users to manage large, complex, and high-value projects. Most packages, such as the one offered by PM, integrated planning and scheduling capabilities along with a facility for cost management. PM's products were widely used in the construction industry to manage large-scale construction projects; they were also used extensively by major utilities to assist in the management of outages.

Like all project management packages, PM's core product allowed product managers and their subordinates to construct a precedence diagram or network, illustrating project activities and their sequential relationships. It also determined the critical path[2] of a project and calculated the slack time, that is, the allowable slippage on paths other than the critical path. Users could also input cost data for the activities of a project in order to calculate crash costs or other cumulative costs associated with that project.

PM's product was considered one of the better project management software packages on the market because of its sophisticated functionality, its outstanding performance capability, and PM's excellent support services. PM's system had the leading number of installations in the mainframe IBM marketplace, and its domination here showed no signs of weakening.

In recent years, however, PM had run into significant problems with some of its other offerings. During the early 1990s many organizations shifted their hardware configurations to personal computers and client/server technology. But PM's PC product, introduced in 1989 and upgraded in 1993, had not been well received by personal computer users. The product had much of the same robust functionality as the mainframe version, but many users found it too difficult and cumbersome. Thus, PM was definitely not the first choice for organizations looking for project management software for the PC environment. This hurt sales growth and profit margins. For example, the company's revenue growth slowed to about 3 to 4 percent a year during the 1992 to 1995 time frame.

However, PM was determined to rebound from its current slump. It was working on a revised PC version of its software with a much improved, easier to use graphical interface. In addition, PM was putting more emphasis on marketing and was planning a foray into several new industries. Thus, the company was projecting an optimistic 7 to 8 percent sales growth in 1996 along with a much improved profit margin.

MAUREEN PRESTON

Maureen Preston recently received her MBA in marketing from a major midwestern university. Prior to her MBA studies she had worked for several years in the software industry as a programmer/analyst for a small company that produced financial management software packages. She heard of PM Software during her previous employment and was delighted when she learned that they were hiring in her field.

During the recruiting season she began the interview process with PM Software's Tom Cohen, the Vice President of Marketing. Cohen had been given authorization to expand his department because of the company's more aggressive sales objectives. Cohen was looking for individuals with marketing acumen along with a technical background. He was quite impressed with Preston and invited her back to Seattle for a second round of interviews. These interviews went quite well and 2 days later Cohen offered her the position of Senior Marketing Analyst. She would report directly to him and would be supervising a staff of six support personnel and analysts. Her group had responsibility for researching market trends, analyzing customer prospects, international market analysis, and competitive analysis.

During the interviews Cohen bluntly pointed out to her that the firm's president, Jeff Michaels, had almost a fanatical obsession with knowing as many intimate details about his competition as possible. This was reinforced during her brief meeting with Michaels when she visited the Seattle office. PM's archrival, Harris Software, Inc., located on the banks of the Charles River in Cambridge, Massachusetts, had recently won some major deals in head to head competition with PM. Michaels was determined to find out "what was going on." Preston felt uneasy about this apparent obsession. Consequently, she did have some reservations about taking the job, but when the employment offer finally came, it was far too attractive to turn down. Besides, she figured, this was a respectable company that would not risk its reputation by engaging in unsavory or illicit tactics to learn about the moves of its competition. Thus, Preston eagerly accepted the position at PM and reported for work in early July after a well deserved month long vacation.

A CHALLENGING ASSIGNMENT

The marketing department at PM was loosely organized with two supervisors who were responsible for all aspects of marketing communications, market research and analysis, along with pre- and postsales product support. One of these supervisors, Dave Wilkins, who ran the research arm of the department, now reported to Preston. He did most of the competitive analysis with the help of another staff person and one of the department's administrative assistants. Wilkins was not trained in marketing, but he knew the product line extremely well since he was a former project manager. In addition, he worked for several years at PM as a customer service analyst. As a result, he was also quite familiar with the nuances of project management software. He had prepared a competitive survey of the major players in the industry several months ago but since then moved on to other assignments.

During Preston's second meeting with Cohen, he mentioned nervously that Michaels was particularly apprehensive about a new product that Harris was bringing to the marketplace. He explained that Harris was focusing more intensely on the growing market for personal computer project management software where it had already established itself as the market leader. It was introducing a new product, code named EZ-PRO. This product supposedly not only outperformed PM's PC product but also had more robust security and cost analysis features. Also, it had a slick and easy-to-use graphical interface that insulated the users from the need to learn any sophisticated or arcane commands.

Michaels wanted some verification of this in a hurry so he could decide on his next move with his own PC product development team. They were in the midst of preparing an improved PC version of PM's flagship product that would fix the flaws of previous PC products and be more appealing to personal computer users. Like EZ-PRO, PM's new PC product would also have an improved graphical user interface so that it would be easier to use than command driven products.

Cohen suggested that Preston get together with Wilkins to prepare a comprehensive report on EZ-PRO within the next 2 days. "I realize that you're new here and that this is a tough assignment," he said, "but it's essential that we get this information as quickly as possible. Michaels won't rest until he gets some answers."

Later that day Preston met with Wilkins in her office to discuss this project. "This is so typical of Michaels," Wilkins told her. "He is paranoid about new products and will do anything to find out about them before anyone else." Preston discussed with Wilkins a possible strategy for gaining some background knowledge about EZ-PRO. "What tactics have you used in the past?" she asked Wilkins. "Does the company have any guidelines about this?"

"Guidelines! You've got to be kidding," Wilkins exclaimed. "We do whatever it takes to prepare these reports for the top brass."

Wilkins proceeded to sketch out for Preston the various methods which the company had recently employed to gather this sort of sensitive information. He reported that PM sometimes conducted phony job interviews hoping that a competitor's employees would disclose inside information to impress the interviewer. On occasion, PM hired people away from the competition and heavily relied on them as a source of competitive information. Michaels himself sometimes met with these individuals shortly after they were hired, and once their guard was down he would pump them for information usually over drinks and dinner. Another common practice, according to Wilkins, was to misrepresent oneself as a potential customer looking for product information. On rare occasions PM might hire a consultant to do its "dirty work," but this was not a preferred solution since it was too costly and somewhat risky.

Wilkins also pointed out that another valuable and rich source of information was PM's own customer base and that such an approach might work for this particular case. Some of their biggest clients were always being courted by Harris and sometimes became privy to proprietary information about the Harris product line.

Wilkins remarked that he heard through the grapevine that the EZ-PRO product manager had recently visited a major aerospace manufacturer in Denver, Colorado where she conducted a presentation and a "sneak preview" demonstration of this new product. The meeting was highly secretive and confidential and its participants were all required to sign nondisclosure agreements which enjoined them from divulging what they saw to any third party. One of the aerospace company's project managers who attended the meeting was a loyal PM customer. He was usually willing to share competitive information, and Wilkins conjectured that he could be the best source of information about the Harris PC product. "Besides," commented Wilkins, "he owes us a big favor. We recently provided his division with several days of free consulting services to help them with a particularly troublesome application. He has been a very good customer and Cohen has always done his best to keep him satisfied by doing him favors like that. So I think he'll help us out." Wilkins felt that an in-depth interview with this individual would provide considerable insight into the features of EZ-PRO and Harris's future plans for this product.

Preston's initial reaction to this proposal was skepticism and concern. "That sounds all well and good," she said to Wilkins, "but should we be encouraging this guy to violate a nondisclosure agreement?"

"I wouldn't worry about that," replied Wilkins. "Nobody takes those things seriously any more. Everyone signs them so frequently that they have lost their value. Besides, I know this guy, and that won't bother him in the least. Also, frankly, I don't see any other options."

MAKING A DECISION

Preston was still not convinced about the ethical propriety of this approach but said that she would think it over and give him an answer in the morning. Wilkins reasserted that this appeared to be their only option and that they should move fast. Clearly he felt elated that his contacts provided such an expedient solution for his new boss! He shook her hand and told her that a good report on EZ-PRO would get her career off to a great start. However, Preston was not so elated. She felt uneasy about some of PM's tactics for gathering information and she was not sure that encouraging key customers to divulge proprietary information was such a good idea. On the other hand, her options were really restricted. She reflected, if someone's willing to talk about the competition's products why shouldn't she listen? Isn't that the way this game is played? This isn't graduate school. When she left the office that evening she was still not convinced, but her resistance to Wilkins's pragmatic suggestion was softening.

Now as she traversed the Sound on this quiet and foggy July morning Preston realized she had some important decisions to make that might set a precedent for her whole career at this company. To begin with, she had to decide about the EZ-PRO report. Should she let Wilkins interview his contact or should she pursue another avenue? If so, what would that be? How else could she get the information necessary to keep Michaels happy?

In addition, Preston was a firm believer in policies and unambiguous guidelines. She felt that it was especially important for the Marketing Department to have such guidelines in the murky area of competitive analysis. She was reluctant, however, to propose this to Cohen given PM's past practices and its apparent lack of concern about the ethical suitability of those practices. Was this the most propitious time to bring the issue of proper guidelines to Cohen's attention? Clearly, there was much at stake here, and there was little time for any soul searching or thoughtful analysis.

Case 3.2   Fare Game or Foul Play?

In a 1994 lawsuit filed in federal court in Minneapolis, American Airlines alleged that one of its competitors, Northwest Airlines, pilfered proprietary information relating to its "yield-management system." According to this lawsuit, confidential data made its way into the hands of Northwest managers when it hired away from American Airlines as many as 17 technical experts who specialized in the science of fare-setting and yield management.

All of the major airlines have recently been preoccupied with the issue of yield since their revenues have not kept pace with increases in travel. At the same time, the entire industry has had a hard time generating profits. During 1994 the industry earned "just $100 million on revenues of $54 billion—barely 2 cents for every $10 in revenues."[3]

The "yield" is defined as "the number of cents earned in revenue from each passenger mile."[4] Many factors affect the yield, including the length of the flight, the type of service (coach vs. first class), and so forth. It is estimated that in the past 30 years "the overall yield of the world's airlines declined by 2.6 percent a year, from 19 cents per passenger kilometer to about 8 cents per passenger kilometer."[5]

Since airlines are now earning less for each passenger, it is essential that they increase their load factor, that is, fill as many seats as possible and above all increase their yield. Sophisticated yield management computer systems are indispensable for helping airline managers to accomplish this objective. They project and forecast demand for an airline's hundreds of flights. Also, these programs automatically adjust the pricing and seat availability within each price category so that a particular flight will have a high load factor *and* yield the most profit. As a result, these programs also facilitate the monitoring of the fare structure which changes constantly. It is now estimated that those fare changes can number as many as 120,000 per day.

It was well known within the airline industry that American Airlines had developed one of the best and most effective yield management systems. American estimated that by using this system it realized about $300 million in incremental revenues each year. Thus, this system clearly gave American a significant competitive advantage over other airlines, and as a consequence American had been loath to sell or to lease the system to any of its competitors despite some attractive offers. American regarded this as a valuable company asset and hence attempted to be as vigilant as possible about guarding the formulas and computer algorithms that formed the core of its yield management programs.

It could not prevent its employees, however, from bringing some of these key formulas to one of its major competitors, Northwest Airlines. Northwest and American compete aggressively on many of the same routes and the two airlines have long had an intense rivalry.

According to American Airlines, Northwest induced some of American's most capable managers to jump ship. American contends that when several of these managers left they took with them diskettes containing formulas and other data that they used in their work at American as yield managers. It is further alleged that experts at Northwest relied heaviiy on these formulas and programming techniques to construct a viable yield management system for Northwest. Indeed, shortly after this employee migration from American, Northwest did revise and rewrite its outmoded computerized demand-forecasting system. This system known as AIMS allegedly relies on the five basic techniques employed by the American Airlines System. For example, the AIMS forecasting formulas relied quite heavily on booking information from future flights. This technique was one of the fundamental features of American's pioneering system.

Moreover, according to the *Wall Street Journal*, one American employee took five related documents to Northwest when she joined the company in 1991. One was entitled "Seminar on Demand Forecasting," and it presumably was utilized to help two Northwest experts write their own paper entitled, "Demand Forecasting: Summary of Existing Techniques." This paper concluded with the suggestion that Northwest upgrade its system by "using ideas from the A1 approach." The *Journal* reports that "although the Northwest paper didn't mention American, it did make mysterious references to 'A1' techniques." In addition, one of the authors testified in a deposition that "A1" referred to American; he observed that "Northwest's operations director told him to remove all references to American, [and so] 'A1' was substituted."[6]

For its part, Northwest Airlines has steadfastly denied American's allegations. A spokesperson for Northwest did admit that data was taken from American but the company contends that none of this information was really "proprietary" or the intellectual property of American. Northwest maintains that the documents which were acquired were not marked "confidential" and that the "secrets" they supposedly contained were mathematical formulas that are common knowledge and part of the public domain. The Northwest spokesperson also pointed out that the company simply collected and used the "knowledge and experience" of the workers who transferred from American.[7] One should not expect that these employees would bracket or ignore the knowledge they gained from years of experience just because they moved to another job at a different organization. It is unclear whether or not these employees had signed formal nondisclosure agreements for American Airlines.

In preparation for the trial, Northwest decided to find out who developed or uncovered the original formulas used in American's yield management system. Northwest's lawyers recently managed to locate a mathematician who once worked for American Airlines developing algorithms for this system. He maintains that the formulas which he used were public knowledge. Northwest is hoping that this "may prove that American's secrets weren't so secret after all."[8]

Regardless of the court's decision, this incident vividly illustrates the vulnerability of critical data or "trade secrets" when employees transfer to other firms within the same industry. This dispute also implies some provocative questions about property rights and the methods utilized to acquire and assimilate valuable information into one's organization. Can companies such as American Airlines really differentiate between general knowledge and expertise and proprietary information resources that belong to the firm? Also, what is a fair procedure for drawing on the expertise of employees who have migrated from competitors while still preserving respect for the intellectual property rights of those competitors?

Case 3.3   E-Mail Policy at Johnson & Dresser

Jason Perry left the executive office suite of Johnson & Dresser shortly after 3:30 PM and returned to his own office on the floor below. He had made a rare visit to the company's Chief Operating Officer (COO) in order to discuss the company's questionable e-mail policies. The meeting had gone reasonably well and Perry was wondering about his next steps. As he checked over his notes and waited for his next appointment he reviewed the events leading up to this meeting.

Perry had joined Johnson & Dresser, a moderate sized retail brokerage firm, about seven years ago. He was hired as a senior systems analyst but within two years he was promoted to the position of Information Systems (IS) Director. He was relatively well known in the industry and aspired to work for one of the major brokerage houses on Wall Street.

A year or two after Perry's promotion he oversaw the purchase and installation of an advanced electronic mail system that would be used throughout the company. Although many were slow to make the transition to an on-line communication system, within a short time almost the entire organization became dependent on e-mail.

The new product had been introduced at several training sessions where electronic mail was frequently compared to regular postal mail and where the confidentiality of one's communications was certainly intimated. Users were not told that all of the company's e-mail messages were archived and available for future inspection at any time. Moreover, users were strongly encouraged to use e-mail for communicating with their fellow employees. The firm clearly saw this form of electronic communication as preferable to the use of phone calls or quick office visits.

Perry did not expect that Johnson & Dresser would make much use of the archived messages, but when an insider trading scandal broke at the firm it was decided to check the e-mail of several brokers who had been implicated. All of the brokers involved resigned quietly and nothing further came of the matter. The brokerage house had a strong reputation on Wall Street for integrity, and always acted quickly when there were problems of this nature. The company was keenly aware of the importance of an unimpeachable reputation in order to maintain its current clients and attract new business.

In the aftermath of this potential scandal senior managers at the firm decided to routinely inspect employee e-mail. This was to make sure that no one else was involved in the insider trading scandal and to ferret out any other compliance problems or suspicious behavior. As a result some managers regularly asked for a compilation of e-mail messages before an employee's annual review. In the vast majority of cases they found nothing incriminating or damaging in these messages and the individuals never knew that anyone had been checking their electronic mail messages.

But there were some exceptions to this. One incident that bothered Perry a great deal involved a young analyst named Lisa Curry. She was a 10 year veteran at the company responsible for following the utility industry. She worked closely with brokers providing reports and advice on various utility stocks. Like others at Johnson & Dresser, she was a little wary at first of using the e-mail system. Soon, however, she came to heavily rely on electronic mail for a large portion of her communications with her fellow employees. Indeed over time she felt much less inhibited when she composed e-mail messages. Thus, although she was usually pretty diffident around the company, she found herself engaging in some intense e-mail discussions with one of the few women brokers at the firm, Margaret Leonard. She often sent Leonard messages that complained about sexist corporate policies or messages that conveyed the latest company gossip. None of these messages were especially incendiary or provocative but they were fairly critical of Johnson & Dresser. Also, on occasion she criticized her boss for his lack of sensitivity on certain issues; she was perturbed, for example, at his condescending attitude toward some of the other women analysts.

Curry never dreamed that anyone would ever see these messages. Leonard assured her that she promptly erased the messages right after she read them. Curry let her know that she did the same with Leonard's messages. Both of them assumed that when they hit the delete key the messages would be permanently erased from the system. When Curry was due for her annual review her manager decided to check her e-mail communications and found the messages which she sent to Leonard. He was furious that she was so critical of Johnson & Dresser and also chastised her for wasting so much time sending "trivial, gossipy" e-mail messages. He told her that she did not seem to be a real team player and that maybe she should look around for a company that had a philosophy closer to her own. The end result was that despite her excellent track record as an analyst Curry received a small salary increment and a mixed performance review.

Curry was completely shocked by this. She could not believe that her messages were not considered completely confidential. She expected such confidentiality especially since she was not told anything to the contrary. Indeed, in her view she had been led to believe by the IS department that her privacy would be protected.

Among those she called in the company to complain about her treatment was Perry. She told him that his department's training sessions had duped people into believing that their e-mail messages would be confidential. She also pointed out that users should be told that messages would be archived and might be available for future scrutiny. Finally she stressed that she would be loath to continue using e-mail if everything she wrote would one day be scrutinized by her manager and "God knows who else at this paranoid company!"

Perry was sympathetic. He had received a few other complaints, and was beginning to question the company's fairness. He told Curry that he would look into the matter and try to craft a more open and responsible policy. He could make no promises since he knew that others in the company would need to be involved in any such policy emendations. Perry felt sorry for what happened to Curry, and he did not want to see other employees get blindsided in the same way that she did.

Consequently, Perry decided to ask for a meeting with the Chief Operating Officer in order to broach the issue of a revised e-mail policy that would better protect the privacy of Johnson & Dresser employees. During this session Perry argued that the company should probably at least take steps to inform employees that their messages were being stored and might be intercepted. However, while the COO did not disagree, he was worried about the ramifications of announcing to everyone that e-mail was being monitored. For one thing users might be less inclined to use e-mail, and the productivity gains realized by adopting this technology would be lost.

When asked about the legal implications of all this, Perry noted that according to current law the company was well within its rights to read an employee's e-mail. He wondered, however, if the company was living up to its high moral ideals by inspecting these messages. Isn't it a violation of confidentiality to read someone's postal letters? Why should electronic mail be any different? Should the company be proactive and declare electronic mail off limits except under unusual circumstances? Should it even continue to collect and store the large volume of e-mail messages generated by its many employees?

The COO was ambivalent about these suggestions, and he pointed out to Perry how the policy of archiving and inspecting e-mail helped the firm to uncover the insider trading scandal and take swift action. Maybe it needed to compromise employee privacy sometimes in order to protect the company against such abuses in the future. The more sources it could tap, the better it could discover problems and ensure that everyone at Johnson & Dresser was complying with the regulations of the Securities and Exchange Commission (SEC).

As the meeting came to a conclusion Perry was told to propose and defend a tenable and responsible e-mail policy that could be presented to the Executive Committee. He now began to think about what that policy should be. Clearly, there were many complex issues to untangle and key decisions to make.

Case 3.4   The Topper Travel Agency[9]

> Too many employers practice a credo of "In God we trust others we monitor."[10]

Katherine Davis arrived early for work on a bright, sunny Friday morning to read over a long report and a petition from disgruntled workers documenting her company's alleged violations of their right to privacy. As she pulled into the empty parking lot of the corporate headquarters of the Topper Travel Agency, Katherine realized that the situation was quite volatile and must be handled with extreme care. She had only recently taken the job as Topper's Human Resources Director and this was her first major crisis. The company's president, Robert Donaldson, wanted her recommendations on the matter by the close of the work day. She had already discussed the situation at some length with the company's attorneys but they were not very helpful. After that conversation yesterday afternoon Katherine realized that the key issues in this dispute were not legal ones; rather, they were difficult and nettling ethical questions that defied easy answers.

THE COMPANY

The Topper Travel Agency was founded in 1962 by Gerald H. Topper and his brother, William. The company began in a small suburban office with only four travel agents and a secretary for Gerald Topper. But within a few years the agency had already added three new offices to handle its growing business. Because of its reputation for superior service, the Topper Travel Agency continued to attract new business especially from corporate clients. As a result, the company expanded quite vigorously in the 1970s and 1980s and by 1992 its revenues had grown to almost $800 million.

Topper's corporate headquarters was located in a large mid-Western city. The company continued to specialize in providing fast, reliable, efficient service to many of this area's largest and most distinguished corporations. The agency's growing revenues were matched by high profits as well. Indeed, the company had shown a profit every year since its inception. However, recently because of the recession in the early 1990s and other forces there were pressures on its profit margins. During the past year Topper's profit margin declined from 6.7 to 5.5 percent. The company was forecasting little growth in revenues or profits for 1993 because of the slow economy and more competitive pressures in the mid-West market.

A MONITORING SYSTEM

In response to these revenue and profit projections company president Robert Donaldson decided to focus on improving efficiency and reducing costs in order to prevent any further erosion in profit margins. The company wanted to be certain that its travel agents were working at maximum efficiency so it decided to install a sophisticated monitoring system produced by Rockwell International. In selling its monitoring system to Topper, Rockwell salespeople emphasized the productivity gains that could be achieved by faithful use of this system. They pointed out that 1 second shaved off 1000 agents' calls each year could save the company $1,000,000 in labor costs.

The Rockwell monitoring system would be used primarily with the travel agents serving Topper's large corporate clients. The system measured the duration of each agent's phone conversation with a client. The company's standard for completing a simple airline reservation and processing the tickets was 108 seconds. Sometimes, of course, a client would make airline and hotel reservations along with arrangements to rent a car. In these cases Topper used a different time standard but the same procedure for calculating variances. Variances were duly noted and summarized in a monthly report which was sent to supervisors and the Human Resources Department. If an employee had a record of consistent negative variances he or she received a reprimand from the department supervisor. A meeting was also scheduled with the employee in order to uncover an explanation of the problem and work out a tenable solution. A representative from Human Resources might be asked by the department to attend a follow up meeting if the problems persisted. At that time the employee would be given a warning that he or she would be dismissed if the problem was not corrected within 3 months. So far only one employee had received a warning whereupon she resigned from the company.

The monitoring system had other features besides its capacity for measuring the duration of phone conversations. The system could also detect when an employee left his or her desk to go to the bathroom, take a break, and so forth. The duration of these "interruptions" was also measured, thereby allowing a supervisor to monitor whether the employee was spending too much time going to the bathroom (a 3-minute standard was set), or exceeding the time limits for a break (15 minutes) or lunch (45 minutes). The travel agent could not leave his or her desk for any other reason. Finally, the system enabled supervisors to listen in on employee phone calls. This would permit them to determine if employees were following the company's rigid instructions for booking reservations by phone. Once again, if employees failed to follow the correct protocol or received and made personal phone calls during company time, they could receive a reprimand and eventually a termination warning.

EMPLOYEE REACTION

Electronic monitoring was not well received by most employees at the travel agency. Most of them regarded this computer system as an unwarranted and odious intrusion of their privacy. Employees felt that it was especially unfair for the company to listen in on phone calls. Sometimes incoming or outgoing personal calls were a necessity particularly in cases of an emergency or family crisis. Since the company monitored *all* phone conversations, managers were often privy to private, intimate details about an employee's personal life. Travel agents also complained bitterly that incessant monitoring of their phone calls was causing considerable stress and anxiety. According to one agent:

> This monitoring system is nothing more than a digitized whip to make us work faster. It produces incredible stress and I'm afraid sometimes that I'm going to crack under the strain.

One other long time employee of Topper made the following observations:

> This new technology is terrible! It invades my privacy—this company knows everything I do even how long I spend in the bathroom. Also, if the clients knew that they were being listened to, they wouldn't like it

one bit. And they wouldn't be happy that we are under constant pressure to get the call over with and move on to the next customer. It makes it real difficult sometimes to be courteous and thorough with each of our clients.

Despite these complaints, Topper's management steadfastly defended its right to monitor its employees in order to ensure that they were performing up to company standards. Indeed, as Chairman William Topper observed at the most recent Board of Directors meeting, since installing this system productivity for the corporate travel agents had increased by almost 15 percent. If these productivity gains could be sustained, it would enable Topper to eliminate several positions by attrition and thereby cut costs and improve its profit margins. When Katherine Davis pointed out the high level of employee dissatisfaction with the new system, Topper's response was quite peremptory and defensive:

This company has a right and an obligation to shareholders to manage this workplace with the most effective tools available. No company can succeed unless it changes with new technology, and this means that the employees must learn to adapt. We need this technology to stay competitive, to maximize profits, and to deliver quality service to our customers with greater efficiency.

DAVIS'S DILEMMA

Shortly after this meeting, Davis received the petition from the travel agents outlining their complaints and requesting that the monitoring system be removed. About 75 percent of the agents had signed the petition. Since Davis was seen as a manager with some humane empathy and had been sympathetic to various agents who had complained in the past, many saw her as their only ally among upper level management. Thus, Davis had a difficult decision to make. Should she become an advocate for the employees and press the issue with Donaldson or defend management's right to monitor its employees and measure productivity?

Before deciding on a course of action she had to carefully weigh some "philosophical" and practical questions. For example, does the employee's right to privacy take precedence over the employer's right to monitor its employees, to check up on them and see how they're doing? Were the company's practices really unfair or did employees simply resist the pressures to become more productive? Furthermore, was there a way to strike a better balance between these competing interests? Also, was the monitoring too intense? Should it be modified in some way to lessen the anxiety of the travel agents?

Regardless of how these questions were answered, something would have to be done. Davis was apprehensive that the decline in morale would soon lead to other problems such as increased turnover or higher health insurance costs as a result of the enhanced stress level. These negative effects might in the long run offset the productivity gains achieved by the monitoring system.

As Davis arrived at her office on the fifth floor of the Topper building she began to prepare her report and recommendations to company president Donaldson. She recalled the words which concluded the agents' petition:

> We used to enjoy working at this agency and helping its customers. Now we find this workplace to be an uncomfortable and hostile environment. We don't object to management checking on us, but we do object to this electronic straitjacket that has brought so much stress and anxiety into our lives.

Thus, Davis had to sort through many conflicting feelings and different perspectives in preparing her final recommendations to Donaldson.

Case 3.5   The Franklin Trucking Corporation

The Franklin Trucking Corporation is a medium sized transportation company located on the outskirts of Chicago. It is a nonunion regional carrier founded in 1965 and has a distinguished history of providing service to many small and midsized manufacturing firms in the greater Chicago area. Franklin currently has a fleet of over 100 trucks that service these various routes. It has demonstrated remarkably stable earnings and revenue growth thanks to its conservative but highly competent management team.

As the company expanded and its operations became more complex, the management of its information resources became more challenging. As a result, in the late 1980s Franklin hired a data manager to manage its data bases and other computer systems. The data manager reported directly to the Vice President of Administration. In addition to his other duties this individual was responsible for handling the company's client/server network. The server functioned as the primary repository for a customer data base that was developed by programmers in the early 1980s. It effectively maintained basic information about Franklin's clients. It also supported accounts receivable and accounts payable applications to facilitate the company's cash flow. Thus, Franklin's executives were satisfied that the company had adequate control over its customer information.

However, other forms of information were not tracked and maintained as carefully. One serious problem area was the company's maintenance records for its sizable trucking fleet. Franklin did not track in any systematic way the mechanical problems or down time of its trucks.

When drivers reported problems, the truck in question was immediately taken off the road and fixed. Also, all trucks received regular preventative maintenance and were subject to frequent safety inspections by Franklin's mechanics. But, despite the company's diligence there was acknowledgment that little effort was made to identify trucks with a long history of problems and repairs. Several managers observed that if they could have access to repair data in a better organized and more structured format, they could get problem trucks off the road and do a better job of replacing trucks in the fleet with chronic difficulties.

For instance, several trucks with a history of leaks in their compressed air systems recently had brake problems while on overnight trips. Perhaps these potentially damaging incidents could have been avoided if someone was monitoring and assessing each truck's repair history. Once trucks with chronic problems were properly identified, the company could take steps to replace them. Allowing such trucks to remain in the fleet was not only dangerous but costly. Breakdowns and the need for repairs often caused appreciable delays in getting shipments to their destination, and this impaired the company's efforts to sustain a high level of customer service. Thus, the data base proposed by Franklin's Administrative Vice President would give the company's operations managers a much better handle on the overall reliability and safety of its expanding trucking fleet.

Within a week after this proposal, the company's data manager presented to the operations committee the specifications of this new data-base system. All were impressed with the technical features of the system and were convinced that a truck maintenance data base could solve a pressing need. Also, it was evident that the cost of developing the system would be fairly minimal, since the company already owned the software tools necessary to build it. Further, it was pointed out that the company's one programmer had adequate time to code this project and complete it within a few months. Hence, there seemed to be no compelling reasons for delaying it any longer.

But several committee members raised some troubling questions about the potential problems of developing such a system. It certainly made sense to collect this information more systematically so that it could be profitably shared *within* the company. But, they conjectured, wouldn't this information now be more readily available to outsiders as well? For example, would it have to be shared with a plaintiff in a lawsuit if there was an accident? Could the data-base records be subpoenaed in such a situation, and, if so, could they be used to incriminate Franklin? Clever attorneys could probably find many ways to manipulate this data. Even if the truck involved in the accident had a reasonably good safety record, the aggregate safety data revealed more clearly through this data-base system could be powerful ammunition for some attorneys.

Others considered what damage might occur if the data-base records were demanded by regulatory agencies or the firm's insurance company. Or, what if competitors got hold of this data thanks to an unscrupulous Franklin employee? The general problem, then, could be characterized as follows: If Franklin chose to collect and structure information on the reliability of its trucking fleet it would improve the.company's ability to develop maintenance procedures for the fleet; but it might also magnify the company's liability if this data was shared with certain external parties. Maybe it was more prudent to leave this data in its current, unstructured state, shrouded in ambiguity, an amalgam of unreliable paper records and the tacit knowledge of the employees responsible for maintaining the trucking fleet.

Clearly, the objections posed by these executives had some merit. Moreover, the discussion on this issue underscored the need for Franklin to develop a clear and coherent data policy on what types of information the company should collect and codify. Specifically, should Franklin gather this data about the maintenance records and reliability of its trucks and, if so, under what circumstances should they make this information available to outsiders? Would it be irresponsible *not* to construct this maintenance data base given the obvious need and the opportunity? Wouldn't this data base help to improve the fleet's safety record and doesn't Franklin have an obligation to optimize the safety of its fleet?

Franklin's managers needed to make a specific decision about this project. It would also be necessary to think through a data policy that addressed these questions of data collection and data sharing before determining how to proceed.

NOTES

1. Pamela Samuelson, "Is Information Property?" *Communications of the ACM,* March 1991, p. 16.

2. A "path" is a sequence of activities that leads from the beginning to the end of a project; the "critical path" is the longest path and any delays on this path will delay the entire project.
3. Howard Banks, "Recovery," *Forbes,* March 27, 1995, p. 79.
4. "A Survey of the Airline Industry," supplement to *The Economist,* June 12, 1993, p. 4.
5. Ibid.
6. William Carley, "Did Northwest Steal American's Systems? The Court Will Decide," *The Wall Street Journal,* July 7, 1994, p. A8. Reprinted by permission of *The Wall Street Journal,* © 1994 Dow-Jones & Company, Inc. All rights reserved worldwide.
7. Ibid.
8. Ibid.
9. This case originally appeared in *Ethical Aspects of Information Technology.* Englewood Cliffs, NJ: Prentice Hall, 1995.
10. Marlene Piturro, "Electronic Monitoring," *Information Center,* July 1990, p. 31.

4

Information Access

Chapter 4 considers the pivotal question of accessibility to information. Once organizations have determined the type and scope of the data that they will collect and synthesize, they must make decisions about who can access that information. Also, in some situations they must determine who should profit from the subsequent uses of this information in future applications. For example, should personal information provided to vendors or government agencies be considered proprietary, off limits for subsequent utilizations? Or can this information be sold or rented to others for marketing or other commercial purposes without permission?

Clearly, a key consideration in resolving these matters is respect for privacy rights. Almost everyone recognizes the importance of the right to privacy but there is less consensus on its scope and exact meaning in the information age. Nonetheless Alan Westin offers a cogent definition of privacy as "the claim of individuals, groups, or institutions to determine for themselves when, how, and to what extent information about them is communicated to others."[1] Privacy is also often characterized as the right of the individual to be left alone.

An individual's right to privacy is protected by law, specifically by the First, Fourth, Ninth, and Fourteenth Amendments. Only the Fourteenth Amendment provides some basis for protecting an individual's "informational privacy." There are also numerous laws to protect privacy such as the Fair Credit Reporting Act (FCRA) of 1971 and the 1974 Privacy Act. The FCRA sets standards for the legitimate use of credit reports and specifies a consumer's rights in challenging those reports.

Moreover, according to some philosophers, these legal rights are grounded in a *natural right* to privacy. While certain proponents of this view argue that privacy is a fundamental, irreducible right, others have maintained that privacy is not a separate right but is derived from other rights such as the right of freedom or rights over our property. We can certainly appreciate the intimate connection between privacy and freedom and the argument that some degree of privacy is a necessary condition of freedom. When I watch someone or monitor their activities I change the context of their actions and perhaps even their behavior, since many people become more self-conscious and inhibited under these circumstances. Surveillance or monitoring, then, becomes an encumbrance which restricts one's mobility and basic human freedom. The right to privacy, of course, must be a *prima facie* one since under certain circumstances legal authorities may have the need to violate the right to privacy for the sake of the common good of protecting the welfare of citizens. Privacy, therefore, is not an absolute right but must be balanced against other rights and interests.

The erosion of privacy has been an important issue for consumer advocates. They are concerned about the proliferation of marketing data bases built on the personal information of consumers and the free exchange of this information with other vendors and information brokers. This information may be collected from various sources such as point-of-sale scanning devices, data left behind after a credit card purchase, and so forth. Some advocates claim that consumers retain some property rights in the personal information that they provide to vendors and hence ought to be compensated accordingly. This statement by Anne Branscomb is typical of those who propound this reasonable, albeit controversial, point of view.

> Our names and addresses and personal transactions are valuable information assets worthy of recognition that we have property rights in them. Unless we assert those rights we will lose them. If such information has economic value, we should receive something of value in return for its use by others.[2]

Corporations, of course, would argue that they have exclusive property rights in the information that they collect, but this assessment is far from self-evident.

All of the cases in this chapter which focus on accessibility concern to some degree this critical issue of privacy. The first case study, *Micromarketing and Customer Information Systems,* describes the widespread use of consumer information systems and examines the ethical implications of using the increasingly popular technique of micromarketing which relies heavily on the detailed information in those systems. Do these systems jeopardize the privacy rights of consumers? If so, can we articulate guidelines for how consumer information systems can be used more responsibly?

The next case, *The Lotus "MarketPlace: Households" Product Controversy,* continues with various themes that emerge in the micromarketing case. This data base was designed to enable small businesses to purchase targeted mailing lists for direct mail campaigns. The data was derived from the credit files of Equifax, and was made available on a compact disk. This case examines the ethical and privacy issues triggered by the introduction of this new species of data base products. Should the data in credit files be made so readily accessible? What gives this question added urgency is that this product represents a movement in the direction of on-line access to personal data. There were privacy safeguards but their adequacy was a bone of contention. Thus, this is a rich case study that offers a unique perspective on how companies like Lotus and Equifax should manage and control accessibility to personal data.

While these two cases primarily concern external information sharing, the next case, *Southern Midland Bank: A Case for the Data Policy Committee,* focuses on the sharing of information *within* an organization. In this difficult situation a bank must decide which departments (if any) should have access to depositor information. The challenge is to craft a comprehensive data policy that does not compromise the bank's business opportunities while respecting the depositor's right to a meaningful level of privacy.

The next case study, entitled *United Industries International, Inc.,* shifts the axis of discussion to the employee and his or her medical or "lifestyle" data. To what extent can an employer have access to this information in order to make decisions about disability payments or even employment related matters? Is there a need for a Chinese wall between the employee's department and a company's "wellness center" that stores confidential medical and lifestyle information?

The focus changes yet again for the final case, *Note on Data Protection in Sweden,* which dwells on how the country of Sweden has dealt with some of these challenges. This case study explicitly considers the reassessment of Sweden's Data Act, the world's first national data protection legislation. This case also raises many public policy issues such as whether or not there is a need for comparable data protection legislation in the United States.

Case 4.1   Micromarketing and Customer Information Systems

THE CONSUMER INFORMATION SYSTEM

One of the most effective marketing techniques to be developed in recent years is a form of target marketing known as *micromarketing*. Micromarketing relies on specific information that will help vendors to identify who is most likely to want or need their goods or services. In recent years companies have been slowly migrating from mass media advertising campaigns to more direct marketing techniques that contact targeted groups through more personalized advertising, including direct mail and telemarketing.

There are several reasons for this shift. To begin with, most companies regard conventional advertising as expensive and ineffective. This is because of the development of many new media outlets which has fragmented the audience. The problem of relying on traditional mass marketing approaches is also exacerbated by the proliferation of new products and product variations. According to the *Economist,* in 1994 "20,076 new consumer goods appeared on the shelves of America's supermarkets and drug stores," representing a 14.3 percent increase over 1993.[3] Consequently, advertisers must struggle to make their products visible in this crowded and noisy marketplace. The alternative is a more targeted and selective approach that pitches products to those consumers who are most likely to be interested in them.

In order to accomplish this task, manufacturers and retailers have been developing comprehensive and detailed customer information systems. In recent years they have invested heavily in these systems in order to collect basic personal data along with demographic and lifestyle information about as many consumers as possible. Once this data is assembled, companies can use it to market directly to their customer base; it can also be used to ascertain potential market segments. The ultimate goal is to "integrate this mass of information into a concrete understanding of what products different customers want and what they're willing to pay."[4] An extensive and detailed customer information system will thereby enable companies to tailor their marketing messages to many different consumer groups or segments. They can engage in classic niche marketing despite the large scale of their operations or their substantial customer base.

American Express is one of many companies that uses its customer data base to target special offers to carefully differentiated groups of cardholders. These offers might include airline tickets, car rental deals, clothing specials, or restaurant discounts. For instance, it may send a special promotion to customers who tend to dine out frequently (as determined by their credit card transactions) who live in the vicinity of a new restaurant. The company credits these "data-base techniques" with helping it generate profits of $1.4 billion in 1994.

Another company that has had great success with this technique is Capital One, a credit card provider with five million accounts and $9.6 billion in credit card transactions in 1994. Its customer information system is composed of millions of customer records that have been established from years of credit card transactions. Capital One continuously mines this data in order to gain insights about its customers and to test market new credit card or loan offers to different segments of its customer base. Also, it can offer these targeted groups of customers a wide variety of options. According to *Computerworld*, "the firm offers secured and unsecured cards, student cards, joint account cards, and affinity cards, each with various combinations of interest rates, fees, terms, and conditions."[5] Thus, through data mining Capital One can target a certain group of customers or potential customers and present to them a customized product offer, such as a low interest student credit card with special repayment terms.

The primary advantage of this "data-base marketing" phenomenon is clear enough: companies can deal with customers or prospects as distinct groups of individuals rather than as an undifferentiated mass. Also, marketers can use these systems as a valuable consumer feedback mechanism and as a means of collecting empirical data about the success (or failure) of their products. They can learn a great deal about possibilities for new products, the efficacy of various promotion techniques and pricing schemes, and so forth.

INFORMATION SOURCES

Unfortunately, the use of these techniques is not risk-free. Data-base marketing has generated controversy in some circles because of its potential threat to consumer privacy. To a certain extent, this controversy stems from the *sources* of consumer information used to construct a customer information system. In some cases, data may come from public records such as birth certificates, census records, and property records. Usually it comes from various private commercial transactions. Those transactions might include credit card purchases, mail order purchases, or magazine subscriptions.

Let us consider the first source of data, which is generally *external* to the corporation and often consists of various public records. During the past decade governments at the state and local levels have been computerizing much of their data and then selling it to information brokers. As a result, these brokers provide widespread access to computerized government records such as county records, bankruptcy records, lawsuits, real estate records, and so forth. For instance, a company know as Metromail acquires and resells detailed real estate records. These records include data regarding the sale and purchase of property along with consumer mortgage information. The records might be purchased by organizations which intend to target new home owners with certain products or services. Car registration and license information is another major source of marketing data that can also be utilized to reach certain groups of consumers. The Department of Motor Vehicles (DMV) in many states routinely sells drivers' information for a fee. This information usually includes a driver's height and weight along with other basic data elements such as name, address, age, vision, social security number, and the make and model of the driver's car. This data is sold to data brokers such as Dateq which in turn sell it to other companies for their targeted marketing campaigns.

Thus, one method of building up or supplementing an extensive customer information system is the purchase of these consumer records garnered from diverse public sources.

The second source of data for these systems is the information generated by various commercial transactions such as telephone or mail orders, memberships, warranty cards, or even rebate coupons. This data too can serve as the building blocks for richly detailed customer records. According to the *New York Times,* "Virtually every time a person orders from a catalogue, makes a donation, or joins an organization, that person's name becomes part of a list that can be rented or sold. Marketers can choose among tens of thousands of lists collected by nearly 1000 companies acting as brokers and compilers."[6]

Most companies find that they have a plethora of valuable information about their own customers, and consequently they do not purchase data from outside sources such as information brokers. However, this decision to rely primarily on *internal* records depends upon the objectives a company has for its customer information system. The main objective may be to keep existing customers by developing stronger relationships with them. In highly competitive markets "pushing up the 'lifetime value' of the customers you already have is just as useful as bringing in new ones."[7] On the other hand, the objective may be to win many new customers. Obviously, if a company has this goal in mind it will be necessary to rely on outside sources of information about prospective customers.

It is also possible to run certain promotions for the explicit purpose of generating information for a marketing data base. Some companies, for instance, have given away free samples of their products to customers who call a certain 800 number. When consumers call in with their requests they are asked a few questions about product preferences and a list is usually compiled of their answers along with their name, address, and telephone number. This list can be used by the vendor for future promotions or it can be sold to other companies which are selling similar products.

Johnson & Johnson implemented this technique to help sell Serenity pads, a product for women who have a problem with incontinence. Interested customers could call an 800 number or write for a free sample. Johnson & Johnson, however, "did not tell the 4.4 million people who responded that it was compiling a list of their names, addresses and telephone numbers."[8] The company used a list broker to try to rent this list to other companies selling "adult health products," but backed off because of pressure from a Congressional subcommittee investigating such dealings. Johnson & Johnson still runs this promotion and is continually adding to its list.

PRIVACY CONCERNS

While many companies attest to the efficacy of data-base marketing methods, there are some doubts and concerns about whether or not some or all of these practices violate a consumer's right to privacy. Recent polls reveal that consumers are profoundly concerned about this issue. For example, in a 1993 Louis Harris poll 67 percent of the consumers surveyed indicated that the confidentiality of their credit card transactions was "very important."[9]

The primary problem from the consumer's point of view is an increase in unsolicited offers usually through junk mail. The more lists one is on, the more frequently one will receive promotional material in the mail or receive phone calls pushing certain products or deals. For example, "a single magazine subscription . . . could lead to unsolicited mail from 25 companies twice a year."[10] But are there additional adverse consequences for consumers? For example, could these lists and data bases be used for nonmarketing or even insidious purposes? Some consumer advocates envision the use of this data as a basis for screening potential customers. They worry that perhaps insurance companies will begin buying certain lists to screen clients who participate in dangerous leisure activities or have other habits that make them a bad risk.

The key question revolves around determining when access to customer information is fair and proper and when it is clearly inappropriate. If customers have voluntarily offered information for a specified purpose, for example, inclusion in a customer information system, and they are informed about how that information will be used, then there is probably no problem. Legitimate questions arise, however, when information is gathered and exchanged without the customer's knowledge or consent. Further, is it acceptable that public sources of information be so readily accessible as the building blocks of marketing data bases? Or should companies rely exclusively on internal, proprietary sources of data for constructing and enhancing these systems? Also, should the data collector obtain permission from consumers before selling or renting their records to other vendors?

Customer information systems facilitate target marketing which can be a powerful tool for companies seeking to make their marketing efforts more cost effective. These questions about privacy, however, must be carefully considered in order to ensure that customer information is handled in a responsible and prudent fashion.

Case 4.2   The Lotus "MarketPlace: Households" Product Controversy[11]

INTRODUCTION

When the details of the Lotus MarketPlace product were made public in April 1990, no one at the well-known Cambridge computer company could have anticipated the vehement protests that were to come. Consumers and computer users beseiged the company with letters and electronic mail messages, claiming that MarketPlace: Households would be an irresponsible intrusion into their lives and a violation of their personal privacy.

Lotus was working in conjunction with Equifax Inc., one of the three major credit bureau companies in the U.S. The proposed software package would enable small businesses and other organizations with limited resources to purchase targeted mailing lists. These lists could be used to solicit new customers through direct mail marketing campaigns. But in the face of the controversy and firestorm of protest generated by this announcement, both companies had to decide whether there was a future for this innovative product.

LOTUS DEVELOPMENT CORP.

Lotus Development Corp. was founded in 1981 by computer wizard and entrepreneur, Mitch Kapor. Its objective was to produce business productivity software for personal computers. In 1983, the company introduced its most popular and successful product, *Lotus 1-2-3*, a spreadsheet software package. Despite many competitive products such as Microsoft's *Excel*, *Lotus 1-2-3* dominated spreadsheet products since its first appearance in the PC software market. In 1991 its share of the PC spreadsheet market was still 60%. Lotus also marketed business graphics and data-base products. It combined its three major application packages, graphics, data base, and spreadsheet in another popular product known as *Symphony*. The company's other major businesses included CD-ROM products, financial information products for personal computers, and electronic mail packages for local area networks.

Lotus was one of the fastest growing PC software companies during the decade of the 1980s. Its five year (1986–1990) compound average growth rate in revenues was 28.8%. In 1991 Lotus reported healthy net earnings of $43.1 million. Its revenues for the same year were $828.9 million, a 19.7% increase over 1990.[12] But despite its financial success in 1991, Lotus stumbled in its introduction of *Lotus 1-2-3* for Windows, Microsoft's popular new operating system for the IBM PC and compatible systems. In addition, as the market for spreadsheets became increasingly saturated, Lotus aggressively sought to market new products such as "Marketplace: Households" in an effort to sustain its high growth rate and propel it into the next generation of software products.

Lotus had no experience in marketing such information-based products or developing targeted mailing lists. Hence its role in this collaborative effort was to provide its considerable technical expertise in software development.

EQUIFAX

Equifax, a billion dollar credit bureau, was founded in 1899 in Atlanta, Georgia. It was first known as the Retail Credit Company. Equifax grew quickly in the 1980s thanks in large part to the acquisition of many smaller, regional credit bureaus. Equifax was one of the "big three" credit bureaus which dominated this industry along with TRW and Trans Union. During the 1980s its annual return to investors had averaged an impressive 31%.[13] In 1990 Equifax reported profits of $63.9 million on total revenue of $1.08 billion. (This was up sharply from net income of $35.6 million on revenues of $840 million in 1989.)

Equifax collected data on consumers from a variety of sources including a consumer's credit history acquired from banks, employment history, and payment records from credit grantors. It also received data from the U.S. census bureau and periodically purchased drivers' license data from the Department of Motor Vehicles in most states. It also purchased data from other direct mail companies on automobile and appliance purchases along with data about those making mail order purchases. The company tracked this information on approximately 150 million individuals. Some of this information was compiled into a credit report that was sold to banks, retail stores, or other organizations granting credit. The sale of such credit reports was the main source of revenue for Equifax and the other players in this mature industry. The more marketing-oriented data was used for other purposes such as its mailing list business.

A controversial practice of Equifax, TRW, and Trans Union was their participation in the mailing list business. At one time all three of these companies sold names, addresses, and limited financial data to direct mail organizations or directly to companies initiating targeted direct mail campaigns. In 1990 the mailing list business for Equifax totaled about $11 million. This practice had been heavily criticized as a violation of personal privacy. The direct mail business fell under a gray area of the Fair Credit Reporting Act. According to this law, credit data can only be sold for "legitimate" business purposes. But the word "legitimate" is obviously ambiguous, and according to the credit bureau industry, should not have precluded the sale of this data to junk-mailers. Thanks to considerable public pressure all three credit bureaus have recently abandoned this business.

Equifax played a pivotal role in the development of this joint product with Lotus, since it was the primary source of information on 80 million U.S. households. The company also used its extensive files on American consumers to compile the demographic and life-style information that was to become an essential component of the "MarketPlace: Households" data base.

THE PRODUCT

In April 1990, Lotus and Equifax announced the impending introduction of the new Lotus MarketPlace product at the beginning of 1991. This CD-ROM (compact disk—read only memory) data-base product would have two main components: "MarketPlace: Households" and MarketPlace: Business. The MarketPlace: Households product consisted of the names, addresses, gender, age, marital status, shopping habits for over 100 products (including luxury cars, vacations, gourmet foods), and estimated income levels, for 80 million households. The product also included 50 psychographic categories ranging from "accumulated wealth" to "inner city singles." Both companies, however, had reservations about using these psychographic categories, and so this data field was excluded from the final product specification. All of the actual data came from Equifax's voluminous credit files.

MarketPlace was "aimed at small and mid-size businesses that want to do inexpensive, targeted direct mail marketing."[14] Lotus sought to take advantage of CD-ROM's substantial storage capability and thereby bring the direct mail marketing industry to the world of personal computers and desktops.

The MarketPlace: Households product would enable small businesses and non-profit organizations to purchase targeted mailing lists for a direct mail marketing campaign. If used correctly this product would help these organizations to identify prospective customers (or donors) in a cost effective and efficient manner.

The minimum list size was 5,000 names. The categories of information listed above could be used for the basis of selecting the names. Thus, for example, a small vendor such as a luxury car dealer might want to do a localized targeted mailing to consumers with incomes greater than $60,000. The dealer might utilize the following criteria to generate the list: all the individuals in Fairfield County (Connecticut) who are over 40 years old, who have an income in excess of $60,000, and who have a propensity to purchase expensive cars and other luxury items. Using these criteria a list of names and addresses would be generated, and this list in CD-ROM format would be the permanent property of the dealer. In other words, the dealer would have unlimited use of these names. This differs from other consumer data-base mailing list products which were rented to vendors for one-time use. The price of "MarketPlace: Households" was $695 for the program and the first 5,000 names, and $400 for each additional 5,000 names.

PRIVACY CONCERNS

Both Lotus and Equifax steadfastly maintained that they had addressed consumers' concerns about privacy. Hence they did not include on the disks available to vendors telephone numbers or personal financial data. They also made it impossible to query an individual name. One could not type in "Peter Brown" and expect to get his age, income level, and purchasing habits. Of course, if Brown is part of the targeted group selected according to broader criteria, then one would have this information. Lotus also promised that the product would not fall into the wrong hands, since it would be sold only to legitimate businesses. Businesses intending to purchase the product would be carefully screened in order to ensure that only respectable companies had access to this product. As a result, companies selling speculative investments or peddling pornography would not be allowed to subscribe to MarketPlace: Households. Also, the product would not be sold to individuals. Furthermore, a carefully worded contract would limit the product's use by the purchaser and prohibit that company from reselling the names to another vendor. Finally, consumers would be given an opportunity to have their names excluded from this data base by informing either company or the Direct Marketing Association (DMA). Both companies felt confident that these safeguards would protect confidential information about a consumer and hence not violate his or her privacy.

Critics of "MarketPlace," however, were not satisfied by the announcement of these safeguards. If the product were widely disseminated how could Lotus *really* control how it was used. Could the company monitor and enforce the contract prohibiting the resale of the data? There were also concerns that consumers would not be able to delete their names from the data base or make corrections in a timely manner. After all, by the time such corrections or deletions were implemented, inaccurate versions of the data base would already be on the market.

Some of the criticism became quite heated as thousands of individuals wrote strong letters of protest to Lotus' corporate headquarters in Cambridge. Some of the letters were transmitted electronically and copied on hundreds of networks; this further fueled the controversy and provoked others to join in the protest.

In response to these protests Lotus agreed to delete immediately the names of anyone who contacted the company. In a short period of time it received over 30,000 such requests. However, this did not silence Lotus' critics who seemed to be growing more militant as the controversy intensified. In addition, organizations such as Computer Professionals for Social Responsibility added their voice to the chorus of protests; they were especially concerned that there would be no way to guarantee that everyone in the data base had freely consented.

Finally Lotus and Equifax capitulated to these criticisms and reluctantly agreed to cancel the product. It was reported that Equifax and Lotus made this decision in the interests of consumer privacy and economics; both companies feared that a consumer backlash would affect their core businesses. The MarketPlace: Business software package, offering marketing information on seven million American businesses, was not cancelled. Under a licensing agreement with Lotus this product is being sold by a start-up company, the MarketPlace Information Corporation in Cambridge.

POSTSCRIPT

Despite the abrupt cancellation of MarketPlace: Households, some of the product's supporters were surprised and confused by the criticism and hostility which it generated. They pointed out that the product could be a significant benefit to small and mid-size businesses which need to use targeted direct mail campaigns to find new customers and increase revenues. It should be noted that the same information is purchased by large companies for higher fees for the purpose of DBM (Data Base Marketing) campaigns. MarketPlace made the process of purchasing data less expensive for small businesses, and hence gave them an opportunity to do their own DBM campaigns. Further, Lotus and Equifax did take great pains to address the privacy concerns. Thus, some in the industry felt that this was a valuable product with adequate protection against breaches of confidentiality.

An executive at a well-known consulting firm made the following observation:

> I'm quite sure that "MarketPlace: Households" or a similar version of that product is not dead yet; it has only been postponed. Lotus or some other company will bring it back in some form or another. There is already a vast amount of this information for sale, and the data available in MarketPlace is not that different from what is already available in other electronic data bases of consumer information. With some minor changes and additional safeguards, this product could be quite successful.

Only time will tell if he is correct.

Case 4.3   Southern Midland Bank: A Case for the Data-Policy Committee

January 18, 1996

Memorandum

To: Data-Policy Committee Members
From: Arthur F. Beaton
           Chairman
Re: Agenda for January 22nd Meeting

I have called a special meeting of the Committee in order to consider a controversial proposal for a request for customer deposit data for the Investor Services Division. The Committee must consider who gets access to the main customer data base and especially to its deposit information. Such data has usually been shared freely with several other departments in the bank, specifically those that market other products or services. But, as you may know, Mr Wilson has asked us to reexamine this policy and to make a recommendation on the request of the Investor Services Division. We should attempt to settle this troublesome matter once and for all at our next meeting.

Please be prepared to propose and defend an appropriate policy. The document containing details of the Investor Services request is enclosed.

cc: D. Wilson
enclosures
afb/mp

Mary Benedict was certainly familiar with the request described in Mr. Beaton's succinct memo. She was the vice president of Customer Relations and had recently fielded several complaints from some of the bank's biggest depositors. They were complaining about receiving excessive promotional material from the bank about investment opportunities. She also served on the bank's new data policy committee and sought to conscientiously represent the best interests of the bank's customers. She had always felt strongly that there should be strict limits on the sharing of customer deposit information, but she was rethinking this position in preparation for the meeting.

SOUTHERN MIDLAND BANK

Southern Midland Bank (SMB) was a major commercial bank located in a large southeastern city. It was established in 1887 by a prominent southern family. Through a series of recent takeovers the bank had expanded to $5 billion in deposits. Its commercial loan portfolio in 1995 was about $2.1 billion. Southern Midland had over 100 branches located throughout the city and its environs. It had experienced many years of consistent growth in both profits and revenues.

Southern Midland was considered a progressive institution within its community. It often took the lead in philanthropic activities and had an aggressive affirmative action policy. Its chairman and CEO, Douglas Wilson, was a major figure and recognized leader in the community. The bank was quite conscious of its reputation and it was always circumspect to make sure that its image was not tarnished by improper actions.

In 1995 Wilson decided that many of the bank's most controversial and difficult decisions were being made in the area of information policy. Some employees, for example, were upset at some of the bank's surveillance policies which they considered to be intrusive. In light of such employee resentment, the policy was modified. Also, Southern Midland had a lucrative credit card business and was re-examining its long standing practice of selling the names and addresses of its credit card customers to direct mailers for various marketing solicitations. This was a common practice among other banks and for the time being Wilson decided to let it continue despite his reservations.

However, he formed the data policy committee to scrutinize these issues and to consider other policies about the accessibility or dissemination of the information in the bank's vast data-base repository. The committee was composed of several vice presidents and other representatives from various departments such as marketing and information technology. It included the bank's Management Information Systems (MIS) director who was the primary custodian of information in the bank's centralized data bases. Its chairperson was the vice president of the Credit Department, Arthur Beaton.

THE INVESTOR SERVICES DIVISION

During the early 1990s Southern Midland established a subsidiary known as SMB Investor Services, Inc. It employed brokers and financial advisors and functioned much like an investment house. It offered a broad array of no-load mutual funds investing in stocks, bonds, and money market instruments. These funds included the SMB Treasury Money Market Fund, the SMB Income Fund, the SMB Short-Term Income Fund, and so forth. Clients could also buy and sell stocks or bonds through their SMB brokers or "counselors." Customers of the bank who maintained a minimum deposit of $10,000 in their checking or savings account received a discount on these purchases.

Financial counselors helped their customers to develop a feasible investment plan. They often recommended appropriate funds to investors to help meet the income and long-term growth needs consistent with their financial plan. They solicited business from SMB's customers through a number of channels. Most major branches set up offices for a financial counselor; this was a great source of walk-in business. Promotional flyers and ads were also available in these branches. In addition, the company sent out mailings to all of the bank's customers, including depositors, credit card holders, and those with mortgages or installment loans. This too generated considerable investment business.

In late 1994 Investor Services marketing executives decided to try more creative ways of soliciting the bank's existing customers for new business. They decided to target the bank's largest depositors with a series of promotional mailings describing the value of investing in mutual funds. The head of the Investor Services marketing department approached the central MIS department which controlled access to the main customer data base and requested a list of depositors with combined deposits of over $25,000. The MIS director initially questioned the legitimacy of the request, but after some discussion agreed to generate the mailing list sorted by deposit size for the Investor Services division.

In general, Southern Midland looked favorably on the internal sharing of information across departments and product groups. The bank's implicit policy was that any group that had a justifiable business need for the information should be given access to it. Thus, there was really no basis for turning down the request.

The results of the mailing were impressive, and as a result Investor Services decided to attempt a more aggressive strategy. Shortly after these mailings were concluded they requested a list of depositors with certificates of deposit of $10,000 or more that matured within the next four weeks. The list would eliminate those depositors who indicated their intention of renewing or rolling over their CDs. The plan was to use the list as the basis for an ambitious telemarketing campaign. Financial counselors would call the depositors in their respective areas and pitch various mutual funds or promote one of their new bond offerings.

This time the MIS Director was extremely reluctant to comply with this request and he referred it to the senior vice president for Operations. He was responsible for all the branch operations and would have to contend with any backlash from the marketing campaign. He too had some reservations and eventually the proposal was sent to Wilson's office for a final resolution. After some consultation with the parties involved Wilson decided that the data policy committee should expeditiously make a recommendation about this unprecedented request for targeted depositor information.

CUSTOMER BACKLASH

Some of Midland's customers were already resentful that they were being "bombarded" with mail about investment opportunities and mutual funds. These complaints were referred to the Customer Relations Department, headed by Benedict. She listened sympathetically to the several vocal customers but consistently defended the bank's policy. She offered customers an opportunity to opt out of future mailings and directed the MIS department to make a provision for this option when they supplied customer data to other product groups. When Benedict learned of the new proposal she approached Wilson about the matter. She told him that customers were already complaining and that a telemarketing campaign directed at some of the bank's best customers could lead to considerable backlash. He was noncommital, however, and told her that the committee needed to really debate the matter and work out a tenable solution that "everyone could live with."

Benedict estimated that about 75 customers complained about the frequent promotions, deciding to opt out of future mailings. Although these customers were annoyed at the mailings, they had not alleged that there was any breach of confidentiality. Among the executives of the bank there was considerable division of opinion about the appropriateness of these marketing campaigns of the Investor Services Division. Clearly, the division was a huge success and a growing profit center, and much of its success could be attributed to its ability to market its products effectively to the bank's prosperous customer base. As a consequence, most of Benedict's colleagues wanted to continue the data sharing practices, though some argued that modifications and safeguards would need to be introduced. But Benedict was quite apprehensive about the long-term effects on customer relations.

On the eve of the January meeting Benedict was reconsidering her stand on the issue. She still felt skeptical about the more frequent use of customer data by the Investor Services Division, but she liked a culture that encouraged cooperation and information sharing. On the other hand, she did not want to encourage policies that exploited the trust of SMB's customers. As she prepared for this important meeting she reflected on the most viable options, considering them as objectively as possible. Also, she thought about the pressing need for this committee to develop some coherent management principles that would help SMB's evolving information culture.

Case 4.4   United Industries International, Inc.

Dave Gibson was quite distraught as he left a long and embittered meeting with the company's union representatives. Salary negotiations were going poorly and on top of this several vocal individuals accused the company of consistently violating employee privacy. They charged that United's new "wellness program" was a pretext for gathering sensitive medical data about employees which could be used against them in certain contexts. Gibson answered the allegations with some indignation, pointing out that this was an expensive program and that United had the best interests of its employees in mind. There were no ulterior motives as they had suggested. At issue was the access to information supplied by employees at the Wellness Centers. As the meeting ended Gibson agreed to review corporate's plans for its popular wellness programs and discuss them at the next round of negotiations.

UNITED INDUSTRIES INTERNATIONAL

United Industries International (UII) manufactured a plethora of industrial products such as compressors, air conditioners, electrical equipment, and transportation equipment. United entered many of these businesses by means of acquisitions during the 1970s and 1980s. By 1995 UII had become a large multinational organization and was listed among the 500 largest industrial corporations in the United States. Its revenues in 1995 were close to $3 billion with net earnings of $165 million. Despite steady but unspectacular sales growth, profit margins had not improved during the last 3 to 4 years.

Dave Gibson was president of the Air Conditioning Division (ACD) located in a small city in Michigan. This division manufactured commercial air conditioning equipment for buildings such as small factories, schools, office buildings, and so on. It employed close to 2000 individuals who worked two shifts. Gibson had been the president and chief operating officer here for the past 6 years. During this time the ACD's contribution to corporate profits had improved steadily because of his cost cutting and organizational skills. Gibson was considered one of UII's top division managers.

Also, when Gibson arrived he replaced many of the ACD's middle managers whose management "style" had led to serious morale problems. As a result worker morale improved dramatically and Gibson became quite popular with the workforce. Moreover, he prided himself on being a hands-on manager who spent much time on the factory floor getting feedback from his workers.

However, the congenial atmosphere at ACD appeared to be changing. Business had slowed a bit in 1995 and orders for the first half of 1996 were off by 12 percent. Hence, corporate headquarters had told Gibson to hold the line with salary increases for the next union contract. For the first time in many years there was palpable friction between management and the union laborers.

THE WELLNESS CENTER

In 1991 Gibson decided to authorize the opening of a Wellness Center for his division with the blessing of corporate headquarters. United was encouraging all of its divisions to open such centers. The company payed about $5000 a year for an employee's health insurance and hoped that by improving the lifestyles and health habits of its employees it could begin to control its spiraling health care costs. The Wellness Center included a small state-of-the-art gym along with a medical clinic and a health counseling office. A wellness program was also established in conjunction with the center. This program provided counseling and mini-courses on hygiene and other health-related issues. The courses and workshops provided by the center were usually popular and well attended.

As an incentive for joining the Center qualified employees would receive a 5 percent discount from their health insurance co-payment. In order to become a member it was necessary to fill out an extensive Health Appraisal form. The form asked many personal questions about the employees' lifestyle and health habits. For example, did they have marital problems, how much did they drink or smoke, what were the sources of stress and anxiety in their lives, did they suffer from sexual difficulties, what was their medical history, did they ever suffer from depression or other mental disorders, and so on. This information was utilized by the center to create its extensive member data base, which was chock full of this sensitive information about employees' behavior patterns, habits, and medical history. Thus, for example, information in this electronic file might include the fact that a particular worker had scarlet fever at age 7, has 20/200 eyesight, smokes 15 cigarettes a day, gets little exercise, drinks moderately, and currently lives in a stressful home environment.

By 1994 about 60 percent of ACD employees took advantage of the program and provided this information. Most of them were happy to get the 5 percent discount and were delighted to have access to the gym during their lunch breaks. Membership continued to increase steadily until most recently when the union began receiving complaints about how the medical data was being used.

OPEN SECRETS

When the center was established neither Gibson nor the center staff gave much thought to how this sensitive medical data might be utilized. In addition, there were no guidelines or explanations from corporate headquarters on this matter. However, during the spring of 1994 an incident occurred that greatly disturbed Gibson. One of the company's best employees in the shipping department filed a worker's compensation claim with the benefits office for a chronic back problem. He claimed that many years of heavy lifting had led to a serious back problem including a slipped disk. The individual was 58 years old and unable to work because of his injury. The worker was a member of the Wellness Center and hence there was extensive medical data on file. The corporate benefits office considered the disability claim but refused to pay. They accessed the worker's file and unearthed some potentially incriminating information that cast doubt on whether the injury was really work related. The worker listed hobbies such as gardening and also mentioned that he liked to spend a lot of time fixing his own house along with the houses of his children. Those evaluating the claim pointed out that there was no way of knowing whether the back injuries were caused by his employment or by these "hobbies." Consequently, the claim was denied and the employee received no worker's compensation. The union protested on his behalf but to no avail. Union officials argued that confidentiality had been breached. In response to this charge, the company pointed out that release forms signed by the employee during his application for worker's compensation insurance gave it legitimate access to *all* of his medical records. In the company's view, this included those records in the Wellness Center data base.

Gibson and union leaders were also informed of an impending corporate policy to make membership in the Wellness Center mandatory. All employees would be required to fill out the Health Appraisal form and take a "wellness exam." Those workers who manifested health problems such as high-blood pressure, lack of exercise, weight problems, excessive drinking, and so on, would be asked to pay higher premiums for their health insurance. Those who refused to take the test would be subject to a surcharge on their health insurance. In this way United could shift some of its expanding health care costs to those employees who were not making an effort to be more health conscious.

Union leaders wanted Gibson to do something about this "misuse" of their health data to deny paying disability claims or to establish higher health insurance premiums for high-risk employees. As one union official observed during the last negotiating session, these practices were beginning to create an Orwellian atmosphere that undermined trust and morale. Gibson shared some of these concerns but was not sure if he would have any leverage with those at corporate headquarters who were imposing these unilateral decisions on the various divisions.

Gibson felt that some clear policy decisions should be made about the confidentiality of this health data. This sentiment was reinforced after a recent luncheon meeting with a group of managers. One of the managers mentioned to him that he had suspicions that one of his employees had a serious alcohol problem. He was often late for work, had a high record of absenteeism, and took long lunches. Also several of his colleagues reported smelling liquor on his breath on at least two occasions. When the manager confronted the employee he vehemently denied that he had any such problem and resolved to improve his attendance and be more careful about his performance. His behavior, however, did not change. The manager knew that the employee frequented the Wellness Center and he contacted one of the counselors for information. She pulled up his record on the computer screen and divulged to the manager the employee's medical history and lifestyle details—a past problem with alcohol, financial problems, a recent divorce. Armed with this information the manager confronted the employee once again and this time insisted that he take a paid leave of absence and get some help for his problem.

Gibson was happy that the employee in question was treated compassionately by his manager and that his alcohol problem was being addressed. However, he was concerned with how freely such sensitive information was released to the employee's manager without the employee's consent. Gibson was convinced that ACD needed a clear policy on access to the data in the Wellness Center's file. Obviously, this data could be used to help employees experiencing difficulties, but what about the worker's right to privacy? He was worried that the use of this information could get out of hand, but wondered about how to articulate an appropriate policy. Also, he questioned whether it would be feasible to confront corporate executives on their plans to utilize this data as a basis for charging higher health care premiums. Clearly, a strong stand on this contentious issue would help him with his own union. The next negotiation session was 2 days away and Gibson needed to shape some sort of response to the deeply felt concerns and apprehensions of ACD's union leaders.

Case 4.5   Note on Data Protection in Sweden[15]*

> In Sweden, when talking about privacy we begin with Warren and Brandeis and their idea of a right to be let alone.[16]
>
> —*Ingela Halvorsen, Legal Adviser*
> *Data Inspection Board, June 1991*

In 1991, Sweden's Data Act was being reassessed. The Swedish Commission on Data Protection, appointed in 1989 by the Ministry of Justice to revise the Act, had issued a preliminary report laying out basic principles to guide the next stage of its work. Its primary objective, as stated in the report, was to create more effective safeguards for the individual's right to privacy.[17]

The world's first national data protection legislation, Sweden's 1973 Data Act, had been enacted to prevent "undue encroachment on personal privacy." It had established the Data Inspection Board (DIB), an independent agency whose primary function was to license keepers of automated personal data files and to supervise the controllers of those files in accordance with guidelines laid down in the Act.[18] In 1982, the Data Act had been revised to make licensing less burdensome and to focus the Agency's efforts on the data files most likely to pose a serious risk to personal privacy, those containing sensitive information. In 1991, once again, the Act and the role of the Agency were being reconsidered.

In 1991, the DIB was governed by a six-member part-time Board of Directors, including three members of Parliament, one representative of industry, one professor of sociology, and one representative of the media.[19] The agency was staffed by 39 full-time employees, about 20 of whom were law school graduates.

DEFINING PRIVACY

Although its stated purpose was to guard privacy, the Data Act had not attempted to define privacy. And wisely so, according to Ingela Halvorsen, legal adviser to the DIB: "Integrity and privacy are what a person feels. They cannot be defined in general for everyone or for every situation." Indeed, one political scientist who interviewed board members about the meaning of "undue encroachment upon personal privacy" found diverse views among them.[20]

As elaborated by Warren and Brandeis in 1890, the right to privacy protected "the privacy of private life."[21] It protected thoughts and sentiments, sayings and actions performed in private, personal appearance, as well as personal writings and other products of the intellect or emotions. It protected from publication various kinds of information: facts about certain domestic occurrences, information listing the letters a person has written or the contents of a personal art collection. Underlying this diverse list of protected information rested, according to Warren and Brandeis, the principle of an inviolate personality which could be invoked to "protect the privacy of the individual from invasion either by the too enterprising press, the photographer, or the possessor of any other modern device for recording or reproducing scenes or sounds."[22]

Warren and Brandeis had invoked a right to be let alone in the face of advancing technology and changing business methods in 1890.[23] One hundred years later, the DIB was continuing the tradition within a radically different technological and business environment. Although the DIB had not developed a definition of privacy and did not do systematic empirical research to find out how Swedish citizens felt about privacy, it did receive complaints and concerns of all types in its ombudsman and supervisory functions. Halvorsen explained some typical complaints:

> One common complaint concerns incorrect information. For example, one person called because of hospital records which identified her as having a psychiatric condition which she did not have. In the case of incorrect information, the DIB will raise the issue with the file keeper, who is expected to investigate and change incorrect records. The procedure is an informal one, and file keepers generally resolve problems without further action. If necessary, the DIB may do an inspection to gather facts, but the DIB has neither staff nor authority to do criminal investigations or to adjudicate disputes.
>
> A second type of complaint concerns unsolicited mail. In those cases, unwilling recipients are advised to consult the State Personal and Address Register (SPAR), the source of most names and addresses used for direct mailing. SPAR has a name removal service for those who request it. In practice, most mail stops after that, though some may continue from past requests and from companies with whom a person has had a customer relationship.
>
> In other cases, people complain about being registered at all. They do not wish to have their names on the SPAR, for example. Some people do not understand that certain functions are necessary in society. But mostly, the public doesn't fully understand what is going on with information technology or what information is actually collected. People often assume that if someone has your address, they can get any information about you.

The DIB did not advertise itself widely, though its staff distributed brochures to visitors and to audiences whenever they made presentations. The main way people learned about the DIB and name removal possibilities was through the media. Said Halvorsen, "In practice, every five years or so, the press tends to raise the privacy issue and people become more aware."

THE LICENSING FUNCTION

Even though the licensing process had been simplified under the 1982 revisions of the Data Act, the main function of the DIB continued to be licensing keepers of data files. This function accounted for about 35% of the agency's budget in 1989.[24] Anyone wishing to maintain an automated personal data file was required to notify the DIB to obtain a license and to pay an annual fee.

A license was automatically granted unless sensitive data was involved. "Sensitive data" was a broad category including information about social welfare payments, health, criminal investigations or convictions, race, religion, political opinions, or evaluations or appraisals such as those found in letters of reference.[25] In cases involving sensitive data, special permission was required to maintain the file unless there was a specific connection between the controller of the file and the person registered. For example, a special permit was not required for organizations to maintain files on members, employees, clients, or customers.

Special permission was also required to integrate personal data from two files unless authorized by the data subject, status, or the DIB.[26] This so-called "cross-matching" or "joint processing" was thought to entail particular risks to privacy. Practically speaking, however, requests for permission to match data had declined over time because of the difficulty of comparing data based on different definitions and criteria. Personal data files set up by decision of the Government or Parliament were exempted from the permission requirement, although the Act provided that the DIB would issue opinions concerning such files if they contained sensitive information.[27]

The DIB was authorized to set conditions on special permits if needed to avoid undue encroachment on privacy.[28] These regulations might govern, among other things, the purpose of the file; collection of data for the file; data processing procedures; technical equipment; the dissemination of data; security; and procedures for maintaining accuracy. The DIB could also issue regulations specifying what operations could be performed on the personal data in a file, such as matching it with data in other files. Applicants for permits who wished to contest the imposition of special conditions or other aspects of the DIB's decisions could appeal to the Ministry of Justice.

There appeared to be a low level of compliance with the licensing requirement. The DIB reported about 38,500 licensed file keepers and an estimated 200,000–500,000 files in Sweden.[29] According to Halvorsen, part of the problem was that many companies were not aware of the DIB and the licensing provisions. In theory a company's failure to obtain a license or its violation of regulations issued by the DIB could subject its director to a fine or an obligation to pay damages. (In Sweden, fines were imposed on individuals and not on companies.) As with other penal fines in the Swedish system, the amount was related to the director's income and other factors affecting ability to pay, such as number of children and other liabilities. In practice, however, the prospect of penalties was remote. The DIB lacked the staff and resources to undertake investigations of unlicensed data keepers. Instead, DIB resources were used to inform possible file keepers of their obligation to secure a license. According to the preliminary report of the commission on Data Protection, fines or damages were imposed in only a handful of cases each year.[30]

GENERAL RULES AND POLICIES

Besides providing for licensing, the Data Act also laid down rules for file keepers. These rules provided that files could be kept only for specific purposes and that data could not be disseminated or used for purposes other than specified without permission of the registered person or in accordance with law.[31] In general, a public agency or authority could not sell a file without the permission of Parliament or the Government, although there were exceptions. For example, it was possible to buy names and addresses from the register of landowners. Private organizations could also buy information, such as an individual's name, address, marital status, number of children, and land holdings, from the SPAR.

In the private sector, information could be forwarded without permission of the data subject if the recipient of the information had a need accepted by law. Under Swedish law, according to Halvorsen, the desire to do direct mail marketing would not be recognized as a legitimate business need. Hence, permission of the registered persons would have to be secured before data collected for other purposes, such as granting credit, could be sold to direct marketers.

The rules also obliged file keepers to satisfy requests from persons seeking to know what personal data concerning them was on file,[32] to make corrections and inform third parties about them,[33] to maintain the confidentiality of certain information in the file,[34] and not to transfer files if there was reason to assume that data processing contrary to the law would occur.[35] The permission of the DIB was required for the transfer of data to countries that had not acceded to the Council of Europe's 1981 Convention on personal data protection.[36]

SUPERVISION AND INSPECTIONS

The DIB supervised the controllers of files and the application of the Act through inspections. However, on-site inspections were made only in some twenty cases a year. Most were "desk-inspections" carried out by correspondence.[37] Some inspections were the result of complaints by the public. Others were initiated by the Agency.

Despite the smaller number of inspections and the paucity of penalties actually imposed, the Agency was perceived, at least by some, as a serious constraint on information processing. One Swedish banking executive reported, "We must be prepared to show the contents and uses of our databases at any moment."[38] He went on to explain that the DIB had rejected two requests by his bank. One would have provided merchants using the bank's point-of-sale systems with aggregate information about the purchasing habits of its customers. The other would have created a data base of information about the customers of competitors who used the bank's branches on an occasional basis. In both cases, the bank sought and was denied permission for these projects.

PUBLIC POLICY ISSUES IN 1991

Although the DIB issued regulations for individual files, it was not primarily a policy-making body. It was not organized for and lacked the resources to carry out continuous work on policy issues. Nevertheless, the Agency was frequently involved in policy debates concerning various aspects of information privacy in Swedish society. In some cases Parliament asked the DIB to develop research or recommendations. In others, the DIB would take up issues on its own initiative. Halvorsen noted that the DIB's agenda was strongly influenced by what journalists considered interesting and chose to write about it.

In 1991, several issues were being debated and discussed at the DIB and in Swedish society. The first concerned the creation of a national data base of insurance payments for illness. The planned data base sought by 26 local bureaus of the medical insurance system would include information about illnesses, visits to the doctor, and diagnoses, as well as daily payments of insurance to individuals. Parliament had created a commission to investigate the proposal and recommend a policy response.

A second debate had centered on Parliament's decision to transfer the population registry from the Church of Sweden to the Swedish tax authorities on July 1, 1991. Since the sixteenth century, the Church of Sweden had maintained a record of the Swedish population showing births, immigrations, and deaths of individuals along with family affiliations, both adopted and biological. The record also indicated whether or not an individual belonged to the Church of Sweden, though it did not include affiliation with other religions. Only those whose names appeared in the registry were eligible to secure a driver's license or any other social benefits.

The use of the Personal Identification Number (PIN) by private companies was also on the DIB agenda. Assigned by the tax authorities for use in dealing with public authorities, the PIN had been found to be a useful identifying device by private companies as well. In response to public opinion opposing the use of the PIN by private companies, the government had passed legislation restricting the private use of the PIN beginning January 1, 1991. The DIB was charged with figuring out what these restrictions should be and how they should be implemented. Although many people wanted the use of PINs by private companies eliminated entirely, this was not, according to Halvorsen, a possibility. There were cases in which an existing legal obligation required the reporting of the PIN. For example, companies were required to use PINs in reporting certain sources of their income.

The DIB was also working on a set of recommendations for employers concerning employee privacy. According to Halvorsen, these were in large measure modeled on the Council of Europe's recommendations on the subject. After a period of comment by employers, the DIB's proposal would be reevaluated and decided on by the board. It was likely that compliance with the recommendations would be made a condition of obtaining a license.

LIKELY CHANGES IN THE DATA PROTECTION ACT

The preliminary report of the Swedish Commission on Data Protection described the main lines of likely reform. Strengthening the Agency's supervisory and regulatory functions and abolishing the licensing and special permissions system were central. The Commission was also proposing to clarify the concepts of "right to privacy" and "undue infringement."[39] Study of international developments, particularly the Finnish, Dutch, and U.K. Data Protection Laws, had influenced the Commission's deliberations, according to the report.

The Commission's main proposals included the following points:

- abolish the system of application for permission;
- develop regulations for different sectors of the economy, including rules for joint processing, and provide for supervision by state agencies already regulating those sectors;
- introduce a system of obligatory notification for sensitive files;
- intensify the Agency's supervisory activities with focus on files with sensitive information.

- strengthen the Agency's role as ombudsman and authorize Agency to issue injunctions and influence prosecutions;
- continue to finance Agency activities through annual fees paid by controllers of files;
- maintain the present system for administering Government Personal Data Files, but strengthen supervision.[40]

Although the next report of the Commission had been expected in early 1991, it had not yet been issued in June.

NOTES

1. Alan F. Westin, *Privacy and Freedom.* New York: Atheneum, 1967, p. 7.
2. Anne Wells Branscomb, *Who Owns Information: From Privacy to Public Access.* New York: Basic Books, 1994, p. 29.
3. "How to Turn Junk Mail into a Goldmine—or Perhaps Not," *The Economist,* April 1, 1995, p. 51.
4. Jim Bessen, "Riding the Marketing Information Wave," *Harvard Business Review,* (September–October) 1993, p. 152.
5. Gary H. Anthes, "Customer 'Data Mining' Pays Off," *Computerworld,* May 15, 1995, p. 28.
6. Deborah Jacobs, "They've Got Your Name. You've Got Their Junk," *The New York Times,* March 13, 1994, sec. F, p. 5. Copyright © 1994 by *The New York Times Company.* Reprinted by permission.
7. "How to Turn . . . ," p. 52.
8. Jacobs, "They've Got Your Name . . . , p. 5.
9. Mitch Betts, "Records Privacy Concerns Grab Citizen Attention," *Computerworld,* October 11, 1993, p. 64.
10. Jacobs, "They've Got Your Name," p. 5.
11. This is a revised and updated version of a case which appeared in *Ethical Aspects of Information Technology.* Englewood Cliffs, NJ: Prentice Hall, 1995.
12. "The Datamation 100," *Datamation,* June 15, 1992, p. 96.
13. Laurie Kretchmar, "How to Shine in a Sullied Industry," *Fortune,* February 24, 1992.
14. John Wilke, "Lotus Product Spurs Fears about Privacy," *The Wall Street Journal,* November 13, 1991, pp. B1, B5. Reprinted by permission of *The Wall Street Journal,* © 1991 Dow Jones & Company, Inc. All Rights Reserved Worldwide.
15. Unless otherwise indicated, the information in this note is based on the author's June 19, 1991 interview with Ingela Halvorsen, Legal Adviser to the Swedish Data Inspection Board.
16. The reference is to an article entitled "The Right to Privacy," which Samuel D. Warren and Louis D. Brandeis published in the *Harvard Law Review,* vol. iv, no. 5 (December 1890), pp. 193–220.

17. English Summary, First Report of the Swedish Commission on Data Protection, (Skärtptillsyn, SOU 1990:61) (hereafter, Commission Report), p. 201.

18. Files created at the direction of the Government or Parliament were exempted from the licensing requirement. The Data Act (as amended with effect from January 1, 1989, hereafter "The Data Act"), (1973:289) sec. 2a.

19. A fuller description of the Board can be found in David H. Flaherty, *Protecting Privacy in Surveillance Societies.* Chapel Hill: University of North Carolina Press, 1989, p. 101.

20. Mentioned in Flaherty, p. 103.

21. Warren and Brandeis, p. 215.

22. Ibid., pp. 205–206.

23. Ibid., p. 195.

24. Commission Report, p. 2.

25. The Data Act, secs. 2, 4.

26. The Data Act, sec. 2.

27. The Data Act, sec. 2a.

28. The Data Act, sec. 6.

29. Commission Report, p. 199.

30. Commission Report, p. 201.

31. The Data Act, sec. 7.

32. The Data Act, sec. 10.

33. The Data Act, sec. 8.

34. The Data Act, sec. 13.

35. The Data Act, sec. 11.

36. Ibid.

37. Commission Report, p. 200.

38. This interview is reported in Henry Jefferson Smith, Jr., *Managing Information: A Study of Personal Information Privacy,* doctoral thesis on file at Baker Library, Harvard Business School (1990).

39. Commission Report, p. 201.

40. Commission Report, pp. 202–203.

5

Information Stewardship

This chapter focuses on another dimension of information management, which is known as stewardship. It seems reasonable to presume that those who collect and aggregate information for various purposes share responsibility for how that information is used and disseminated. This matter is obviously related to the access issues discussed in the previous chapter, but it goes beyond concerns about the sharing of information. Data managers are custodians of information, and they must be committed to the prevention of unauthorized access. They must also verify and maintain the accuracy of their data and exercise some control over how that data is matched or recombined with other data.[1]

It is instructive to reflect on the precise meaning of "stewardship" and its application to a valuable but intangible resource such as information. According to the traditional view, stewardship implies that one has been entrusted with another's property and has an obligation to protect it: "if you are a steward, you have property that has been entrusted to you to take care of by the owner, and it is your duty to make sure that it is well maintained, well used by those who use it, improved as appropriate, self-sustaining, and profitable."[2] Clearly, providing a vendor or an organization with one's personal information is not the same as giving someone property to take care of. However, consumers who provide such information do have an interest and a stake in how that information will be maintained and utilized.

For example, if sensitive information about an embarrassing medical condition is supplied to a doctor or pharmacist but then carelessly falls into the wrong hands, the end result could be considerable harm for an individual and his or her family. Thus, when one provides that information one trusts those who take it to exercise great care about how it will be stored, processed, and distributed. If they do not treat it appropriately, then it seems fair to say that they have not lived up to their obligation as "stewards."

Moreover, the obligation of information stewardship can be deduced from the general moral duty to prevent injury to others. Recall from the discussion in Chapter 2 that this was one of the seven primary *prima facie* duties described by Ross. If the careful handling of information will prevent harm, it must assume the status of a secondary moral duty. The scope of this duty, however, is a matter of some debate and controversy.

Those who do have such stewardship obligations, then, must ensure that the data for which they have responsibility is secure and accurate. It must be well protected from unauthorized users and kept as up-to-date and error-free as possible. The latter obligation is sometimes overlooked, but the negative impact of data inaccuracies can be quite severe. Consider the possible adverse consequences if a consumer's credit report has false or outdated information: the denial of a mortgage or some other form of credit and perhaps even the loss of a job opportunity. Finally, custodians of information must be cognizant of how it could be matched and recombined with other data. Since the results of such data matching in some circumstances could expose individuals and destroy their privacy, data managers have some obligation to be vigilant about the potential results of the data recombination process.

The first case in this chapter, *It's Not Your Job to Be a "Data Cop!"* introduces us to some of these themes and serves as a fitting transition from Chapter 4. It deals with the question of whether or not a data broker is responsible for how a client uses or misuses data. Where does the responsibility for one's product end, especially when that product is a commodity such as information?

This is followed by *Data Accuracy and the Credit Bureau Industry,* a case which focuses primarily on the theme of accuracy. It considers how far companies in this industry must go to ensure the accuracy and integrity of their data. Obviously, erroneous credit information can be a nightmare for consumers, but the volatility and volume of credit data make the goal of accuracy difficult to attain. Can the major credit reporting companies do a better job of improving accuracy and serving their customer base?

The issue of accuracy also plays a critical role in another case called *Medical Records Privacy and the MIB*. This case examines the Medical Information Bureau (MIB), which is a counterpart of the credit bureau industry for those in the health and life insurance business. The MIB collects detailed medical information and sells it to those insurance companies. Are there sufficient safeguards in this context to ensure the accuracy of the information which will be used to make important underwriting decisions? Also, who should be allowed access to this sensitive information?

A related case, *Physician's Computer Network and the Mining of Patient Records,* deals with a new cottage industry that specializes in the collection of prescription data from the computerized files of physicians and pharmacies. This data is then leased to pharmaceutical companies eager to see how their products are doing. Patients' names are presumably deleted during this process, but critics argue that physicians have no business entrusting this sensitive data to an unregulated industry. Does this practice represent a failure of stewardship on the part of those physicians supplying their data for this purpose?

The final case, entitled *Government Computer Matching,* deals explicitly with the issue of data recombination or data "profiling." This is usually achieved by comparing and matching data from unrelated or disparate data bases. The case discusses some current examples of matching and considers its efficacy as a technique for detecting fraudulent behavior. It also considers the pros and cons of this questionable practice. The primary issue suggested by this case is the extent to which custodians of information in government agencies should promote and cooperate in data recombination and matching practices.

Case 5.1   It's Not Your Job to Be a "Data Cop!"[3]

Robert Wessell works for a well-established and highly profitable corporation that has carved out a niche as an information broker. Wessell is currently the manager of the direct mail division in Chicago. This division rents out various mailing lists to direct marketers. Companies and other organizations usually purchase these data lists in order to develop and target a direct mail marketing campaign for certain products or services. Most of the company's customers are reputable organizations which use this data conscientiously for legitimate purposes. For example, some of Wessell's best clients are major charities which rent these lists in order to help raise money for worthy causes.

However, Wessell has just received a substantial request from a new customer, a west coast mortgage company which specializes in second mortgages. He recognizes the company's name because it has recently gained some notoriety for targeting vulnerable segments of the population. It has allegedly "suckered in" some of these customers by allowing them to get some equity in their property in exchange for taking out a second mortgage at exorbitant interest rates that sometimes exceeded 19 percent. The current market interest rate for a 30-year second mortgage is about 9 percent. Despite the negative publicity, the mortgage company has steadfastly denied any wrongdoing. Several states have made these accusations and have initiated investigations, but so far no charges have been filed.

This mortgage company has asked Wessell's division to download a data base that lists personal demographics by ZIP code in several major eastern cities. Given the company's history, Wessell is convinced that it will use this data base to target low-income areas for its direct mailing and telemarketing campaigns. Wessell is loath to respond to this request, and he decides to articulate his concerns with his boss, Jane Manning, who is the vice president for Information Services. She listens attentively to Wessell's reservations about this request, but for the most part she is unsympathetic. She advises Wessell not to worry about how the company's customers will be using this data. She points out that the mortgage company is a new client and that this could be a lucrative account. "Further," she tells Wessell, "this organization just can't possibly control how data lists will be used. Besides, the charge against the mortgage company is only an allegation and perhaps it isn't even true. Also, you have no proof that they will be targeting low income families; your suspicions may be completely unfounded." Wessell offered a mild protest and rebuttal of her arguments, but to no avail. Manning ended the meeting by exclaiming, "Look, Robert, it's not your job to be a data cop!"

Wessell was still unsatisfied, and he now felt perplexed about the scope of his responsibility. Should he try to get more information about how the mortgage company will be using this list? Or, are these concerns really not his responsibility? After all, maybe his boss was right: he can't possibly be a watch dog for all of his customers. Nevertheless he felt quite uneasy about complying with this client's request and wonders what he should do especially in light of the indifference of Manning.

Case 5.2   Data Accuracy and the Credit Bureau Industry

The purpose of the credit bureau industry is to provide information to organizations which routinely grant credit to their customers: banks, automobile dealers, credit card companies, retail stores, and so on. Any of these organizations can request a credit report on a client or a prospective customer and thereby assess which of those customers might be bad credit risks based on their past history. These reports can also be used for other "legitimate" business purposes and hence are routinely made available to employers, landlords, and insurers.

Credit reports usually contain detailed information about an individual's employment and credit history. They include information about one's credit cards and other credit accounts, bank loans, and student loans. For each loan listed, the report reveals salient facts about the individual's payment history and highlights any late payments or other problems. The report will also include information about the subject's mortgage amount, terms, balance due, and payment record over the past year. It will usually reveal the presence of outstanding property taxes and whether or not there are any liens against the property. The report might even contain information from various public sources regarding bankruptcy proceedings, divorce proceedings, marriage licenses, civil lawsuits, and so forth. The report will list any occasions when one's credit card has been reported as lost or stolen, since this may imply that one is careless and perhaps a bad credit risk. Finally, the report lists one's present and past employers along with previous addresses.

Hence, the credit report is a comprehensive lens on the creditworthiness of a consumer who is a candidate for a mortgage or some other form of credit such as an installment loan. Most organizations which extend credit consider it to be an indispensable tool for making day-to-day credit decisions.

A BRIEF HISTORY

The first local retail credit bureau was founded in 1860 in Brooklyn, New York as an association of merchants who exchanged information about their customers. The growth and expansion of such organizations, however, was quite slow prior to World War I, primarily because only a relatively small segment of the retail business was conducted on a credit basis at that time. After the war, as credit became more popular, local credit bureaus began to emerge throughout the country. In 1906 the Associated Credit Bureaus of America (ACBA) was established in order to provide for closer cooperation and exchange of information between local credit bureaus.

These small community-based credit bureaus became a formidable force in American society since they were the most important sources of consumer credit information. These bureaus, which were located in nearly every city with a population in excess of 10,000, operated on the principle of "give and get." Creditors were charged a fee for the credit bureau's service but were also expected to contribute information to the bureau's files. Information on consumers came from a plethora of sources including employment records, public records, other credit bureaus in the ACBA network, collection services, and so on.

Some bureaus resorted to more unorthodox techniques to acquire information on consumers. As recently as 1971 a Washington, DC credit bureau hired hostesses to greet new arrivals to the community. After welcoming the newcomers with pleasant conversation and nice gifts they would politely and subtly make inquiries about the family's income, outstanding debts, and other relevant information.[4]

The dominance and autonomy of the "friendly" local credit bureau has changed dramatically within the last two decades as the industry has consolidated. At the national level, the industry has become an oligopoly, and is currently dominated by three large and puissant companies: TRW Credit Data of Long Beach, California, Equifax of Atlanta, and Trans Union Corporation of Chicago. These companies grew large by rapidly acquiring smaller credit bureaus. In the late 1980s, the remaining larger companies were swallowed by the "big three." Thus, TRW acquired Chilton, and Equifax formed an alliance with CSC Credit Services to complete the rationalization. The largest of the three companies is Equifax with 1994 operating revenue of $1.5 billion and 14,200 employees. All three organizations annually provide about 550 million reports to creditors based on the information in their substantial data bases. The bureaus assess a monthly fee to their clients and also charge a fee for each report that is ordered.

In addition to this radical consolidation, technological changes have also helped to transform this industry. Any remaining local credit bureaus are linked electronically to the sophisticated computer networks of the "big three." Creditors subscribe to reports from one or more of these three national companies; they can get these electronically generated reports directly or through a local bureau linked to one of the national bureaus. The principle of "give and get" remains in effect, since creditors seeking information must share their files with the bureau. Hence, banks and other businesses periodically file reports of their active credit accounts with the credit bureaus.

The downside of these changes and technological advancements is that credit reports have essentially become a low-price commodity. It is difficult to differentiate this product when the report issued by the three major credit bureaus looks almost identical. This resulted in slow revenue growth and stagnant operating income through the early 1990s.

These companies are now expanding into new businesses and are beginning to "reinvent" themselves as information providers rather than simply credit bureaus. Equifax, for example, has moved into health care; it recently purchased several companies that handle claims processing. Also, Equifax has begun selling information solutions that add value instead of a mere credit report. Thus, a bank or car dealer can now receive a recommendation from Equifax on whether a customer should be given a loan or line of credit. All of this creative expansion has helped Equifax to appreciably improve its bottom line; in 1994 the company earned about $214 million or about $1.60 a share which is more than twice the $.73 per share it earned in 1989. TRW and Trans Union have made similar forays into new businesses and information services.

ISSUES OF ACCURACY

It is estimated that each of the three national players in this industry has files on approximately 150 million consumers or 89 million households. Also, these companies are inundated with fresh credit data on a daily basis, and consequently they must make billions of updates and changes on individuals' records each month. Equifax has estimated that its data entry staff must input 65 million updates each day in order to handle new incoming credit data. In addition, it performs 130 million updates annually of drivers' license data. Other major updates are required whenever there is new U.S. census data.

Further, as consumers rely more heavily on credit, demand for credit reports has grown at a breathtaking pace. An industry spokesperson reported recently that the industry now sells about two million credit reports a day to insurers, banks, mortgage companies, car dealers, and other organizations where consumers expect to pay on credit.

Hence, given the overwhelming volume and volatility of this data, it is not surprising that these credit reports are prone to errors and inaccuracies. The extent of those errors is difficult to estimate and a bone of contention between the credit bureau companies and consumer groups. The system was most recently scrutinized by an independent source in 1991 when *Consumer Reports* commissioned a study of the industry by James Williams of Consolidated Information Service. This company analyzed a sample of 1500 reports from the three major bureaus and it found errors in 43 percent of those reports. Equifax, TRW, and Trans Union have disputed this extraordinarily high-inaccuracy rate. They point to another 1991 study funded by Associated Credit Bureaus, the industry trade organization, and conducted by Arthur Andersen, that found errors in only 1 percent of the consumer files.

They do admit that there are certainly some errors lurking in their files but contend that many of these errors stem from careless reporting procedures of banks, retail stores, and other vendors that are the sources of this data. Often these businesses have shoddy record keeping practices and this results in flawed credit reporting. Also, part of the blame for certain inaccuracies lies with consumers themselves who sometimes use different versions of their name when applying for credit or supply vendors with inadequate and inaccurate information.[5]

The credit bureaus contend that they cannot be held responsible if their sources of information are not so careful about the records which they submit. Currently most of the data received is not independently verified and is assumed to be accurate. Any sort of independent verification would be too time consuming and probably prohibitively expensive. Thus, if a bank reports erroneously that a consumer made three delinquent car loan payments, there is usually no effort made to verify or confirm this potentially damaging information.

CONSUMER CRITICISMS AND INDUSTRY RESPONSE

In the past several years, the credit reporting industry has faced intense criticism from consumers about these persistent inaccuracies and its inferior customer relations. During the early 1990s the industry became the number one source of customer complaints in America according to the Federal Trade Commission (FTC), which handled almost 9000 of these complaints in 1992. There are numerous examples of such problems, but an especially embarrassing incident in 1991 generated considerable adverse publicity for the industry along with increased pressure for reforms. In the summer of 1991 for no apparent reason all of the residents of Norwich, Vermont were reclassified as high-credit risks in TRW's data base of credit records. Several individuals could not use their credit cards and the town clerk received frantic calls from local area banks. Meanwhile mortgages and loans were denied even for the town's most respectable citizens with unblemished credit records. After numerous complaints to a beleagured customer service staff at TRW the mystery was solved. Apparently a part-time employee for a small Georgia company that looks up public records for TRW made a serious mistake. While checking over the records in Norwich she asked for a list of property tax delinquents but instead was given the list of those who had paid their property taxes in full. The employee inadvertently wrote down the entire list of 1400 residents. The situation was quickly rectified, and TRW referred to its mistake as an isolated situation. However, in October 1991, TRW admitted that similar errors had occurred in Woodstock, Vermont and several other New England towns.

Consumer groups also maintain that such foul-ups are not so isolated. They claim that the industry keeps inaccurate, shoddy data, has deficient security measures, and makes it difficult for consumers to inspect and correct their credit records. Finally, they note that when consumers do get a copy of their credit report, they cannot understand it. These reports tend to be so arcane and elliptical because of the use of codes and abbreviations that the industry has sold guides for deciphering them.

Some inaccuracies, of course, such as an incorrect address are not problematic. But other forms of invalid information can easily disqualify consumers from credit cards, insurance, and mortgages; these might include false late payment or outstanding debt information that can ruin one's credit rating. Another type of error that can lead to problems results from mixing up the credit information of two individuals with the same name.

Consumer advocacy groups also contend that credit bureau firms are slow to change their reports and to delete inaccurate information from reports even after consumers have complained. In addition it has been common practice to dispute a consumer's version of the facts; moreover, while this dispute is going on the questionable information is usually left in the file until some final resolution is reached.

In response to this mounting criticism TRW, Equifax, and Trans Union have argued that their procedures are essentially sound and secure. They claim that errors are the result of credit grantors and even consumers themselves. They also point out that new regulations might bog down and encumber the credit system. That system enables U.S. consumers to buy 5000 homes, 40,000 cars, and 300,000 appliances daily. As a result, they argue, tampering with this industry could have a negative impact on the whole economy.

Currently, however, the industry has mollified its defensive posture. All three credit bureaus have recently discontinued the practice of selling names from its files to junk mailers. Also, in October 1991, TRW agreed to give consumers free copies of their credit reports. TRW, along with Equifax and Trans Union, charged $15 for these reports. In a press release, TRW indicated that they would offer one free report a year upon a customer's request. Equifax and Trans Union still charge a fee of $8 for residents of most states unless the consumer is denied credit. They maintain that no business should be required to give away its product free of charge. The practice at all three companies is to send credit reports only upon the explicit request of a consumer.

Finally, in a 1994 settlement with the FTC, Equifax has agreed to investigate a dispute within 30 days, and if the company cannot verify the disputed information within that period it must be deleted from the file. Equifax pointed out that it had "voluntarily" adopted this practice long before the agreement with the FTC had been worked out.

Also, Equifax has consistently emphasized its commitment to protecting the confidentiality of its data and its need to sustain high information standards. The following is a brief statement from a 1990 company report on this issue:

> As we looked at the ways information technology has developed and is making possible more extensive and sophisticated uses of consumer information, it became clear to us that information integrity and confidentiality is our company's most important asset.[6]

Thanks to recent policy changes, the company has arguably done a better job of living up to these standards.

Some still complain that these changes do not go far enough to help ensure more accurate and up-to-date files on consumers. They argue for more careful verification of information that is received from banks and retailers and for more diligent edit checking. A large part of the problem, however, is the sheer size of the data bases that are maintained by the big three. It is axiomatic that as data bases become larger the chance of anomalies and errors goes up and the opportunity for the detection of those errors is reduced.

Furthermore, making progress in the area of accuracy is difficult since clients often do report erroneous information to the credit bureaus. Currently there are no sanctions or penalties imposed on companies that report false credit information, regardless of the reason. Moreover, banks and retailers have steadfastly resisted any regulations that would leave them with extra liability for credit report inaccuracies. Since these organizations are the paying customers of the credit bureaus, the bureaus have not opposed their intransigent position on this issue.

A key question, then, is whether or not the three major credit bureaus should be more proactive and aggressive in their efforts to detect and correct errors in their voluminous credit files. Are they fulfilling their stewardship obligation to maintain accurate and up-to-date information on the millions of consumers who rely so heavily on their ability to make purchases based on credit? Or should consumers take more initiative to check on their files? Those files are more easily accessible and correctable, so perhaps some of the burden should fall on consumers to be more vigilant about the contents of their credit reports. According to David Flaherty, the privacy commissioner of British Columbia,

> the usual Equifax type of defense makes sense: they store and report only information the consumer gave to the credit grantor in the first place, plus detailed information that is supposed to reflect the realities of credit performance. Thus, it's imperative for consumers to check their own credit reports regularly to make sure the information is accurate.[7]

Case 5.3   Medical Records Privacy and the MIB

The most sensitive information maintained about any individual is undoubtedly his or her medical records. We constantly entrust information about our medical background and history to physicians, hospitals, and insurance companies. Furthermore, we assume that this delicate material will be kept confidential. This case concerns the stewardship responsibilities of an organization which is the counterpart of credit bureaus. It is known as the Medical Information Bureau or MIB, and it tracks medical data for millions of Americans. A key issue here concerns the adequacy of its safeguards for protecting this data from falling into the wrong hands and especially for maintaining and verifying its accuracy.

THE MEDICAL INFORMATION BUREAU

The Medical Information Bureau was founded in 1902 by a group of physicians who also happened to be directors of several life insurance companies. It is a nonprofit trade association of approximately 700 life insurance companies "formed to conduct a confidential exchange of underwriting information among its members as an alert against fraud."[8] Whenever someone applies for life or health insurance a background check and investigation is usually initiated in order to verify the medical information and history that has been provided by the applicant. The results of this investigation are reported to the MIB.

Member companies can also request information from the MIB in order to assist their own investigations. Thus, in this regard the MIB functions in the same way that credit bureaus do, since the same philosophy of information sharing prevails. Its primary purpose and mission is to help life insurance companies detect fraudulent applications and to thereby minimize their risk. According to the industry, without this data bank the likelihood of weeding out fraudulent applications would be appreciably diminished.

The agency's only source of revenues is the $.25 access fee which is charged for each report that is requested. Insurers also pay an annual membership fee. It is important to note that under the terms of membership, the MIB report cannot be used as the sole basis for denying anyone insurance coverage. It can only function as a red flag device, that is, a warning that further investigation is necessary.

The MIB currently has a data base of about 15 million records. The information maintained by the MIB in this electronic data base is in a coded format. Medical conditions are delineated by over 200 different codes. For example, the code "150GTY" might indicate that the person has a serious health problem such as a chronic heart condition. The bureau also tracks certain "nonmedical hazards" but has never revealed what these are. The use of these cryptic codes is designed to protect these files from inspection by outside intruders. Only certain MIB employees along with the member insurance companies have access to the code books which explain the meanings of these esoteric strings of numbers and letters.

Approximately 15 percent of individuals applying for insurance coverage will be "reported" to MIB usually because they have an above average risk or because there is some potential for fraud. The information collected by the insurer for its report comes from myriad sources including the policy application itself. Other sources include the applicant's physicians, hospitals, employment records, the Department of Motor Vehicles data base, and even interviews with friends or associates from work. However, none of the information received by MIB is independently verified; it is virtually always assumed to be accurate, complete, and up-to-date. Thus, if an insurer reports erroneous information to the MIB it will become part of the subject's file along with the factual information.

The MIB does take precautions to ensure that this information does not inadvertently fall into the wrong hands. Information in these files is only provided to member insurance companies. It is not made available to any third parties such as employers, government agencies, or others who might be seeking out medical data about someone for illegitimate reasons. The agency feels that this strictly enforced policy protects privacy while providing necessary information for those who must underwrite insurance policies.

DATA ACCURACY AND PRIVACY

Despite these precautions and safeguards, this organization seems to have many critics. They are concerned that the MIB does not adequately fulfill its obligation of stewardship. Some argue that more stringent standards are necessary in order to protect privacy and ensure greater accuracy of the sensitive data in these files.

Privacy advocates obviously worry about who will get access to the information stored in the MIB data base. The danger that MIB employees will leak information is probably slim, but "there are few guarantees that an insurer or the investigator it hired would not disclose such information."[9] In other words, how can MIB be so sure that its clients will always exercise careful stewardship of this information?

Another key concern is data accuracy. Obviously, the ramifications of misinformation lurking in one's file are quite serious, since this could disqualify a person from insurance coverage for some spurious reason. Errors can happen in several ways. As with credit reports medical records themselves are often inaccurate; they may include misdiagnoses that were never corrected or incomplete information about a patient's condition. Sometimes a physician may send the wrong record to a prospective insurer who in turn sends it along to the MIB. Also, even if all the information that is submitted is correct, something may get encoded incorrectly. This could occur through carelessness or through misinterpretation. The latter seems to be a distinct possibility in some cases given the difficulty of reducing all mental and physical ailments to 210 codes. How well do our illnesses and complicated physical conditions translate into these simple codes? Are there risks in having a medical record consisting of such unnuanced data elements?

Finally, according to another informed observer of the MIB, "another potential area of concern is that, instead of sending just a diagnosis, some physicians submit photocopies of patients' entire medical records to insurance carriers, which then pass the information on to the MIB."[10] The problem is that these files often contain the physician's notes which patients assume to be quite confidential.

MIB does have a procedure for correcting errors. Any consumer can write to this organization to determine if there is a report on file containing his or her medical data. If someone gets this report and detects an error, they can contact the company in order to get it corrected. However, if a file is challenged MIB will not take the consumer's word but will instead contact the organization that submitted the report and ask them to verify the accuracy of the information in that report. If that insurer is unwilling to admit that there is a mistake, the error will not be corrected in the MIB data base.

In these "stalemate" situations the consumer's only recourse is to get a physician to write a letter along with supporting documentation which will support his or her position and clear up the mistake. Thus, the task of getting errors corrected can be dauntingly complex. Also, most consumers have no idea that MIB even exists so they would not know enough to get a copy of their files in order to check for such inaccuracies. They do not automatically receive a copy of the MIB report when they are denied insurance.

SPECIFIC CASES

In his book, *Privacy for Sale,* Rothfeder documents several cases of individuals who have apparently been victimized because of errors present in their MIB files. For instance, he describes the unfortunate case of David Castle who was turned down for disability insurance at several major insurance companies. When Castle investigated the matter, he determined that his medical file at MIB indicated that he had AIDS. It appears that a doctor erroneously wrote on a medical record that Castle was HIV positive. This was uncovered by one of the insurers to whom Castle had applied, and in turn it was passed along to MIB. The doctor's notation was the result of an erroneous report from a radiologist. The doctor also wrote that Castle was gay, but this too was untrue, and apparently had been deduced from the mistaken notion that he was HIV positive.

Castle's doctor has attempted to rectify this misinformation by writing a letter to MIB. According to Rothfeder, MIB will not delete the erroneous entry; rather, it will add the correction to its file and note that there was a mistake. The notation that Castle has AIDS and is gay will remain as part of his permanent record in the MIB data base.[11]

There is also the infamous case of Charles Zimmerman. His MIB medical record included the notation that he was an alcoholic, but this was inaccurate. Apparently, Zimmerman had told an insurance investigator that he attended AA meetings not because he had an alcohol problem "but thought the program's 12 step approach to addiction would help him stop smoking."[12] The insurance investigator sent a report to MIB indicating that Zimmerman attended AA meetings. There is a code for this activity which was entered in the MIB data base, but of course there was no explanation of *why* Zimmerman was going to these meetings. Zimmerman dropped his first application for disability insurance but when he applied to another company several months later they picked up this data that he attended AA meetings and reasonably concluded that he was an alcoholic. As a result of this Zimmerman was charged a 25 percent premium on his disability insurance policy. Zimmerman's record was finally corrected after a year or so of phone calls, correspondence, and investigations.

CONCLUDING REFLECTIONS

Both of these incidents illustrate how mistakes can inadvertently become part of one's medical record along with the difficulty of correcting those mistakes. The company has consistently maintained that these situations are anomalies and that its records are accurate. According to a company spokesperson, in 1993 MIB released 17,000 files to inquiring consumers and corrections were required in fewer than 500 of those files.[13]

No one disputes the insurance industry's right to guard against fraud and its need for the sort of information available in the MIB data base. However, some legitimate questions seem to have been raised about MIB's system and its safeguards to ensure that this data is as confidential and accurate as possible.

It is worth noting that unlike companies in the credit bureau industry that are regulated by the FTC, the MIB is completely unregulated. It is not subject to any federal or state laws that restrict its practices or policies. Thus, there are no external guidelines that the company is compelled to follow regarding data accuracy, the preservation of confidentiality, or the distribution of the information in its files.

As this little known company receives more attention and its policies are subjected to more intense scrutiny, MIB's managers must consider whether they have adequately addressed the issues of privacy and accuracy raised by some anxious critics and consumers.

Case 5.4   Physician's Computer Network and the Mining of Patient Records

COMPANY BACKGROUND

Physician's Computer Network, Inc. (PCN) is a small, privately held corporation located in Laurence Harbor, New Jersey. The company is owned in part by several corporate giants such as IBM (which has a 23% stake) and MacMillan, Inc. PCN has been a pioneer in capitalizing on the emerging medical-data network that includes hospitals, private physicians, HMOs, and pharmacies. It is estimated that thousands of doctors form a crucial part of this network.

PCN's primary business entails the collection of pharmaceutical data from the computer files of several thousand doctors who have agreed to participate in its program. Every week or so PCN dials into these computer files and carefully searches through these confidential patient records for certain information. It collects data about patient illnesses along with which drugs have been prescribed for those illnesses.

For instance, it might determine that Digoxin has been prescribed for a particular patient with congestive heart failure. The patient's name and other personal data is automatically stripped away from the record when it is captured by PCN.

Once this valuable data is gathered from these files it is compiled into a marketing data base which is then rented for a lucrative fee to the major pharmaceutical companies. With this market feedback, they can readily determine how their drugs are faring with rank and file physicians. In addition it gives these companies insightful competitive information since they also get a good indication of the success (or failure) of their competitors' products.

As one might expect, this practice has come under some scrutiny by those concerned with the potential for abuse. However, participating physicians and PCN itself defend this business by insisting that patient privacy is fully protected since names are never included with the data. Moreover, the recipients of this data, the pharmaceutical firms, have no interest in getting names. As Rothfeder explains those firms are primarily seeking data about product use and more general information such as the following: "50 percent of hypertensive patients in the Northeast with a systolic reading of 140 are prescribed a beta blocker and 25 percent are told to take nothing—information that's worth its weight in gold to drug manufacturers."[14]

This data collection method employed by PCN is based strictly on the honor system. In other words, PCN officials give their word that names and related personal information will be deleted. There is no way, however, to monitor what pieces of data have been taken from a physician's file. It's *possible* that names could be collected without the knowledge of the physicians or their patients. There are no regulations or safeguards to ensure that PCN or other companies engaged in similar data capture procedures are abiding by this verbal and informal agreement to respect patient confidentiality.

Despite these concerns PCN is a rapidly growing business in an embryonic industry with excellent prospects. It has been able to attract many new doctors with some appealing incentives. It usually approaches doctors with an offer to lease them a "top-of-the-line personal computer and software for about one-third what these would otherwise cost."[15] The computer can be used to operate the physician's business and it becomes the repository for the market data that PCN will be gathering.

OTHER PLAYERS

PCN is not the only company involved in garnering pharmaceutical and medical treatment data. Pharmacies are a gold mine of such information and there are several key data collection organizations that profitably exploit that information as well. Two such companies are IMS International (owned by Dun & Bradstreet) and a British company, Walsh International, Inc. According to the *Wall Street Journal* these companies buy information from drug wholesalers such as FoxMeyer. For instance, pharmacies that purchase their drugs from FoxMeyer agree to let this company "scoop up computerized prescriptions once a week over telephone lines."[16] Foxmeyer in turn sells this data to IMS and Walsh. Pharmacists who have agreed to this arrangement admit that they do not know which data elements are collected. They too have been told that patient names are deleted but cannot verify this assertion.

In 1993 the U.S. pharmaceutical firm Merck & Company acquired Medco Containment Services, Inc. primarily for the purpose of unrestricted access to its data base of prescription drug purchases. Medco runs a mail order drug business and manages pharmaceutical health plans for different employers. Its extensive files include data on prescription drug use of 38 million people. This data shows "which doctors wrote which prescriptions for which patients and how often the prescriptions were refilled."[17] Merck is using this data to ascertain which drugs are most effective and to increase its own pharmaceutical sales through carefully planned interventions with doctors and employers.

Insurance companies that process and pay claims for prescription drugs also get into the act. For example, PCS, a division of McKesson Corporation, which covers prescription drug payments for many employers, sells all of its data to Walsh International, Inc. PCS records 120 million prescriptions annually in order to process payments for employees who present a PCS insurance card at their pharmacies. The *Wall Street Journal* reports that "though PCS deletes patients' names, it includes their age, sex, and Social Security number, as well as their physicians' federal ID numbers."[18] Walsh has indicated that they do not use these social security numbers since they replace them with their own unique identifying codes. In this way it can track the history of an individual's drug purchases without knowing his or her name. Once again PCS has not verified Walsh's claim and only relies on their word that names and social security numbers are not being passed on to pharmaceutical firms.

MORAL CONSIDERATIONS

The mining of medical data does provide a valuable market feedback mechanism to pharmaceutical companies. It can greatly expedite market research and make possible so-called "outcomes research" that exposes which treatments are most effective for certain illnesses. On the other hand, most would agree that patient privacy should not be sacrificed even for the sake of this research and market feedback.

Physicians, hospitals, and pharmacies are obviously the custodians of this key medical data that is being collected and resold by companies such as PCN. Consequently, they must conscientiously consider the ethical and social implications of providing this data under the conditions previously described. This means coming to terms with at least some of the following questions. Is it morally acceptable for physicians to entrust medical records to these companies without the consent and knowledge of their patients? Or should patients be informed of this practice? Are the obligations of information stewardship fulfilled by relying on blind trust and the verbal agreement that confidentiality will be protected? Or should physicians and pharmacists insist on other safeguards to ensure that names and other personal information are not taken from these files? In summary, what is an appropriate data policy for all of the parties which cooperate in this exchange of information, and how can that policy be structured to prevent misuse of information while also ensuring its potential benefit?

Case 5.5   Government Computer Matching

One of the most common forms of data recombination is the technique of so-called "computer matching." It is often employed by government agencies in order to detect fraud or other irregularities. The two groups most frequently subjected to computer matches are federal employees and welfare recipients.

Computer matching is defined as "a computer-supported process in which personal data records relating to many people are compared in order to identify cases of interest."[19] It has been used since 1977 by many state, city, and federal agencies. For example, the U.S. Postal Service has matched its data base with the data bases of law enforcement agencies in order to determine whether or not its employees have engaged in criminal activities.

Computer matching recombines isolated and separate pieces of data in unrelated data bases in order to create a more complete profile of a certain individual or group of individuals. The premise of computer matching is that when data is maintained separately it does not have as much value and power as when it is combined with other data. For example, if one combines income tax data available on magnetic tape from the IRS with a police file on delinquent fathers, one now has a powerful tool to reveal which "deadbeat dads" can really afford to make payments to their deprived families.

Computer matching functions as follows: records are selected (according to certain criteria) from two separate and distinct data bases; the records selected from these data bases based on certain criteria are then matched or compared to each other and during this process there will be a number of "raw hits" or data matches. Some analysis is done on these raw hits which results in filtering of the remaining records and some resultant "solid hits"; based on these solid hits a new record is created containing the data from both of the original records, and these new records comprise a whole new data base. If warranted, action is then taken against the data subjects included on these records.

Consider the following example of a recently implemented computer matching operation in the New York area. New York City along with the states of New York and New Jersey now compare their data bases in order to ferret out "double-dippers," that is, those who are collecting welfare benefits in more than one of these particular jurisdictions. According to a report in *Computerworld*, this computer matching project uncovered 425 Newark, New Jersey residents who collected welfare benefits in both the city of Newark and New York City during 1993.

Computer matching has been done for many reasons but this is "the first concerted effort to use computer matching to nab welfare double-dippers from neighboring jurisdictions."[20] In this case, the solid hits will be also inserted into a data base that will be sent to New York state officials in Albany who will conduct further investigations on those who are allegedly culpable of this double-dipping.

PROS AND CONS

Since its inception in the late 1970s computer matching has provoked considerable debate. Many critics question the suitability of this activity, claiming that it is an intrusive violation of individual rights such as the right to privacy and the right to due process. On the other hand, supporters of computer matching argue that it is a necessary and efficient mechanism for dealing with fraud and other illicit activities. Does computer matching represent a threat to our privacy by Big Brother or is this a legitimate way to deal with those who seem unwilling to abide by society's laws and regulations? Let us briefly consider both sides of this thorny issue.

Critics of computer matching techniques contend that it gives too much power to the state and it violates basic human rights such as those guaranteed by the Fourth Amendment which protects against unreasonable searches and seizures. This includes so-called "fishing expeditions" directed at a whole class of individuals in order to determine if they might be doing something wrong or untoward. Some might argue that this was the case with the search for "double-dippers." Essentially, the law has supported the position that generalized fishing expeditions (e.g., a massive dragnet or house-to-house search in a given area for no specific reasons) violate the Fourth Amendment because they are unreasonable searches.

In addition, as Shattuck argues, computer matching may violate the principle of presumption of innocence. According to Shattuck, "once a computer match has taken place, any person whose name appears as a 'raw hit' is presumed to be guilty; in part, this is because the technology of computer matching is so compelling and in part because its purpose—the detection of fraud and waste—is so commendable."[21]

Others have found fault with computer matching because it is a blatant infringement of privacy rights. Matching records and its product, recombined data, yield new information about data subjects. What right do federal or state authorities have to such personal information? Does government really have the right to cull information from unrelated data bases so that it can get a better profile of its citizens and perhaps find those who are supposedly cheating the system in some way? Should information that has been supplied in good faith for one purpose (such as personal data provided to the Registry of Motor Vehicles when applying for a driver's license) be used for these other purposes (such as tracking down deadbeat tax payers) without an individual's knowledge or consent?

Moreover, through computer matching and data recombination individuals could lose control of information about themselves. Also, what if an erroneous impression is created by this recombined data? As Clarke perceptively points out, "Of particular concern is the extent to which the digital persona that arises from the matching process may be a misleading image of the individual and his or her behavior."[22]

Finally, opponents of computer matching make the case that it violates an individual's right to due process, the right to confront one's accuser, and to be given an opportunity to defend oneself. The problem is that on some occasions actions (such as terminating welfare benefits) have been taken against those who are on the "hit list" without any further investigation. According to Shattuck, this approach is quite unfair and "makes a mockery of due process."[23]

There are also, of course, powerful arguments on the other side of this question. Supporters observe that it is one of the few methods available to deal with both errors and fraud, which cost state and federal governments billions of dollars each year. Further, they contend that governments have a responsibility to taxpayers and other stakeholders to check as diligently as possible for the misuse of funds and entitlement payments. The use of various data bases for this purpose does not reflect a failure of stewardship, but this *would* be the case if they did not take steps to ensure that citizens are only receiving what they are legally entitled to receive.

Those who advocate and support computer matching *do* note that government agencies must be careful not to violate one's due process in their haste to find cheaters or double-dippers. All "solid hits" should be subjected to further examination and investigation in order to ensure that no errors are made. The matching procedure is only the beginning of the process. Programs that did not include such investigation and manual checking would be considered irresponsible by most government officials and supporters of computer matching.

Defenders of computer matching also contend that it is important for government agencies to use the most effective audit procedures available. They should not be compelled to confine themselves to purely manual techniques when automated ones are available. As Kusserow observes, "computer matches have not created new areas of audit or investigation, but they have allowed agencies to improve their methods."[24]

Kusserow also addresses the common objection that these match projects are fishing expeditions that violate the Fourth Amendment. He classifies most computer matches initiated by government agencies as "eligibility reviews," that is, their purpose is to determine if someone is eligible for a certain entitlement payment or other benefit. According to Kusserow, "an eligibility review can hardly be characterized as a 'fishing expedition.'"[25] This implies that an individual's Fourth Amendment rights are clearly not violated, since a computer matching endeavor is not a dragnet searching for suspected criminals but an inquiry into one's eligibility for certain government benefits or payments.

CONCLUSIONS

The technique of computer matching has become more widespread through the 1990s but it remains highly controversial. Some see it as a misuse of information, a violation of privacy, and other rights guaranteed by the Constitution. They are apprehensive that its use will grow and that the success of this technique will lead to the entrenchment of a "Big Brother" mentality within certain sectors of the state and federal government.

Others see it as an effective, proactive, and relatively harmless way of dealing with the massive problem of government fraud and waste. In their view, it is not intrusive nor unfair, and it does not violate any rights. Data is recombined in order to clarify who is eligible for a certain benefit, and if the findings reveal a problem or a question only then is an investigation or action warranted.

The fundamental issue in this case is the control of data recombination. Should this practice be more tightly controlled by the cooperating agencies of the state and federal government? Should it be more circumscribed for the sake of protecting privacy? Or is it acceptable to let government agencies and other organizations share their data freely and openly in order to create a comprehensive digital persona for various social purposes? Or, perhaps the answer lies in the middle: should only some types of data recombination be permitted? Whatever the answer, the controversy of computer matching is unlikely to subside any time soon.

NOTES

1. I am indebted to the brief discussion of stewardship issues in James I. Cash, et al., *Building the Information Age Organization.* Homewood, IL: Irwin, 1994, pp. 248–250.
2. Lisa Newton, "Gambling: A Preliminary Inquiry," *Business Ethics Quarterly,* October 1993, p. 406.
3. This case originally appeared in *Ethical Aspects of Information Technology.* Englewood Cliffs, NJ: Prentice Hall, 1995.
4. For background information about credit bureaus see Robert H. Cole and Robert Hancock, *Consumer and Commercial Credit Management.* Homewood, IL: Irwin, 1984, p. 211 ff.
5. For more discussion on this see Michael W. Miller, "Credit: An Open Book— With Typos," *The Wall Street Journal,* March 27, 1991, p. B1.
6. Excerpt from "The Equifax Report on Consumers in the Information Age," 1990, p. II.
7. Simson Garfinkel, "Separating Equifax from Fiction," *Wired,* September 1995, p. 106.
8. H. Jeff Smith, *Managing Privacy: Information Technology and Corporate America.* Chapel Hill: The University of North Carolina Press, 1994, p. 33.
9. Gary A. Seidman, "This is Your Life, Mr. Smith . . . ," The New York Times, August 1, 1993, p. F7. Copyright © 1993 by The New York Times Company. Reprinted by permission.
10. Jill Andresky Fraser, "Medical Intelligence," *Bloomberg Personal Magazine,* December 1994, p. 21.
11. Jeffrey Rothfeder, *Privacy for Sale.* New York: Simon & Schuster, 1992, pp. 183–185.
12. Seidman, p. F7.

13. Fraser, p. 21.
14. Rothfeder, p. 193.
15. Michael Miller, "Patients' Records are Treasure Trove for Budding Industry," The Wall Street Journal, February 27, 1992, p. A1. Reprinted by permission of The Wall Street Journal, © 1992, Dow Jones & Company, Inc. All Rights Reserved Worldwide.
16. Ibid., p. A6.
17. Gina Kolata, "New Frontier in Research: Mining Patient Records," The New York Times, August 9, 1994, p. A21. Copyright © 1994 by The New York Times Company. Reprinted by permission.
18. Miller, p. A6.
19. R. A. Clarke, "The Digital Persona and Its Application to Data Surveillance," *The Information Society*, vol. 10 (1994), p. 84.
20. Mitch Betts, "Computer Matching Nabs Double-Dippers," *Computerworld*, April 18, 1994, p. 90.
21. John Shattuck, "Computer Matching Is a Serious Threat to Individual Rights," *Communications of the ACM*, June 1984, p. 539.
22. Clarke, p. 84.
23. Shattuck, p. 540.
24. Richard P. Kusserow, "The Government Needs Computer Matching to Root Out Waste and Fraud," *Communications of the ACM*, June 1984, p. 545.
25. Ibid.

6

Software Ownership and Intellectual Property Issues

The case studies in this chapter concern the moral question of software ownership and the scope of intellectual property rights. During the last decade or so there has been a steady erosion of respect for intellectual property laws. Many end users and professionals seem to have few qualms about making illegal copies of commercial software, and several studies confirm that such unauthorized copying is widespread.[1] In addition, in a recent *Computerworld* poll, 53 percent of the information professionals surveyed indicated that they had made unauthorized copies of software programs.[2] Most of these individuals rationalized their behavior by saying that they were just "trying out" the software.

Of course, intellectual property issues are more complex than pilfered copies of software and, given that complexity, it is instructive to consider briefly the whole conception of property and its subset, intellectual property. Most contemporary analyses equate the notions of "ownership" and "property." Hence, the statements, "I own that house," and "that house is my property," are equivalent, since they convey the same information. Further, those analyses define ownership as "the greatest possible interest in a thing which a mature system of law recognizes."[3] Simply, ownership of property implies that the owner has certain rights and liabilities with respect to this property, including the rights to use, manage, possess, exclude, and derive income.

Intellectual property rights imply that someone has the right to certain concepts, knowledge, or ideas. However, as we observed in Chapter 1, there are serious difficulties with the notion that one has property rights in an idea, since this would mean the "right" to exclude others from using and building on those ideas. Rather, it is generally recognized that one has property rights in the way one expresses ideas, whether it be in the form of a book, a play, or a software program. Thus, the distinction between an idea and its expression serves as a fundamental basis for making legal and moral decisions about intellectual property protection.

Software is a basic form of intellectual property but *how* it should be legally protected has been subject to extensive debate. Copyright laws, patents, and trade secrets can all be used to protect software programs, but the efficacy of these forms of protection has been heavily disputed. Patents cover unique processes and functions, but since virtually all software is derivative, patent protection seems inappropriate for software programs. Copyright protection may be more suitable since it does distinguish between ideas and their expression. However, the extent and scope of that protection is unclear, and when a competitor has stepped over the line and infringed on another's property rights can sometimes be difficult to determine.

From a moral point of view a compelling case can be made for a *natural* right to property. Philosophers often invoke Locke who claimed that labor and effort engendered at least some sort of property rights. Those who work, who invest their time and energy in a project, have a right to the fruits of their labor. Thus, if software companies invest heavy resources and labor in creating a product they should have a limited moral right to the returns which will be generated by this investment by controlling the use of that product. To a certain extent, American copyright and patent laws are grounded in this Lockean conception of property, since they confer long, heavily protected monopolies for product innovations that preclude competitors from cloning or otherwise imitating the protected product.

What we have been describing is the traditional Western conception of *private* property rights. It should be remarked, however, that other countries and traditions adopt a very different approach to property. In general, they put more emphasis on common property whereby some sort of access is granted to all. This is especially true with intellectual property which is conceived by many developing countries as common property. According to Steidlmeier, "developing countries argue that individual claims on intellectual property are subordinated to more fundamental claims of social well-being . . . [and] that while people may have a right to the fruit of their labor, they have a duty to reward society which practically made the very fruitfulness of labor possible."[4] This divergence of opinion on intellectual property between American businesses and some of their competitors throughout the world has sometimes been the source of intractable moral problems.

Another source of moral conundrums is the difficulty of differentiating between the property rights of employers and their employees. For example, what portion of an information asset or a software program belongs exclusively to one's present employer and which portion constitutes part of the employee's general knowledge and expertise that can be utilized without impunity in another organization? Does the employee's creative work on a project engender any sort of property rights or are these always surrendered to the employer?

This chapter begins with a relatively straightforward case called, *Piracy on the Internet.* It describes a well-publicized incident in which software products were disseminated on the Internet without permission. There may be agreement that a serious moral transgression has occurred but there is less consensus on the locus of responsibility and a fitting penalty for this misdeed in cyberspace. This case also provides a vehicle for discussing the unconventional viewpoint that software should not be considered as anyone's property.

The next case, *"It's Never Right to Copy Software,"* raises similar issues. A young teacher in a poor school district must decide about making unauthorized copies of a software program; unless he does so, the school's new computers will be virtually useless. This case asks the question implied by its title: Is the moral injunction against making illegal copies of software programs absolute or does it allow for exceptions in extenuating circumstances?

In the next two cases the question of ownership is perhaps less clear. In *Whose Program Is This?* an employee takes portions of a successful accounts payable program to her new position. Does her labor on this effort confer any right to appropriate some of this program for her own use, especially when there are no adverse consequences for her employer? And in the case entitled, *Doric Conversion Technologies, Inc.,* a software program is no longer marketed by a company, but is it acceptable for its developer to use this discarded program for his own personal gain?

The next case study, *Software Compatibility and Reverse Engineering,* focuses on two major ongoing legal controversies in the software industry which have significant ethical implications. Both disputes deal with the theme of compatibility. The user community is looking for standards in software, yet standardization sometimes conflicts with the notion of intellectual property protection which may permit a particular company to have exclusive rights to a technology that is emerging as an industry de facto standard. Can we have common standards and some degree of compatibility without pulverizing the laws that are designed to protect intellectual property? The debate about standards comes to the forefront in the legal dispute of *Lotus v. Borland,* where the primary issue is how much similarity should be allowed between user interfaces. The second conflict which is discussed in this case is the one which took place between Sega Ltd. and Accolade, Inc. The central question here is the following: What can a vendor do to obtain information needed to write software programs that will work on another vendor's hardware platform. In other words, to what extent should reverse engineering be permitted?

The chapter concludes with a provocative case study that adds another layer of complexity to these problems. In the Harvard Business School case, *The IBM-Fujitsu Dispute,* we are forced to consider how the American notion of intellectual property which sets up a temporary monopoly as an incentive to innovation clashes with the more socialistic Japanese view of property that emphasizes its communal nature. This notion becomes the basis for Japan's stress on the diffusion of knowledge in order to stimulate incremental innovations. As a result, two giant companies are caught in the middle of conflicting paradigms of intellectual property protection.

Case 6.1   Piracy on the Internet

In March 1994, the U.S. Attorney in Boston announced that charges would be filed against a Massachusetts Institute of Technology (MIT) student, David LaMacchia, for computer fraud. It was alleged that this 20-year-old student operated a computer bulletin board on the Internet which distributed copies of various copyrighted software programs. LaMacchia was not accused of actually uploading or downloading any of the programs. Also, the indictment made it clear that he did not collect any money or materially profit from this activity in any way.

The problem of "piracy" and pilfered software programs has become quite serious and expensive. According to the Software Publishers Association, worldwide losses from stolen software amounted to a staggering $7.45 billion in 1994. Moreover, downloading from bulletin boards is now considered to be one of the most common and costly forms of software piracy. Shortly after LaMacchia's indictment Daniel A. Goldman, a student at Brown University, was arrested for alleged computer fraud. He too was accused of disseminating copyrighted software over the Internet.

In the MIT case authorities acted quickly in order to send an unambiguous signal that they would not allow computer bulletin boards to function as depositories and distributors of free software. Given the growing number of users on the Internet, copying could happen on a scale that would greatly magnify losses for software companies. LaMacchia's bulletin board was known as CYNOSURE. It was in operation from November 1993 through January 1995. It is estimated that approximately $1 million of software was illegally copied from CYNOSURE during this time frame. It remains unclear who uploaded the software for purposes of its illicit dissemination to various users. Both the uploading and downloading took place through an "anonymous server" in Finland which deleted the addresses of the users involved.

There are many questions and twists about this case that will make it difficult to get a legal conviction. The most unusual twist is LaMacchia's refusal to collect any money for the software that was allegedly disseminated. If the young student did not wish to profit from this activity, what was his motivation?

Some sources at MIT have reasonably speculated that he was motivated by his beliefs about software ownership, since he rejected the notion that companies should have ownership rights in the commercial software which they have developed. This position is also espoused by Richard Stallman, president of the Free Software Foundation. Stallman, who has never perpetrated or advocated actions like those of LaMacchia, has argued that ownership of software programs is obstructive. He maintains that software should be in the public domain, freely available to anyone who wants to use it. He regards stiff software licensing fees as a disincentive to acquire programs, and thus he concludes that legal ownership of software programs obstructs their utility; expensive, proprietary programs are enjoyed by too few users. Ownership also obstructs software modification and development. According to Stallman,

> Software development used to be an evolutionary process, where a person would take a program and rewrite parts of it for one new feature, and then another person would rewrite parts to add another feature; this could continue over a period of twenty years. . . . The existence of owners prevents this kind of evolution, making it necessary to start from scratch when developing a program.[5]

Stallman concludes that since the ownership of programs is so obstructive and yields such negative consequences, "society shouldn't have owners for programs."[6]

LaMacchia seemed to share this philosophy and apparently decided to do something about it by becoming a "Robin Hood" figure on the Internet, redistributing the ownership rights of copyrighted software programs from large corporations such as Microsoft to individual users.

Regardless of his motivation and the validity of these arguments, LaMacchia's actions were strongly condemned by many in the user community. Software companies praised the indictment as long overdue. But this sentiment was by no means universal. Some civil liberties experts underscored LaMacchia's defense that he did not actually copy the software himself. Hence, what exactly is the crime or transgression that has been committed? According to *Computerworld*, "the student's defense revolves around the assertion that a bulletin board is just a conduit for information and the notion that organizations such as telephone companies, book stores, and newspapers cannot be prosecuted when information they convey is used illegally by others."[7] On the other hand, one could surely argue that he facilitated the use of the Internet as a conduit of criminal activity, that is, the illegal distribution of copyrighted software.

Another protest over the arrest of LaMacchia was voiced by constitutional law expert and Harvard Law School Professor Lawrence Tribe. Tribe argued that the case should not be pursued particularly since there was no attempt to profit from the distribution of the software. He and other civil libertarians have regarded this incident as a free speech case. Tribe noted at the time that an indictment would be problematic since it could "chill the open transmission of information in cyberspace."[8]

This unusual case was carefully watched by major software companies who had a significant stake in this decision. They were disappointed, however, when a federal judge dismissed the indictment, arguing that LaMacchia could not be prosecuted for criminal copyright infringement under wire fraud statutes since those statutes do not cover system operators in cyberspace. Others cheered the decision, since in their view it meant that bulletin board operators could continue to operate their "free speech forums."

Case 6.2 "It's Never Right to Copy Software"

Roger Gleason breezed into the third floor teacher's room to get some coffee before his 8:45 AM meeting with the principal. The room was unusually serene since the first period of classes was already underway. He appreciated the opportunity for some quiet time to prepare for his meeting.

Gleason was a mathematics teacher at City High School, an inner city school with a reputation for academic excellence. City High typically sent 60 to 70 percent of its graduates to college and had a dropout rate of less than 10 percent. It was located on the fringe of an impoverished neighborhood from which it drew the majority of its students. Most of these students came from families who received some sort of public assistance such as welfare. Despite its location and continuing budgetary constraints, the school was especially well known for its math and science departments which were among the best in the entire school district.

Gleason was reassigned to this school several years ago from one of the suburban schools in the district. He was ambitious and felt that this assignment would enhance his career. He also felt privileged to be at a school with such a strong reputation for excellence in mathematics. During his second year here he volunteered to head the math team and under his tutelage it advanced to the semifinals in a statewide math contest.

Teaching at this school, however, was not without its challenges. Many incoming students came from inferior grammar schools and, despite their innate abilities, were grossly underprepared for high school, particularly in the areas of mathematics and English. As a result, conscientious teachers like Gleason were called upon to put in extra hours in order to do remedial work with many students. Many of the faculty were quite willing to expend this extra effort, and, in Gleason's view, this sense of commitment and caring gave the school its special ethos and distinctive character.

Gleason was especially elated these days since he had learned several days ago that a significant gift would be forthcoming to the math department. A local company had decided to donate 22 used personal computers; they were Macintosh IIci's with 40 megabytes of memory. They were scheduled to be delivered within the next few weeks.

The administrators at City High were equally pleased about this magnanimous gesture. The computer science curriculum at the school was severely limited because of the lack of equipment. The school had a meager budget for such items. The science labs were also ill-equipped, and sometimes chemistry teachers were forced to improvise. For many scientific experiments chemistry teachers would use plastic bottles in place of beakers.

Since the principal had actually been anticipating this gift for some time she met with the department on several occasions in order to elicit their recommendation for how these computers should be utilized. The consensus of the department was that some of the computers should be used to set up a special computer laboratory with at least 14 of the 22 systems. These machines would be available for students who needed tutorial assistance with freshman algebra, geometry, or other subjects. It was difficult for the teaching staff to keep up with the demands for such assistance and this lab might help solve the problem. It was also decided that Gleason should be appointed as the coordinator of the new math computer lab. The principal concurred with both of these decisions. Gleason was happy to assume this new responsibility even though it would require more of his time. However, he enjoyed helping students and he saw this as an opportunity to take more of a leadership role in the school.

Gleason finished his coffee and headed down the hall to the principal's office. The principal, MaryLou Duffy, was a 30-year veteran of the school system. This was the beginning of her seventh year at City High School. She was well liked by both faculty and students. She had a reputation for being a no nonsense, pragmatic, and results-oriented administrator, but she had an amiable and engaging personality. Her stature in the school district gave her some clout with the School Board, and many on the Board admired the way she would lobby for the needs of City High with vigor and diplomacy.

As usual, she was right on time for the meeting with Gleason. After the exchange of the usual pleasantries Duffy invited Gleason into her office and promptly began the meeting: "I wanted to get together to talk about your role as the new lab coordinator. This lab is a great addition to the school and I'm grateful that you have decided to take this position. Your background with computers clearly makes you the most qualified person to run this lab." Gleason thanked her for this vote of confidence and inquired about a budget. "I wasn't planning on much of a budget," she said, "since, as you know, our resources here are quite constrained. But what do you need?"

"Well," Roger answered, "our primary need is for educational software for these new computers. I would like to get enough software for at least 10 of these machines. The best program is probably MATH-TUTOR, a series of diskettes that cover algebra, geometry, and even some calculus. This will be invaluable for our students who often need so much extra help in these areas." Gleason sensed some skepticism, and so he elaborated on his request: "Having these machines function as 'electronic tutors' will take a big burden off our faculty; if they don't have to do remedial work they will have more time to prepare their classes and introduce innovative material. Also, the students will be able to work at their own pace. They can spend as much time as they need on practicing problems."

After Gleason finished talking, Duffy rose up in the chair from behind her desk. She checked a file and sat back down. "I notice that we already own one copy of this software. Isn't that right?" she asked Gleason. Gleason explained that the school did have one licensed copy of this software installed on one of the hardware systems in the computer resource center where the programming classes were now taught. "Well, then," responded Duffy, "why not just make copies for the ten machines? No one will ever know."

Gleason looked surprised and there was some hesitancy in his voice. "But that's stealing, isn't it? I know that we don't have a lot of money around here, but it's never right to copy software programs."

Duffy was a bit taken aback by this response, but she was insistent. "Roger, I appreciate your concern, but let's be practical. We just cannot afford to spend all that money for ten copies of fairly expensive software. As I recall, these programs currently sell for $695. That means almost $7000!"

"Well what about asking the software company to make a donation or give us a break on the price?" Gleason asked.

Duffy shook her head. "We tried that a year ago and the company refused. They have a firm policy of no giveaways."

Gleason was silent for a few moments as he mulled over the options. There did not appear to be a viable solution to this problem aside from copying the software. Duffy glanced at her watch and noticed that it was time for her next appointment. "Why don't you think it over a bit," she said. "You *are* the coordinator, so if you refuse to do this, I'll accept that. But keep in mind that I can't give you any money for software and without software these machines won't do us much good. At any rate, let me know by tomorrow what you have decided."

As Gleason was ushered from the office he wondered whether he was being too naive. As he taught his math classes that day he couldn't help focus more intensely on the deprivation of his students and their bleak surroundings. What a stark contrast to the company that produced this software. He recalled reading somewhere that their profits last year exceeded $100 million. Then again, he thought, does this justify taking someone else's property?

Gleason vacillated like this throughout the day. But he was determined to make a decision and move on to planning the other activities associated with starting up this computer lab. When he finished his classes he went straight to his tiny cubicle in the math department. After an hour or so his colleagues had all departed. Gleason picked up the phone and began to dial the principal's extension.

Case 6.3   Whose Program Is This?

Ellen Pederson glanced out the rain-streaked windows at the few remaining cars in the dimly lighted parking lot. She was once again putting in extra hours to finish an assignment on schedule. She was anxious to leave but knew she would need to work a few more hours if she was to make the crucial Friday deadline.

Ellen worked for the Apollo Group, a prestigious organization that specialized in providing employment counseling to executives. Apollo was also a head hunting firm that worked with Fortune 500 corporations to help them find the "right" executive for certain key positions. Ellen began her career at Apollo 3 years ago in the Information Systems (IS) department. When she joined Apollo after graduate school she began working as a programmer on various computer systems for the organization. The department had just expanded and its charge at that time was to construct applications that would provide client information to Apollo account executives, keep track of accounts receivable and accounts payable, and provide a meaningful decision support system for the company's top executives. As Apollo took on more clients and its revenues reached the $250 million mark, the need for these systems was considered critical.

Shortly after Ellen was hired, the IS department quickly moved into action in order to meet these objectives. It purchased a relational data base, a 4GL, and other software tools in order to implement these systems requested by the Apollo executives. The company had a DEC VAX computer system which would be the repository of the applications. Users were equipped with terminals or IBM PCs that could emulate DEC terminals when necessary.

Ellen's primary responsibility became the development of an on-line accounts payable system which became known as U-PAY. Users could go on-line, select the vendor from an approved list, and then key in a description of the product or services provided, the amount of the purchase, and any other pertinent information. The system would automatically generate a purchase order or check requisition while encumbering funds from the department's budget. Payments could also be generated for individuals such as consultants who were not on the payroll but were rendering some service to the company. All approvals were handled on-line as well. Once Accounts Payable received the approved check requisition, it issued a check for the appropriate amount and sent it along to the vendor or the external consultant. The system had many advantages: it expedited the payments to Apollo's many adjunct consultants along with its numerous vendors and it also prevented budget overruns which had been a problem in past years.

Ellen had worked on this system for over 2 years before it was unveiled last August. It was an immediate sensation in the company. Unfortunately, Ellen's boss took much of the credit for the project despite the fact that his input was really confined to its design stage. Ellen was the project leader who put in the long hours to make this application a reality. She did receive a decent pay increase and a small bonus for her substantial efforts, but she was quite chagrined that she did not receive the credit or recognition that she deserved for this project. Now she was working on designing a major new data base system along with some enhancements to U-PAY.

As Ellen became more disenchanted at Apollo she began to look around for a new job. The market for programmers with her skills and experience was pretty strong despite a mild national recession. As a result, Ellen quickly secured several interviews. One of the interviews was with Apollo's chief competitor located in a nearby city. They were far behind Apollo in their systems development work and were impressed with Ellen's achievement. On her second interview at this company, the director of Information Systems asked to see some of her work. Ellen showed him a demo of U-PAY along with some of the code she had written for the system. U-PAY was written for the most part in the computer language PL/1. The director was convinced that Ellen was a consummate PL/1 programmer and he was quite eager to have her on his staff. He offered her an annual salary of $65,000 (she was making $53,000 at Apollo) along with the title of Associate Director.

During this final meeting when this generous offer was made, the director indicated to Ellen that her first assignment would be to build a system "similar to U-PAY." He also pointed out that since she had already done this at Apollo she should be able to expedite this project and complete it within a "pretty short time frame." The more he discussed this topic the more Ellen realized the implication of his remarks. The only way a project of this scope could be completed in such a short period of time would be to borrow heavily from her previous work. To be sure, if Ellen used the same design specs she used at Apollo and certain modules of PL/1 code she could indeed finish the project within a year or so.

When the meeting ended she thanked the director for his offer and told him that she would get back to him with an answer within 24 hours. Ellen was delighted about the high salary and the new title, but she did have some reservations about "borrowing" so much of the work she had done at Apollo. She decided, however, to accept the offer. She also mentioned to her new boss that she would definitely be able to meet his timetable for a new accounts payable system.

Before giving her termination notice at Apollo Ellen made copies of the U-PAY design specs and the PL/1 source code that she and her team had written. Her superiors were sorry to see her go but they did not make a counter offer. Ellen was not surprised. She would be quite happy to leave this ungrateful employer.

As she worked late this rainy night just 3 days before her final day at Apollo she thought of her decision to take with her the design specifications and source code of the U-PAY system. Occasionally, she felt some guilt over this decision, but her guilt was assuaged by her firm conviction that this was *her* work and that she had as much right to it as Apollo. Also, she would not be depriving Apollo of anything. This was a generic application that did not involve any competitive information. As long as Apollo had an efficient U-PAY system what difference did it make if another company, even a competitor, had the same thing? Where was the harm? Also, she knew full well that this was a common practice among software engineers. She was not the only one leveraging the knowledge and experience that had been gained at a former employer. After all, she reasoned, that is the way the game is played these days.

Ellen sipped her diet soda as she continued coding the latest series of enhancements to the revised U-PAY system. She was looking foward to her last day on Friday and the going away lunch that her colleagues had planned for her.

Case 6.4   Doric Conversion Technologies, Inc.

Peter Johnson was late for the software engineering staff meeting in the main conference room. Staff meetings were held each Monday at 3:00 PM and despite his best efforts Johnson always seemed to be late, much to the annoyance of the vice president of Product Development who routinely ran this meeting.

This time Johnson had a good reason for his tardiness. He had been engaged in a heated exchange with someone in the Marketing Department about discontinuing an important software product. As he entered the conference room, the meeting fell silent. Johnson took his seat and the vice president's assistant shot a manila folder across the glimmer of the table. It contained the agenda and supporting documentation for what looked like another long and tedious meeting. As things got underway again, Johnson kept thinking about his latest run-in with Marketing.

Doric Conversion Technologies was a major producer of conversion tools for mainframe and mini computer software products. Under Johnson's leadership, Doric had recently developed a conversion tool for a prominent data base company that converted data and programs from version 4 to version 5 of its Data Base Products (DBP) software package. Version 5 of this popular DBP product represented a major upgrade. As a result, programs and applications written in version 4 could not be used for version 5 without being subjected to a conversion utility. Doric's product, which was sold directly to DBP customers, was designed to provide for a conversion of its applications expediently and efficiently.

This product had been on the market for one and a half years and had been a reasonable commercial success. Approximately 58 percent of the DBP customer base had converted to version 5 and almost all of them purchased the Doric conversion tool. The data base company's customer base was approximately 4500 clients. This meant that Doric had sold about 2600 copies of its conversion utility at a price of $8500 each.

Cynthia Wilson was Doric's Marketing Director, and she was responsible for marketing and selling Doric's rather full product line. She typically had the final say in the company about product longevity. The company sold many types of conversion products that usually had a short life cycle. Wilson was convinced that the life cycle of this product had just about run its course. If Doric customers had not converted by now, she reasoned, most of them would be quite reluctant to convert to version 5 in the near future because they lacked either the resources or interest to invest in this upgrade. In her view, it was not worthwhile to continue marketing, selling, or supporting this product.

The implementation of these conversion utilities such as the one for DBP was usually complicated, and hence required help from the Doric technical support staff. Wilson intended to inform DBP customers this week that support for this conversion utility would be eliminated within the next month. This might provide a major incentive for those clients who had not yet converted. After that point she was unwilling to supply even limited support for this product. In addition, the company had almost run out of manuals and she did not want to assume the expense of a reprint.

Johnson was convinced that the termination of this product was premature. He pointed out that similar Doric tools were given a much longer life cycle and that many DBP customers would buy the product eventually; many "old-time" users he spoke with told him that they would be making the conversion but could not do so at the present time. Thus, Johnson believed that the prospects were promising for selling the conversion tool to a fairly large portion of the remaining 1900 users of DBP who were still running version 4. Potential revenues could be millions of dollars. In his meeting with Wilson he advocated a more intense marketing approach in collaboration with the data base company. However, his plan for more aggressive marketing was rejected by Wilson and her boss. Her preference was to invest Doric's scarce marketing and customer support resources in newer and potentially more profitable products. Further, there was a great deal of turnover in the customer support department and she did not want to spend time teaching new analysts about the DBP conversion tool.

As Johnson listened to his fellow engineers ramble on during the staff meeting, he had an idea about how to deal with this problem and take advantage of an opportunity that was being carelessly discarded by Doric. Johnson reasoned that he could sell the product himself. Perhaps he could start his own company that would initially be devoted to the sale of this conversion program. He could market the product on his own and provide the necessary support. "After all," he thought, "I was the key person in developing this product and I know more about it than almost anyone else at Doric." Johnson had been the project manager for this conversion tool and had supervised the engineering team responsible for its development. Also, as with most of Doric's products, this particular product had no copyright or patent protection. The company's executives felt that this was unnecessary (and expensive) given the product's limited usefulness and short life cycle. Employees did sign nondisclosure agreements which prevented them from using Doric's technology for their own personal gain either while employed at Doric or for 2 years after they departed from the company. The following is an excerpt from that agreement:

> I hereby assign to the Company my entire right title and interest in any processes, techniques, know-how (whether in written, schematic or any other form) or idea, patentable or not, including without limitation any software and software documentation, made or conceived or reduced to practice or learned by me, either alone or jointly with others, during the period of my employment.

However, through an oversight, Johnson and many other veteran employees of Doric never signed such an agreement. As a consequence, there did not appear to be any legal restrictions against appropriating this product and selling it on his own.

After the meeting ended, Johnson returned to his small and crowded corner office overlooking Tottem Pond. The more he thought about this proposal, the more convinced he became that it was quite feasible. Johnson figured that he could make necessary preparations for this during the next month while Doric was still selling and supporting the product. Once it was officially discontinued, he would resign from

Doric and sell the product through his own company. Of course, DBP clients could still buy the product from Doric after this point, but they would not get support or documentation. As a consequence the product would not be very useful under these circumstances. However, Johnson's company would provide both ample documentation and the necessary support. Thus, he would be competing with Doric but the provision of these vital services would give him a significant advantage.

Despite his upbeat attitude about the prospects for success, Johnson did have some ethical reservations about this grand plan. He was apprehensive about telling Doric of his intentions, since he was fairly sure that they would not give him permission to execute this idea. When a colleague had approached the company about a similar scheme a year ago the president emphatically refused to even consider his proposal. On the other hand, why should he allow this product to languish when it could still generate appreciable revenues? Was there anything really wrong with selling a product that Doric had abandoned? Johnson needed to address these questions more carefully before making a final decision about this risky venture.

Case 6.5   Software Compatibility and Reverse Engineering

> the public at large remains free to discover and exploit the trade secret through reverse engineering of products in the public domain or by independent development[9]

In his popular bestseller, *Being Digital,* Negroponte echoes the widespread frustration with current copyright and patent protection for software programs: "Copyright law is totally out of date. It is a Gutenberg artifact. Since it is a reactive process, it will probably have to break down completely before it is corrected."[10] This sentiment is shared by users and producers alike who have been surprised by recent landmark judicial rulings in cases such as *Lotus v. Borland* or *Apple v. Microsoft.*

The software industry itself is sharply divided on the scope of intellectual property protection. On the one side are those who underline the need for common standards and for compatibility between various hardware systems and software programs. Their position is buttressed by the fact that the development of standards acts as a catalyst for economic development. How could the industrial age have succeeded without standard sizes for products like tires and appliances? Hence, they advocate narrow intellectual property protection. Many users and new entrants in the industry would fall into this category.

On the other hand, established software companies oppose this view, claiming that such narrow protection will ultimately stifle investment in new product development. As a result they "work to prevent innovators from making compatible software and hardware; not wanting standards, they fight to maintain rigidly proprietary systems and equipment, an approach that locks out competition."[11] This was the position adopted by Lotus in its protracted intellectual property dispute with Borland, a company which sought to market a spreadsheet similar to Lotus 1-2-3 called *Quattro Pro*. Companies such as Lotus do not want similar products and they regard reverse engineering and the development of compatible products as equivalent to theft of their property. Hence, they seek broad copyright protection.

It is clear that federal copyright law protects not only the source code (the lines of computer code written in a high-level language such as COBOL, BASIC, or C) but also the object code (the binary code created when the source code is compiled) of programs. Thus, copyright infringement would occur if a programmer copied lines of source code and then sold them as his own program. Similarly, infringment occurs if someone makes duplicate copies of the finished product instead of purchasing or licensing one's own copy. What is less clear is whether or not copyright laws are infringed if someone copies the logic, command sequence, general design, or "look and feel" of the program but embodies this in his or her own source code. The key question is this: What is protected beyond the actual source code? If a software program is developed that looks and functions like another software program even though no source code has been copied, has there been any copyright infringement? Also, what methods can be employed, short of copying source codes, to ensure that one's software program will work on a specific hardware system?

The crux of the debate, then, can be reduced to the issue of *compatibility*, that is, compatibility between two versions of a software product (such as a spreadsheet or data base) and compatibility between software and a hardware platform. The key moral question seems to be whether or not there is an inherent contradiction between product compatibility and copyright protection. Among the specific issues that are in dispute and in some form of litigation today, two stand out as especially prominent and controversial:

1. How much similarity can there be between two programs in the screen interface and the command structure?
2. To what lengths can companies go to develop programs that will communicate with a hardware system? Do companies have a "right" to reverse engineer a product?

We will consider two specific disputes which illustrate each of these issues: the *Lotus v. Borland* case and the *Sega Ltd. v. Accolade, Inc.* case. Both of these cases provoke many difficult questions about fairness, rights, and equity that ought to be factored into decisions currently being made about intellectual property.

LOTUS V. BORLAND

Borland International, Inc., located in Scotts Valley, California, is a major software producer known for its data base and spreadsheet products along with programming tools and languages. It was founded in 1984 by entrepreneur Phillipe Kahn and grew quite rapidly. By 1991 its sales had increased to $226 million, up from $91 million in 1989. Also, in 1991 Borland acquired Ashton-Tate, the producer of the popular dBASE product, and this gave it a dominant position in the PC data-base market. More recently, as the result of some management mistakes, Borland has struggled. Its revenues have been declining, and it posted a $45 million loss in 1994.

In the early 1990s, Borland introduced a much delayed version of its spreadsheet product called *Quattro Pro* (QP). The product was available for DOS or Windows operating systems. But QP mimicked some of the commands used in the Lotus 1-2-3 spreadsheet. Borland assumed that it could copy functional features of other products (such as 1-2-3) without infringing on any copyright protection. Lotus, however, a pioneer in the $1 billion spreadsheet market, almost immediately sued Borland for copyright infringement. The Cambridge, Massachusetts company has had the dominant position in the spreadsheet marketplace for many years; its market share in spreadsheets for DOS operating systems is about 89 percent. Hence, the company sought to defend its turf from the encroachment of Borland's new product.

At issue in this case was the protectability of Lotus's command structures. Lotus alleged in its lawsuit that Borland copied its command menus. Those menus included basic commands such as Print, Quit, File, Save, and so on. It maintained that the order of these commands in its pull down menus was a creative decision that should be copyrightable. In addition, Quattro Pro accepted the same keystrokes as Lotus 1-2-3, and this meant that QP had the same "feel" as the Lotus program. For instance, in both programs the "@" key is used to initiate a formula. Thus, "Lotus was the first software developer to make an explicit look and feel claim in a copyright litigation about user interfaces."[12]

The other famous "look and feel" case was *Apple v. Microsoft* wherein Apple alleged that the Microsoft Windows user interface copied the look and feel of the Apple Computer user interface. Apple contended in its lawsuit that Windows was a blatant infringement of its copyrights, especially the copyright covering the on-screen display of overlapping windows. Further, Apple argued that the graphic elements of its popular user interface (such as the use of the trash can icon) should be afforded protection from imitative products such as Windows. Apple lost a series of federal trial court rulings and in February 1995 the Supreme Court refused to hear the case, thereby handing Apple a final defeat in this hotly contested copyright suit.

In contrast to Apple Computer, Lotus was triumphant in the first round of this legal confrontation with Borland. In July 1992 Judge Robert E. Keeton enjoined Borland from selling its Quattro Pro product with its Lotus 1-2-3 compatible menus. According to the judge's opinion, "Borland copied copyrightable elements of 1-2-3 that constitute a substantial part of that program. Lotus has sued and Borland is liable."[13] Emboldened by this court victory Lotus immediately went on the offensive. It ran ads in major newspapers and trade publications with the headline,

There's nothing innovative

about copying.

Lotus innovated. Borland copied.

Lotus defended its lawsuit in this ad, observing that Borland's copying was analogous to someone plagiarizing *The Grapes of Wrath*, changing the ending, and calling it a new novel. For Lotus, Borland's copying of its commands and keystrokes was tantamount to the pilfering of its creative work. Borland, on the other hand, maintained that the arrangement of commands was functional "because it was done to accord with predicted frequency of use."[14] The company also contended that it was unfair to disallow interface similarities and thereby undermine product compatibility that is a significant convenience for end users.

In March 1995, Borland was vindicated as a federal appeals court overturned Judge Keeton's ruling on behalf of Lotus. It ruled that Quattro Pro did not infringe Lotus's copyright on its 1-2-3 product by copying menus of computer commands. The court ruled that the commands are "methods of operation," and hence cannot be copyrighted. The ruling came just in time for this beleaguered company, since most analysts predicted that "Borland might have to be sold or file for bankruptcy if it were forced to pay damages to Lotus."[15] Lotus appealed this ruling to the U.S. Supreme Court and the case was presented in January 1996. The high court's 4-4 split vote affirmed the lower court victory for Borland, but the ruling was not accompanied by an opinion and hence will not serve as a guideline for other cases.

Clearly, the message of this ruling is that commands themselves and the order and sequence of those commands are not subject to copyright protection. The decision, coming so quickly on the heels of the *Apple* ruling, is also another setback for the position that the look and feel of a program should be protected under copyright law.

However, there are some lingering and unresolved questions here. Is it fair and equitable to imitate another program's command structure or is this analogous to plagiarism as Lotus has claimed? This ruling will make it easier for the software industry to develop compatible software and common interfaces. But is such compatibility in any way a form of theft as some companies have insistently contended? Finally, how does society achieve a balance between the interests of innovators and the needs of copiers, and how should this get embodied in the law?

REVERSE ENGINEERING: SEGA V. ACCOLADE

The controversial technique of reverse engineering has become especially popular in the video game industry. The stakes are high since a top video game can generate hundreds of millions of dollars in revenues and profits. For example, in 1994 sales for the video game Mortal Kombat II were $220 million, even though the game was only introduced in October in time for Christmas sales. According to the *Economist*, the worldwide home-video games market is about $20 billion, "of which about two thirds represents the games themselves and one third the machines they are played on."[16] Thus, there is a powerful incentive to develop a hit game on as many hardware platforms as possible.

In this industry there is a perceived "right" to reverse engineer whenever there is no other way to get information that will allow a company to develop a game that is compatible with a specific hardware platform. The only other alternative is to pay stiff licensing fees to hardware vendors. Thus, for instance, Atari decided that it would manufacture and market Nintendo-compatible games without a license from Nintendo. Accolade decided to do the same thing for Sega hardware.

Before considering the methods developed to implement this decision it is necessary to discuss the equity of the decision itself. Is it acceptable, for example, that Atari sells Nintendo-compatible games without a Nintendo license? Atari and Accolade would obviously answer this question in the affirmative and the basis of their rationale is the desirability of free competition. However, Nintendo believed that it should be able to establish the terms for those companies which are developing games for their consoles. Nintendo and Sega only wanted quality games to run on their consoles, and hence sought to control the selection of their game developers. Many of those developers, however, regarded the exclusivity clause as too stringent (for a two-year period the game developer agreed not to adapt the game for other hardware systems). Hence, the impasse and a resort to reverse engineering techniques.

There are many ways to "reverse engineer" a product. An especially controversial form of reverse engineering is the use of a reverse compiler that can reproduce at least some semblance of the original source code. Some legal scholars, such as Clapes, have expressed grave reservations about the use of this particular technique. According to Clapes, "we must recognize that 'reverse engineering' is a term that makes no real sense when applied to software."[17] He further observes that reverse compiling is the same as translating a French novel into English. However, since this cannot be done without explicit permission of the author, translating the novel would have to be an infringement of copyright laws. Also, Clapes points out that decompiling a program is the same process as translating an encrypted text. Isn't the reading and use of another's computer program simply another form of "translation" that infringes copyright protection?

On the other side of this issue stand the so-called antiprotectionists who claim that reverse compiling is perfectly appropriate. They observe that many programmers can decipher an object code even without the aid of a reverse compiler. Moreover, using other programs as the building block of new applications is part of the whole process of the dissemination of ideas that should not be unduly interfered with. It stimulates incremental innovation and broad compatibility between hardware and software products. But how far can companies go to make their video game cartridges work with the incompatible hardware systems of other companies?

This question is surely at the core of the long dispute between Accolade, Inc. and Sega Enterprises, Ltd. Accolade, Inc., located in San Jose, California, is a major producer of video games. Its most popular game was known as "Ishido: The Way of Stones." It had made games for Sega equipment for some time and had never experienced compatibility problems. But its games would not work with Sega's new Genesis consoles. In order to remedy this problem the company disassembled a Genesis console and reverse-engineered a few of Sega's game cartridges.

Through these efforts Accolade discovered the correct setup code and learned how to circumvent a security mechanism that would prevent foreign cartridges from working in the Sega console. With this vital information in hand Accolade was able to program its games to work in the Genesis consoles.

Sega quickly sued Accolade for copyright infringement. According to *Business Week,* in April 1992, "the U.S. District Court in San Francisco issued a preliminary injunction . . . that pulled six Accolade, Inc.'s video games off the market and kept it from introducing eight more."[18] The judge in this case, Barbara A. Caulfield, ruled that this type of reverse engineering was an infringement of property rights. She pointed out that only certain forms of reverse engineering are permissible especially the technique known as "peeling a chip."[19] In this time-consuming method a company can essentially peel off the top layer of the chip and then attempt to make a copy based on what can be seen. Critics of this ruling noted that there is little difference between peeling a chip and the method used by Accolade, Inc. They also argued that if the ruling held, it would establish an unhealthy trend of restricting access to various hardware platforms which would seriously impair the software industry.

When the case was appealed, however, Judge Caulfield's decision was overturned. Accolade's attorneys persuasively argued that the technique which Sega used to make its cartridges work with the Genesis console was the equivalent of an *interface standard,* and unless that technique was discovered and employed in some way by Accolade there would be no way for Accolade's cartridges to work with the Sega consoles. Accolade's position then was that when a product embodies a standard that cannot be circumvented, software developers must have the right to use whatever code is necessary to make their products function with that standard.

The Ninth Circuit Court of Appeals found these arguments to be compelling and it ruled in favor of Accolade. In so doing it also ruled in favor of a wider scope of reverse engineering techniques. The court stipulated that "where the interface is not published and there is no other reasonable way to find the information needed for compatibility, reverse engineering is permissible."[20] Of course, the competitive program cannot be an exact duplicate of the first one—it can only be similar where required by the interface standard.[21]

Despite this decision in the *Sega v. Accolade* case, the debate continues with full force on the suitability of reverse engineering. Is reverse engineering as pernicious as Clapes and the protectionists maintain? Should software products be better protected against the advances of competitors anxious to peek at proprietary code? If so, how can we have greater compatibility and common standards? Further, what are the economic implications of less standardization? Do the economic pressures for compatibility in any way justify the limitation of property rights?

Finally, there are moral as well as legal issues at stake here. Is it *ethically proper* to engage in reverse engineering, to inspect and clone the products of another company without paying it any licensing fees or other compensation? Moreover, what are the limits of such reverse engineering techniques—should programmers be allowed to use *any* reverse engineering techniques or are there moral constraints that should prevail here? Is there any basis for arguing (as some companies do) that there is a right to compatibility and a right to reverse engineer?

Case 6.6 The IBM–Fujitsu Dispute*

In November 1988, after more than three years of negotiations, two arbitrators issued a 43-page agreement settling a long, bitter dispute between IBM and Fujitsu, its largest Japanese rival. The pact ended the battle over IBM's claim that Fujitsu had extensively copied the operating system software that controlled the inner workings of IBM mainframe computers. Fujitsu vigorously rejected this charge, arguing that it had carefully respected IBM's intellectual property rights. The conflict was so acrimonious that one of the arbitrators later commented, "These two parties have hardly been able to agree what color a stoplight is." Observers of the dispute explained its bitterness by noting that the companies were fierce competitors, each governed by different legal systems and responsive to disparate business norms and cultural values.

The settlement governed Fujitsu's future use of material developed from existing IBM materials as well as from new IBM products. Under strict procedures, Fujitsu could inspect strategically crucial IBM materials, but only in a secured facility. It could also develop new products derived from IBM materials. Fujitsu customers who used such products would no longer need fear that IBM would prosecute them. In exchange for access, permission for past and future use, and immunity from liability, Fujitsu agreed to pay IBM a total of $833,251,000, an amount more than double its 1988 net income. Fujitsu would also make

*Copyright © 1990 by the President and Fellows of Harvard College. Harvard Business School case 9-390-168, rev. 5/29/90. This case was prepared by Ilyse Barkan under the direction of Joseph L. Badaracco as the basis for class discussion rather than to illustrate either effective or ineffective handling of an administrative situation. Reprinted by permission of the Harvard Business School.

additional payments of $25 million or more each year depending upon the IBM materials it used in the future. The arbitrators' decision involved no findings of wrongdoing by Fujitsu.

The arbitrators' decision was designed to resolve the parties' dispute completely, binding them outside of U.S., Japanese, or universal copyright law. The agreement required that IBM and Fujitsu maintain the confidentiality of all their proceedings, both during and after the arbitration. The two arbitrators who created the agreement were chosen by the parties' law firms. IBM's law firm chose John L. Jones, a retired executive vice president of Norfolk Southern Corporation. Fujitsu's law firm in the United States chose Robert H. Mnookin, the Adelbert H. Sweet Professor of Law at Stanford Law School and the director of the Stanford Center on Conflict and Negotiation.

Like the arbitration process itself, the agreement gave Jones and Mnookin substantial long-term power over IBM and Fujitsu. For the next 15 years, the two would supervise all disputes arising from the agreement. For the next five to ten years, they could set the prices and terms of any agreement between IBM and Fujitsu over mainframe operating software. Their decisions, unlike judicial decisions, would be final and unreviewable.

THE PARTIES

IBM

During the 1980s, IBM earned 70–75 percent of world mainframe revenues, and these provided roughly two thirds of IBM's profits. By the end of the decade, annual worldwide mainframe revenues were roughly $30 billion. Vast R&D expenditures, a global organization, a large, highly trained sales force, and customer relationships built up over decades had all helped IBM dominate the worldwide mainframe business. (See Exhibit 1 for IBM financial data.) IBM's dominance of the mainframe business originated in the revolutionary System/360 computers it introduced in the early 1960s.

IBM had also litigated actively, extensively, and frequently to protect its rights. *Business Week* said IBM had a history "as one of the world's most ferocious legal combatants." Throughout the 1970s, the company fought a massive antitrust case brought by the U.S. Justice Department, and the government ultimately dropped the case. In 1983, after Hitachi pleaded guilty in federal court to criminal charges that it conspired to transport stolen IBM technical documents to Japan, IBM filed its own civil damages suit against Hitachi for stealing the technol-

Exhibit 1   IBM: Selected Financial Data
Five-Year Comparison* (in millions of dollars)

	1988	1987	1986	1985	1984
For the year					
Revenue	59,681	55,256	52,160	50,718	46,309
Net earnings	5,806	5,258	4,789	6,555	6,582
Investment in plant, rental machines, and other property	5,431	4,312	4,644	6,434	5,507
Return on stockholders' equity	14.9%	14.5%	14.4%	22.4%	26.5%
At end of year					
Total assets	73,037	70,029	63,020	56,983	44,989
Net investment in plant, rental machines, and other property	23,426	22,967	21,310	19,713	16,396
Long-term debt	8,518	7,108	6,923	6,368	4,232
Stockholders' equity	39,509	38,263	34,374	31,990	26,489

* *Source: IBM financial statement, Annual Report, 1989, p. 43. Moody's Industrial Manual, 1989, p. 463.*

Lines of Business Revenue
(in millions of dollars)

	1988	1987
Sales	$39,959	$36,424
Support services	9,285	9,297
Software	7,927	6,836
Rentals and financing	2,510	2,699
Number of employees, 12/31/88: 387, 112		

ogy. Hitachi settled the civil suit in 1983, agreed to pay IBM about $300 million, and allowed IBM to inspect future Hitachi products. IBM's case against Hitachi resulted from a complex "sting" operation devised by IBM and the Federal Bureau of Investigation. The climax of the effort was a payment of more than $500,000 made by a senior Hitachi engineer to a Silicon Valley consultant for IBM technology. The consultant was actually working for IBM and the FBI. IBM's efforts led one observer to write that "the scale of the operation and the publicity it drew were more reminiscent of a high-security Soviet counterespionage program than a mere effort to protect trade secrets."[22]

IBM dominated the world market for operating systems software for mainframes. During the 1980s, the price of IBM systems software products grew at an annual compound rate of 28 percent. This software was among the most complex programs in existence, with millions of lines of code, and IBM had thousands of programmers working continuously to develop it. Cloning this software or developing alternative products was extremely difficult: Amdahl spent six years and $10 million in such an effort and then gave up in 1988 because it concluded customers would not want to risk an alternative to IBM systems software, especially when they already had millions of dollars of customized software written for IBM mainframes and operating systems software.

During the 1980s, IBM's market had begun to change. The computer industry shifted from emphasis on single, large, central processing units, typically mainframes, to networks of computers. Mainframe sales slowed; some forecasts showed them growing only 3 percent a year between 1986 and 1996. Analysts also predicted that the personal computer market would soon surpass the mainframe market in sales volume. Moreover, hardware revenues were expected to grow at only slightly more than a third of the 20 percent annual rate of growth predicted for software revenues in the late 1980s and 1990s. IBM was moving into these new areas, but it faced much greater competition there than in mainframes.

Fujitsu

Fujitsu, Japan's largest computer maker and the third largest in the world, made IBM-compatible computers. In the early 1970s, when the Japanese government targeted computers as a strategic industry, Fujitsu and Hitachi were charged with entering the mainframe business. At the time, IBM's stunning success with the System/370 was driving rivals like GE and RCA out of the computer industry. (By the early 1970s, IBM's position in the U.S. computer market was so strong that its American competitors were referred to as "the seven dwarfs" or "the bunch," and one of its rivals observed that "IBM is not the competition; it's the environment.")

Fujitsu and Hitachi both chose a plug-compatibility strategy. In effect , they cloned the 370's hardware and the operating system software that controlled it. Fujitsu's efforts benefited from a strategic alliance with Amdahl Corporation, a California-based manufacturer of mainframes founded by Gene Amdahl, the engineer who designed the IBM 360. In 1972, Fujitsu paid $54 million to purchase a 49.5 percent stake in Amdahl, and thereby secured access to its technology. Fujitsu's customers could buy its mainframes and then run IBM applications software—programs for payroll, data processing, and other functions—on these machines. Fujitsu could also begin selling mainframes to IBM customers, and they could run their libraries of applications software on Fujitsu machines. The strategy succeeded: By 1979 Fujitsu sales in Japan outstripped IBM Japan's.

Nevertheless, Fujitsu viewed itself, as did many outside observers, as an underdog in its contest with IBM. Even after the success of Fujitsu's plug-compatibility strategy, the sales of IBM's Japanese subsidiary alone were almost as large as Fujitsu's. In the minds of the Japanese, the IBM–Hitachi conflict "symbolized the ever-present threat of an IBM so powerful it could squash its competitors."[23] (See Exhibit 2 for recent Fujitsu financial results.)

By the early 1980s, some Fujitsu mainframes outperformed comparable IBM products on a price-performance basis. Like IBM, Fujitsu depended heavily on mainframe sales (which accounted for more than 60% of its profits and 70% of its sales), it built most of the parts it used, and its culture was said to be a Japanese version of IBM's stern, no-nonsense approach. Fujitsu distributed internationally but had limited influence outside Japan. Its overseas sales amounted to only 23 percent of total revenues (about half of IBM's comparable figures), and its profit margins were less than half of IBM's 9.7 percent. Fujitsu products were sold in the United States by Amdahl.

While Fujitsu's domestic sales were growing very strongly, its foreign sales had suffered from IBM's allegations about Fujitsu's behavior and their protracted dispute. Fujitsu's European distributor, Siemens-AG, stopped selling Fujitsu equipment in 1986 after IBM alleged infringement. According to one press report, some Siemens customers were embarrassed by surprise visits from auditors sent by IBM to deter-

Exhibit 2   Fujitsu: Selected Financial Data
Five-Year Comparison* (in millions of U.S. dollars)

	1988	1987	1986	1985	1984
For the year					
Net sales	16,374.4	12,256.3	9,399.0	6,174.9	5,401.2
Net income	336.9	148.0	216.3	351.9	297.6
Return on stockholders' equity†	6.2%	3.4%	6.4%	20.5%	19.0%
At end of year					
Total assets	18,532.8	13,686.2	10,398.5	6,801.0	5,699.3
Net investment in plant, rental machines, and other property	4,735.4	3,741.3	3,078.2	1,996.2	1,466.5
Long-term debt	2,412.9	2,312.7	1,978.1	998.0	914.8
Common equity	6,616.2	4,660.3	3,535.2	2,405.0	1,934.8

Net Sales by Main Product Category* (in millions of U.S. dollars)

	1988	1987	1986	1985	1984
Computers and data processing systems	10,976.1	8,291.9	6,202.8	3,711.3	3,247.2
Communications systems	2,598.2	1,851.2	1,412.0	833.2	830.7
Electronic devices (semiconductors and electronic components)	2,048.8	1,520.6	1,253.2	1,288.7	972.5
Total other	751.3	592.6	531.1	341.7	350.8
Car audio (and car electronics)	496.6	387.9	366.1	231.3	241.2
Others	254.7	204.7	165.0	110.4	109.6

*All financial data are from Fujitsu's annual reports for current year. The exchange rate used in Fujitsu conversion from yen to dollars in current year ranged from ¥125 = US$1 in 1988 to ¥253 = US$1 in 1985 and ¥24 = US$1 in 1984.
†Each year's return on equity is from *Worldscope® Industries Company Profiles*, 1989.

mine the type of software they were using. Fujitsu executives were angered by these tactics and charged that IBM was continuing a practice that industry observers had nicknamed "FUD": ways of spreading *f*ear, *u*ncertainty, and *d*oubt among computer buyers thinking of buying non-IBM products.

THE DISPUTE

Operating system software stood at the center of the two companies' dispute. An operating system is a collection of software used to assist and in part control the operations of a computer. Operating systems generally manage the computer's internal functions and facilitate the use of applications software. They coordinate the reading and writing of data between the internal memory and such peripheral devices as disk drives, keyboard, and printer; perform basic housekeeping functions for the computer system; and prepare the computer to execute applications programs.

System software is like the phonograph stylus that turns the grooves on a record into music.[24] The better the operating system's design, the more efficiently applications software runs on it. Moreover, the operating system of a mainframe determines whether competitors' products such as disk drives, personal computers, and other software can be used with the mainframe. According to some computer experts, operating systems are the principal products of the industry and are critical to securing hardware orders.

Operating system software contains two kinds of information. One type tells what a computer does. Customers and others get this information so they can determine what peripheral equipment will be compatible with the computer or so they can write applications programs the computer can run. The second kind of information tells how the computer does what it does. Fujitsu had sought the second, more sensitive information because it believed it was necessary for designing IBM-compatible mainframes.

Fujitsu used IBM programming material to create its early operating system programs, including the M-series operating system released in 1976. Fujitsu acknowledged that some of its other early programs reflected substantial use of copyrighted IBM material, as did the successor versions of these early programs Fujitsu released between 1982 to 1987.[25]

IBM objected to Fujitsu's use of this information. It argued Fujitsu should have relied only upon "reasonable and adequate" interface information. This information is like the specifications for plugs and holes in the back of a stereo amplifier that users need to plug in compatible components. It is not information about the internal design of the amplifier. But before the 1988 agreement, IBM did not differentiate its interface information from internal design information. IBM began to copyright its basic systems software in 1978.

THE 1988 AGREEMENT

In October 1982, IBM alleged that Fujitsu operating system programs and manuals contained IBM programming material in violation of IBM's intellectual property rights. Eight months of negotiations followed. In July 1983 IBM and Fujitsu reached a settlement that required Fujitsu to make substantial payments to IBM, even though Fujitsu did not admit to being guilty of copyright infringement. The settlement also contained procedures for resolving future disputes.

But these arrangements soon unraveled. Critics said the agreement was poorly drafted, and new disputes arose about infringement of IBM's intellectual property rights. At issue were the "successor versions" of early Fujitsu programs. IBM claimed that these involved extensive copying of IBM's system software. IBM filed a demand for arbitration in July 1985 with the American Arbitration Association (AAA), a private, nonprofit entity. Arbitration hearings on the IBM–Fujitsu dispute over intellectual property rights began in December 1985. Considering the complexity of the dispute, the initial agreement providing for arbitration was relatively short. One of the two arbitrators later commented, "It didn't take long to write down what these two parties agreed on. . . . The two parties have never agreed on anything, other than to agree that the only way to resolve this was to get us to solve it."

Three years later the two arbitrators produced an agreement to define what information was protected, govern future use of existing programs, permit each firm to inspect some of the other's technology, and provide fair compensation for its use. The agreement created three arrangements: a paid-up license, a secured facility regime, and a way to define protected information.

The Paid-up License

IBM agreed to give Fujitsu the right to continue using and selling products based upon IBM intellectual property. Because the parties disagreed on the value of the material, the arbitrators heard extended testimony from experts representing both parties and then established their own valuation. In the end, Fujitsu had to make a final payment of $237 million to IBM, bringing its total outlay since 1983 to $833 million.

The Secured Facility Regime

To provide each party with access to the other's interface information, the arbitrators created a secured facility regime. Under this system, either party could examine without restriction the other's unlicensed system software material. In contrast, examination of licensed materials was carefully controlled. Fujitsu had to set up a special building in Tokyo in which it could scrutinize IBM system software, once it reached the market. Inside the facility, Fujitsu personnel could inspect and analyze IBM system software as it evolved over the 1990s, but only for the purpose of its own independent software development.

The arbitrators established strict, detailed procedures for the building's security. They would decide what documents could leave the building and how much Fujitsu would pay for the information it used. IBM did not plan to establish a secured facility in which to examine Fujitsu material.

Defining Protected Information

The agreement emphasized the parties' obligation to differentiate between licensed and unlicensed material, and it stipulated criteria for identifying the interface information the other party could use. Under the agreement, IBM had to give Fujitsu enough interface information that it could offer its customers application program compatibility. This meant customers could run the same applications programs on either IBM or Fujitsu equipment.[26] The huge investment in applications programs written for IBM operating systems made such compatibility essential to Fujitsu's existing customers.

The agreement also ensured that customers could communicate and share a reasonable amount of data between IBM and Fujitsu systems. In general, the goal was to permit "any to any connections."[27] This meant any terminal or application in a network managed by Fujitsu operating systems would be able to efficiently and reliably access any terminal or application in an IBM-managed network or vice versa.

Some industry analysts viewed the agreement as a victory—and perhaps a vindication—for Fujitsu. One Japanese analyst said that "Fujitsu got off with a very light sentence." *Business Week* reported that "There were broad smiles at [Fujitsu's] staid yellow headquarters building in Marunouchi, the heart of Tokyo's business district."[28] Analysts in the United States stressed that the resolution might provide IBM with a vigorous rival in a critical part of the mainframe business.

INTELLECTUAL PROPERTY BATTLES

The IBM–Fujitsu dispute was only the most prominent in a long series of commercial and trade battles over technology during the 1980s. Increasingly, these international and domestic controversies focused on protection of intellectual property rights, particularly for software and patents. Conflicting laws on the international protection of investors' and authors' rights created so much ambiguity that they failed to deter, and sometimes even fostered, infringement of those rights. Exacerbating the problem were the increasing costs of developing new products and the increasing ease of copying,[29] cloning, and improvement engineering.

Large-scale, institutional efforts had been made to address the problem of intellectual property generally, but not for computer software specifically. Trade negotiation organizations such as the General Agreement on Tariffs and Trade (GATT) and the U.N.-based World Intellectual Property Organization (WIPO) were focusing on the discrepancies among countries' protection of foreign intellectual property rights.

The most recent round of GATT talks, the Uruguay Round that began in September 1968, emphasized the work of the Committee on Trade-Related Aspects of Intellectual Property Rights (TRIPS). GATT's objective, however, was not to harmonize the laws but to establish three things: "(1) minimum substantive standards for protection of intellectual property rights; (2) measures for the effective enforcement of these rights both internally and at the border; and (3) a dispute settlement mechanism."[30]

Some countries had enacted new legislation to redress infringement. In the United States, for example, the 1988 trade bill made it easier to control and penalize imports of products that infringed upon American patents. Before this legislation, patent holders had to prove that someone had infringed on their patent *and* that the infringement had damaged them financially. The new law made proof of patent violation sufficient.

Not all countries endorsed stronger protection for intellectual property rights. Developing nations, such as Brazil, often opposed these measures. They held that protecting intellectual property was a way to keep them dependent on the technology and creativity of the industrialized world and stop them from developing local capabilities to invent and create. Believing "knowledge was the heritage of all mankind," these countries viewed protection as "denying them the educational and instructional tools available from copyrighted works and the social and industrial contributions of patented products." Protection, they believed, made these tools and contributions too expensive for developing countries and available only under conditions that "violate the sovereignty of those countries."[31]

Disputes between developed nations, particularly between American and Japanese companies, over infringement of intellectual property were numerous, and many resulted in litigation. Some industry observers have suggested that the United States and Japan had established roles in intellectual property development: The United States researches and develops the property, then licenses or sells it to Japan, and Japan then uses and perfects the technology.

Recent disputes included Fusion Systems Corporation's battle with Mitsubishi Electric over patent rights for a microwave lamp; IBM, Intel, and Texas Instruments' litigation against Japanese competitors over patent and copyright infringement; Corning Glass's suit against Sumitomo Electric for infringement of fiber-optic patents; and Texas Instruments' suit against nine companies, including NEC, Matsushita, Fujitsu, and Mitsubishi Electric, for patent infringement after the defendants refused to pay the increase in royalties that Texas Instruments demanded on its microchips. Despite their efforts, American companies lost some of these legal battles. Intel, for example, lost its suit alleging that NEC had stolen ideas, specifically Intel's microcode, for Intel's microprocessors. NEC argued successfully that it developed the product in question, not by infringement but by completely legal reverse engineering.

American computer companies have also fought each other, often over complex reverse-engineering issues and accusations that one company's user-interface software had stolen the "look and feel" of another's. When IBM refused to buy a license for Berkeley Limited Partnership's patent, which Berkeley said covered some basic software operations found in almost all personal computers and word-processing programs, Berkeley sued IBM for infringement. In response, IBM countersued Berkeley for racketeering and extortion, but the court dismissed the countersuit. IBM then settled Berkeley's suit.[32]

Despite these legal efforts, borrowing, copying, and cloning software remained common, in part because companies have grown more adept at crossing legal mine fields. For example, IBM did not sue Phoenix Technologies, Ltd. when it cloned IBM's BIOS software for personal computers, in part because Phoenix's reverse engineering divided its programmers into separate groups: those who dissected IBM's product to determine its tasks and those who took a list of tasks IBM's products perform and developed a new product to do those tasks.[33]

LEGAL PROTECTION OF INTELLECTUAL PROPERTY IN AMERICA AND JAPAN

Legal protection for intellectual property differs between the United States and Japan. Copyright, patent, and trade secret laws in the countries differ, as do the legal theories justifying the protection. Under these laws, protection for computer software is particularly ambiguous.

A 1983 American appeals court decision, which ruled that American copyright law extended to operating system software, was one of a very few legal decisions that had begun to reduce uncertainties about the scope of protection for operating system software under American law. In 1984 Japan considered enacting a Computer Program Rights Law to end ambiguities about computer programs in its copyright law. It would have required binding arbitration to resolve copyright infringement suits involving computer programs. But Japan rejected the Program Rights Law proposal under pressure from the United States. Instead, it chose to amend its copyright law in 1985, leaving the ambiguities for computer programs in place and changing only items such as the duration of copyright protection.

Copyrights

Subject Matter   American and Japanese copyright systems both protect the form of expression, but not the underlying idea, of an author's work. Under both systems, the work must be original and may be within the broad realms of literature, science, fine art, or music to be eligible for protection. Computer programs and data bases were within the general statutory definition of protected literary works under the American Copyright Act of 1976. Whether software falls under the Japanese law remained a matter of interpretation.

Duration   Until 1985 American and Japanese systems' copyright protection differed in duration. Generally, U.S. law gave works created on or after January 1, 1978, copyright protection for life of the author, plus 50 years after the author's death. Japan formerly protected the work for only 20 years from the date of granting of the copyright, but in 1985 it adopted provisions like those in the United States.

Protection from Infringement   Copyright infringement is the violation of any of the copyright owner's exclusive rights. Both systems allow for use of copyrighted works without infringement in situations involving teaching, scholarship, and research. But Japan permits uses of copyrighted material that American law would scrutinize more carefully. For example, under Japanese law a user of a copyrighted computer program may debug and upgrade it, and even modify it for the purpose of replacement. Its copyright law also leaves ambiguous the distinction between upgrading and revising a computer program.

Remedies   When a copyright infringement occurs, the holder of the copyright can take legal action against the infringer. Both American and Japanese legal systems provide for injunctive relief (this requires the infringer to stop the offending conduct), for damages that compensate for lost profits or royalties, and for criminal sanctions.

Patents

Subject Matter   American and Japanese patent-law systems both require that patentable inventions be novel or contain an inventive step, and be nonobvious or useful. Both include processes as well as products, and improvements to either. Japan's patent law defines an invention as "the highly advanced creation of technical ideas utilizing natural laws," a definition that depends on how the terms "natural laws" and "technical ideas" are interpreted.

Japan and most industrialized countries give priority to the first of competing patent applicants to file an application for the patent on the technology. The United States grants the patent to the first to invent the technology.

In general, a Japanese patent covers a single claim or novel advance. American patents, in contrast, often list several independently valid claims. This compels Japanese inventors to file more patents to cover a single technology. In 1983, for example, about 100,000 patent applications were filed in the United States, while more than 250,000 were filed in Japan.[34]

Explanations for these differences vary. The scope of a patent—a single claim versus multiple claims—is one. Another is Japan's "first to file" system. Still another factor is that Japanese law, unlike the United States, permits the government to grant other parties the right to use an invention if an inventor fails to do so or if working the patent serves the public interest. This creates incentives to make a patent as *narrow* as possible to maintain its exclusivity and, hence, its economic value. Multiple, narrow patents are each more likely to be worked sufficiently, and a narrow patent has more limited economic consequences than one encompassing a class of related inventions. Finally, Japan requires that patent applications cover only specific and proven inventions. Under U.S. law, patents could describe an invention more broadly and cover multiple variations of the invention. To cover the possible variations, inventors in Japan had to file multiple applications.

The application process in the two countries also differs. The U.S. system examines all patents in the order in which applicants file them. Japan examines applications only at the patent applicant's request and may defer examination as long as seven years. Confidentiality of the patent application is absolute in the United States; publication follows the grant of the patent, at which time the patentee can take legal action for copying and other infringement on his technology. But patent applications in Japan are published or "laid open" after 18 months, often before the patent is granted, if granted at all. Opponents of the grant of a patent may oppose it during the three months after examination is requested and before the patent is granted in Japan. In the United States, opponents must wait until the patent is granted.

Some analysts believe that Japan's "laying open" of patent applications promotes a practice called "patent flooding" because competitors can file multiple improvement patents to force the inventor to cross-license its technology rather than defend the patent in litigation. Protection of rights in the technology also depends on the length of time between filing a patent application and the issuing of a patent on the technology. That period in Japan averages six years, compared to a 20-month average in the United States.

Remedies   As with copyright infringement, the remedies of injunctive relief, damages, and criminal sanctions are available in both countries for patent infringements. Injunctive relief in Japan includes the right to demand not only destruction of the resulting product of the infringement, but also removal and destruction of the equipment involved in and contributing to the infringement. Japan also allows for measures to restore the patentee's business goodwill.

Trade Secrets

Subject Matter   Most U.S. states define trade secrets as any "formula, pattern, device, or compilation of information used in one's business and which gives him an opportunity to obtain an advantage over competitors who do not know or use it."[35] Examples include chemical formulas, manufacturing processes, machine patterns, and customer lists. Japan does not identify any such trade secrets by statute, but it does protect trade secrets covered by contract. Both systems rely on contract terms to set the duration of the restriction on use of, disclosure of, or access to another's trade secrets.

Protection from Infringement U.S. law provides several ways of protecting trade secrets: trade secret and criminal statutes, explicit contracts such as postemployment noncompetition agreements and nondisclosure agreements, and implied contracts, created by special relationships such as licensor/licensee. Japan relies only on contracts, such as nondisclosure agreements. Japan's strictly contractual approach precludes protection against third parties that wrongfully acquire trade secrets. Protection against third parties is possible in the American system if the third party knows that it is a trade secret and the information is disclosed to it through a breach of duty.

Remedies Generally, damages and criminal sanctions are available in both systems, but the scope of those remedies and the underlying legal theories differ in America and Japan. Injunctive relief against competitive employment is available in the United States and may be permanent; in Japan, the commercial nature of the rights in question makes injunctions unlikely, but not impossible.

Damages are available in both systems. In the United States, one can get attorney's fees, punitive damages (which are discretionary with the judge), and actual damages based upon the trade secret owner's loss, the misappropriator's gain, and/or a reasonable royalty. State and federal criminal sanctions may apply in the United States, under general criminal laws and the Federal Trade Secrets Acts. Japan has no criminal law specifically prohibiting unauthorized disclosure of, or access to, trade secrets. But its criminal code may punish the use of unlawful means such as threat, fraud, bribery, or theft of tangible data.

IMITATION IN JAPANESE CULTURE

The many, heated intellectual-property disputes between American and Japanese companies led some observers to seek cultural perspectives on the issues. The most controversial of these, and perhaps the most common, was the view that Japanese culture sanctioned imitation to a greater degree than the American.

Proponents of this view emphasized that Japan has borrowed extensively from foreign cultures. Through contacts with China, for example, Japan imitated elements of Chinese culture, adopting a Chinese-style legal code (Ritsuryò) as the basis for the criminal and administrative codes of its legal system. During the nineteenth century, Japan emulated European and American technology. Meiji Japan consciously imitated European and American organizational models in developing its postal and police systems and its newspapers. Japan selected its parliamentary system of government from among American and European models, and Germanic law informed Japan's civil law system, as did Anglo-American influences during the postwar occupation period.

Japanese artists have traditionally studied their crafts in apprenticeships and learned technique by copying that of the master. Between 1750 and 1850, Japanese artists, particularly Hokusai and Hiroshige, learned by imitating: Their works and sketches originated in the drawings of seventh-century Buddhist figures. Masters generated schools of artists, whose followers produced works in particular style. Japanese artists did not begin to sign their works until the sixteenth century. The Zen tradition of repetition of a task or skill to yield mastery or perfection also greatly influenced and informed the arts, as well as other aspects of Japanese culture.

Scholars who have studied the history of Japanese fine arts have acknowledged a tendency toward imitation. One wrote, for example:

> It has been remarked that a pupil's training consists in copying and recopying his master's works and that there are model-books which show the proper method of painting various subjects. So much stress upon tradition, at once a safeguard against radicalism and an obstacle to free development, naturally gave birth to pronounced school mannerisms and to restrictions which extend even to choice of subject and result in inevitable repetition. . . . It is probable, however, that the special references in the "Six Canons" [a classic guide to Japanese painting] to copying old masters was not intended to mean mere copying; rather it should be interpreted as emphasizing the importance of preserving that part of tradition which ever lives as an eternal principle and of transmitting it to the next generation.[36]

Explanations of Japan's alleged tendency to emulation are diverse. Some suggest it is Japanese openness to other cultures. The Dutch journalist Karel Van Wolferen, a long-time resident of Japan, asserts that Japanese culture is based on "the notion that there is a perfect way of doing things . . . that mastery is reached by the removal of the obstacles between the self and the perfect model, embodied by the teacher, a view which emphasizes great technical skill with a lack of personal expression; there is no room for the idiosyncratic individual."[37] In this view, imitation of aspects of Chinese, European, or American civilizations is part of Japan's "catching-up disposition," emulation deriving not merely from pursuit of perfection, but also from a self-perception of "falling short."

In contrast, other writers attribute cultural emulation, and particularly its innovative applications and expressions in Japan, to Japanese self-assertion. Some argue that Japanese emulation is an effort to make Japan respected internationally. In other instances, Japan's imitation may have reinforced an even more aggressive strategy. In Meiji Japan, according to this argument, widespread emulation occurred to prevent any one nation from becoming indispensable to Japan's modernization. Japan sought not only to hold its own but ultimately to grow dominant.

The view of Japan as a peculiarly imitative nation is often criticized for cultural bias, dubious methodology, and general offensiveness. Cultural emulation and imitation are hardly unique to Japan. Many other nations have looked to other nations' cultures and civilizations when developing their own. For example, British industrialists were horrified at the quality of the American guns on display at the Great Exhibition in London in 1851. They believed the Americans had unfairly appropriated British designs. In later decades, the British made similar complaints about German and American efforts in synthetic dyes, metals, armaments, penicillin, radar, and computerized tomography. Moreover, by 1986 Japan had a higher percentage of its population engaged in R&D than America, and by the mid-1980s it accounted for 20 percent of new patents in ceramics, 26 percent in communication equipment, and 33 percent in office-computing and accounting machines.

Historical studies also point to Japanese creativity. Japan's postal and police systems and newspapers, according to some studies, are actually examples of rapid, innovative adaptations of overseas models to Japanese circumstances. Numerous schools of artists existed in Japan, often at the same time; new masters often emerged, establishing new schools and traditions. Unique painting often embellished or individualized otherwise identical pottery forms. Even Zen acts of repetition can be viewed differently. The former Harvard professor and ambassador to Japan, Edwin Reischauer, sees these acts as triumphs of individualism and innovation—the application of one's whole being to a task and a reliance on individual will, self-discovery, and self-discipline to master a practice or an idea.

While some debated these cultural tendencies and their effects on Japanese laws and company behavior, others speculated on the longer-term consequences of the IBM–Fujitsu arbitration. Would IBM and Fujitsu somehow learn to collaborate, now that they were joined in this peculiar, coerced strategic alliance? Would Fujitsu now bring serious competition to the system software market? Would IBM prevent this by rapidly changing its systems software or by moving functions from software to hard circuitry, which Fujitsu could not inspect? Would Fujitsu continue its efforts to develop non-IBM systems software or even team up with AT&T in an alliance against IBM? Would other companies use it as a model for managing international intellectual property disputes?

NOTE ON SOURCES

In addition to the documents cited in the Notes, the data in this case was based upon articles in the general business press and more specialized publications covering the computer industry.

The discussion of Japanese culture and emulation draws, in part, upon D. Elanor Westney, *Imitation and Innovation: The Transfer of Western Organizational Patterns to Meiji Japan* (Cambridge, MA: Harvard University Press, 1987); William Watson, ed., *Artistic Personality and Decorative Style in Japanese Art* (London: University of London Colloquies on Art and Archeology in Asia, no. 6, 1976); and Henry I. Bowie, *On the Laws of Japanese Painting* (New York: Dover Publications, 1951).

The section on intellectual property laws in the United States and Japan is intended for background information only and should not be construed as legal advice. This section drew upon the following sources: Jay Dratler, Jr., "Trade Secrets in the United States and Japan: A Comparison and Prognosis," 14 *Yale Journal of International Law* 68 (1989); Michael A. Epstein, *Modern Intellectual Property* (New York: Law & Business Inc./Harcourt Brace Jovanovich, 1989); Tohru Nakajima, "Legal Protection of Computer Programs in Japan: The Conflict Between Economic and Artistic Goals," *Columbia Journal of Transnational Law* 143 (1988), p. 27; Robert P. Benko, *Protecting Intellectual Property Rights: Issues and Controversies* (Washington, DC: American Enterprise Institute for Public Policy Research, 1987); Mary Ann Glendon, Michael Wallace Gordon, and Christopher Osakwe, *Comparative Legal Traditions: Text, Materials and Cases* (St. Paul, MN: West Publishing Co., 1985); Robert W. Russell, compiler, *Patents and Trademarks in Japan (A Handy Book)* (Tokyo, Japan, 1984); Fenwick, Stone, Davis & West, "Legal Protection of Computer Software in Japan," in Miles R. Gilburne, [symposium] chairman, *Intellectual Property Rights in High-Technology Products and Sensitive Business Information* (New York: Law and Business, Inc./ Harcourt Brace Jovanovich, 1982); Earl W. Kitner and Jack Lahr, *An Intellectual Property Law Printer: A Survey of the Law of Patents, Trade Secrets, Trademarks, Franchises, Copyrights, and Personality and Entertainment Rights* (New York: Clark Boardman Company Ltd., 1982); and Tervo

Doi, *The Intellectual Property Law of Japan* (Alphen aan den Rijn, Germantown, Nd.: Sijthoff and Noordhoff, 1980).

NOTES

1. See, for example, S. Solomon and J. O'Brien, "The Effects of Demographic Factors on Attitudes Toward Software Piracy," *Journal of Computer Information Systems,* 30 (3) 1990, 40–46.
2. Mitch Betts, "Dirty Rotten Scoundrels," *Computerworld,* May 22, 1995, p. 1.
3. A. M. Honore, "Ownership," in A. G. Guest (ed.), *Oxford Essays in Jurisprudence.* Oxford: Oxford University Press, 1961, p. 108.
4. Paul Steidlmeier, "The Moral Legitimacy of Intellectual Property Claims: American Business and Developing Country Perspectives," *The Journal of Business Ethics,* December 1993, pp. 161–162.
5. Richard Stallman, "Why Software Should be Free," publication of the Free Software Foundation, Inc.
6. Ibid.
7. Gary Anthes, "Piracy on the Rise; Companies Fear Liability," *Computerworld,* April 18, 1994, p. 12.
8. William Bulkeley, "Two Face Computer-Fraud Allegations over Software Piracy on the Internet," The Wall Street Journal, April 11, 1994, p. B6. Reprinted by permission of The Wall Street Journal, © 1994, Dow Jones & Company, Inc. All Rights Reserved Worldwide.
9. Supreme Court Opinion, Bonito Boats, Inc. v. Thunder Craft Boats, Inc., 109 S Ct. 971 (1989).
10. Nicholas Negroponte, *Being Digital.* New York: Alfred A. Knopf, 1995, p. 58.
11. G. Gervaise Davis III, "War of the Words: Intellectual Property Laws and Standardization," *IEEE Micro,* December 1993, p. 19.
12. Pamela Samuelson, "The Ups and Downs of Look and Feel," *Communications of the ACM,* April 1993, p. 34.
13. *Lotus Dev. Corp. v. Borland International, Inc.,* 1992 US Dist. Ct.11311 (D. Mass. June 30, 1993).
14. Samuelson, p. 34.
15. Lawrence M. Fisher, "Borland Gets Court Reprieve in Lotus Copyright Dispute," The New York Times, March 10, 1995, p. D1. Copyright © 1995 by The New York Times Company. Reprinted by permission.
16. "The Christmas VideoGame Massacre," *The Economist,* November 19, 1994, p. 71.
17. Anthony Lawrence Clapes, *The Softwars.* Westport, CT: Quorum Books, 1993, p. 145.
18. Richard Brandt, "Bit by Bit, Software Protection is Eroding," *Business Week,* July 20, 1992, p. 87.
19. Cf. *Sega Enterprises Ltd. vs. Accolade Inc.,* U.S. District Court, Northern District of California, C-91-3871 BAC, 1991.
20. Davis, p. 24.

21. *Sega Enterprises, Ltd. v. Accolade, Inc.,* 977 F.2d 1510 (9th Cir. 1992).
22. Marie Anchordoguy, *Computers Incorporated.* Cambridge, MA: Council on East Asian Studies, Harvard University, 1989, p. 1.
23. Marie Anchordoguy, *Computers Incorporated,* p. 2.
24. Michael Miller, "Fujitsu Can Legally Clone IBM Software: The Question Now, Will It Be Able To?" *Wall Street Journal,* December 1, 1988, p. B1.
25. *International Business Machines Corporation v. Fujitsu Limited,* American Arbitration Association, Commercial Arbitration Tribunal Opinion, Case No. 13T-117-0636-85, November 29, 1988, p. 8.
26. American Arbitration Association, *Summary of Opinion International Business Machines Corporation v. Fujitsu Limited,* p. 7.
27. American Arbitration Association, *Summary of Opinion International Business Machines Corporation v. Fujitsu Limited,* p. 11.
28. Neil Gross and John Verity, "Can Fujitsu Break Big Blue Grip?" *Business Week,* December 19, 1988, p. 102.
29. Statement of National Planning Association's committee on Changing International Realities, as cited in Helena Stalson, *Intellectual Property Rights and United States Competitiveness in Trade.* Washington, DC: National Planning Association, Committee on Changing International Realities, 1987, p. v.
30. "U.S.–Japan Friction Remains on Patent Issues," *Background Bulletin.* Press Office, United States Information Service, March 2, 1989, text of statement of Michael Kirk (Assistant Commissioner for External Affairs at the U.S. Department of Commerce), testimony before Senate Subcommittee on Foreign Commerce and Tourism delivered February 28, 1989.
31. Stalson, *Intellectual Property Rights and U.S. Competitiveness in Trade,* p. 48.
32. "Will Software Patents Cramp Creativity?" *Wall Street Journal,* March 14, 1989, p. B-1.
33. *The Economist,* December 23, 1989, pp. 101–102.
34. Krista McQuade and Professor Gomes-Casseres, "Fusion Systems Corporation," HBS case 390-021, 1990.
35. Restatement of Torts §757, comment (b)(1939) as cited in Michael A. Epstein, *Modern Intellectual Property.* New York: Law & Business, Inc./Harcourt Brace Jovanovich, 1989, p. 3, no. 3.
36. Kojiro Tomita, "Art—Far Eastern Methods," in *Japanese Art: A Selection from the Encyclopedia Britannica.* New York: Encyclopedia Britannica, 1933, p. 34.
37. Karel Van Wolferen, *The Enigma of Japanese Power: People and Politics in a Stateless Nation.* Knopf, 1989, pp. 378–379.

7

Computer Security and Computer Crimes

This chapter is closely related to the main themes of Chapter 5 which presented several case studies on the obligations of information managers as custodians of data. Recall that the focus in those cases was on information security, ensuring the integrity, confidentiality, and limited accessibility of sensitive information.

In this chapter we expand on the topic of security, considering the responsibility of organizations to protect their entire computer systems from unwanted intruders, damaging viruses, and so forth. This task has become more onerous because of more open systems, the use of computer networks, and the proliferation of personal computers. Security was far less of a problem in the era of the mainframe and the more centralized approach to data management and control which it fostered. It is much more difficult, however, to provide security for client/server systems where, for instance, many PCs are connected by a LAN and tied to other networks including the Internet. According to one diagnosis, "distributed networks virtually beg for intruders; the more distributed the network, the greater the vulnerability."[1]

Security problems are clearly exacerbated by this level of open network connectivity. Particular concerns have recently arisen about the lack of security on the Internet. While many more organizations are connecting to the Internet, computer hackers seem to be finding new ways to exploit its vulnerabilities. For example, a particularly insidious method of intrusion known as Internet Protocol Spoofing enables hackers to bypass security measures by pretending to be a "trusted" computer on a company's internal network; this dupes the host computer network which then allows the intruder full access. According to the *New York Times*, "this new form of attack leaves many of the 20 million government, business, university, and home computers on the global Internet vulnerable to eavesdropping and theft."[2]

Despite this new breed of security problems, organizations must make a concerted effort to make their computer systems as secure and impenetrable as possible. A corporation's security policy should include at least three main objectives: to maintain access control, to preserve the integrity of the system and its data, and to provide recovery and backup if the system should fail or the data become corrupted. Password protection, antivirus packages, encryption, firewalls, and audit control software are some of the mechanisms for implementing this type of security.

Most companies recognize that business demands careful attention to security issues. But it should not be overlooked that there is also a moral responsibility to ensure that systems are secure and that data is adequately protected. This responsibility stems from the fact that careless or shoddy security procedures could allow sensitive data to fall into the wrong hands and thereby cause considerable injury for the data subjects. For instance, if careless security allows intruders access to financial records, innocent people could easily be victimized.

Finally, it is instructive to say a few words about the issue of security from the perspective of the perpetrator instead of the victim. Many security breaches are caused by hackers, and some have maintained that most of their intrusive activities do no real harm and do not constitute a serious ethical transgression.[3] Is there any merit to this claim? Also, how do we measure the damage caused by such intruders? If no files or data have been stolen or corrupted, does this mean that the intrusion should be dismissed as insignificant? Further, what is an appropriate punishment for electronic trespassers and hackers?

In addition, under some circumstances it is difficult to define what constitutes criminal activity in cyberspace. Is it always a crime to act as a conduit for the distribution of copyrighted material? Where does the right of free expression end and criminal activity begin?

The cases in this chapter will take into account all of these issues. They will explicitly consider the moral challenge of ensuring a secure environment along with questions about the gravity of electronic intrusion and the appropriate penalties for those who are culpable of violating another's property rights.

Many troubling questions come to the surface in the first case called *The Disgruntled Consultant*. After an employee is terminated, he corrupts a system scheduled for immediate delivery to a major client. What is the company's liability for the actions of this rogue employee and is there some obligation to compensate the injured party?

In the next case, *Internet Abstinence?* (A, B), a hospital executive must determine whether or not Internet connectivity is really worth the risk particularly when the data maintained on his computer system is of a highly sensitive nature. This case provides an opportunity to develop a cost/benefit analysis in order to resolve this complex problem. It also permits us to reflect on the *process* used to make security-related decisions that affect many stakeholders.

The third case, *A Programmer's Dilemma*, continues with the theme of responsibility to provide for a secure environment. A consultant must decide what to do when his boss demands that he wrap up a project without building in adequate security. Among other issues this case raises the question of what constitutes "adequate" security.

The other three cases in this section have a much different focus, since they deal with how to handle those who have transgressed the norms of acceptable behavior. In the case entitled *A Harmless Prank*, university officials must determine a fitting punishment for a clever but penitent student hacker. Electronic trespassing is a serious offense and it is important to send a strong signal but extenuating circumstances make it difficult to arrive at a just and fair decision.

Similar questions arise in a case called *Interview with a Hacker*, which presents a view of this subculture through the eyes of one of its former members. He articulates the so-called "hacker ethic" that one can look around on the Internet but not destroy someone else's data. Other opinions are expressed in the interview about this culture and its norms of behavior.

Finally, *The Case of Craig Niedorf* deals with a young man's arrest for propagating a secret text file on the Internet, and the government's apparent overreaction to the misappropriation of sensitive information. How much power should the government have to curtail activities and set limits on the mysterious new frontiers of cyberspace? This case bears some similarity to *Piracy on the Internet* in the previous chapter, since it too deals with some key civil liberties issues.

Case 7.1   The Disgruntled Consultant[4]

Donald Chase had just celebrated his tenth anniversary at TTI Consulting when he received the bad news. As a result of declining revenues and a shrinking customer base, he was one of seven consultants who was being dismissed. His boss, Dr. Phillip Bluestein, informed Chase at 11:00 AM on Tuesday that his services were no longer needed. Bluestein had usually been rather abrupt in his dealings with subordinates, and unfortunately this situation was no different. Chase was told to pack his things and clear out of the building by noontime.

Crestfallen, Chase returned to his small office on the third floor of the TTI building. He struggled to suppress his anger and resentment. He had given his heart and soul to this company during the last 10 years and felt betrayed by this sudden dismissal. These feelings were perhaps accentuated because he had just recently completed a major project for one of TTI's established clients, The Northwest Commerce Bank. He had worked long hours and weekends to finish its complex cash management application on schedule. Chase completed this sophisticated program only several days ago, and during a brief internal demo he received considerable praise from upper management including Bluestein. Managers at Northwest were eagerly awaiting delivery since they estimated that this new system would save the bank about $60,000 a month because of more efficient cash management.

However, at the time of Chase's dismissal the application had not yet been delivered to the client. It remained on Chase's IBM PC which was linked to the company's extensive client/server network. Chase kept the only backup copy of this system in his briefcase; this had enabled him to work on the application at home at his convenience.

As Chase began packing his belongings, Bluestein appeared at the doorway. They briefly discussed the Commerce application, and Chase pointed out to Bluestein how the application could be accessed on his PC. This discussion was followed by a cursory overview of the programs that comprised this system. It appeared to Chase that Bluestein wanted to make sure that everything was intact for the system's imminent delivery to the Commerce Bank. Bluestein remained with Chase as he finished packing a few boxes of books and other materials. Chase then put only a few additional items in his briefcase and left his office followed by Bluestein. He did not return the backup copy of the Commerce Bank system. After saying goodbye to a few friends Chase left the building and drove home.

Upon his return home Chase decided to seek revenge on his ungrateful employer. He used his PC to connect to the company computer system, entered his USER ID and password, and accessed the only copy of the Commerce Bank application. He proceeded swiftly to disable several key programs by inserting some code that subverted the display of menu screens and corrupted data. Chase also had the presence of mind to cover his tracks by erasing the audit file that accompanied the program; thus, there was no record of this unauthorized access to this application.

Executives at TTI were not aware of what happened until 2 days later when an associate of Chase proceeded to do one final quality assurance test before final delivery of the program to the bank. When she logged in to the application she quickly realized that it had been tampered with and called Bluestein who strongly suspected sabotage. He immediately and repeatedly called Chase's residence but there was no answer; also Chase's large severance check had already been cashed.

As Commerce Bank waited patiently for its cash management system, the company quickly launched an internal investigation. It was apparent that the layoffs represented a chaotic situation within TTI; as a result, there was inadequate communication between certain departments. For example, the company's security manager was not informed about the layoffs until the day after they occurred. At that point USER IDs and passwords for the discharged employees were revoked. However, this was much too late to save the Commerce Bank application from this deliberate act of sabotage. When asked by the executive vice president about this communication failure the Human Resources manager informed her that his department had never coordinated layoffs and dismissals with the security manager. "We've never had the sense in this company that we should lock the gates and put up barricades when people leave," he said; "our employees are trusted colleagues even after they've been let go."

As the investigation continued, Bluestein faced a difficult decision about how he would deal with his contact at the Commerce Bank who was eagerly awaiting the cash management program that was now overdue. Chase was an especially clever and adept programmer and consequently Bluestein estimated that it would take at least several weeks to unearth the bugs and fix the system properly. Also, all of the other consultants were assigned to high priority projects, so there might be some delay in getting started on this work.

Bluestein wondered what he should tell the people at Commerce. Should he be candid about the company's untimely security lapse? Commerce was one of TTI's most security-conscious customers, and hence this revelation might jeopardize lucrative future contracts. However, Commerce was told last week that the project was done and that they would receive it right on time. How, then, could he explain what could have gone wrong to delay delivery by several weeks and maybe longer? Also, Bluestein wondered about the corporation's legal and moral responsibility for what happened. Chase was clearly the main culprit here but to what extent was the corporation also liable for his transgression? And if the company is liable, should it make some restitution to its customer whose business is adversely affected because of this mishap? Bluestein began sorting through all of these questions as he stared at the pink phone messages in front of him.

Case 7.2   Internet Abstinence (A)

Jonathan Fuller, Director of Operations at Higgins Psychiatric Hospital, was handed a copy of the *New York Times* by his assistant as he entered his spacious office. She called his attention to several relevant stories including one on the business page. As Fuller settled into his chair, he perused the lead story in the business section with the headline, "Experts See Hackers Gaining an Upper Hand in Fight over Security." The article described in some detail why computer security experts were convinced that corporations were losing ground to the electronic thieves who were breaking into public and private computer systems. Every time one hole was plugged up new ones seemed to emerge.

This was the latest in a long series of articles in the press that articulated the same concern. There seemed to be a growing consensus that security on the Internet was a fleeting illusion. Dr. Fuller put the article aside and wondered how any organization could insulate itself from the dangers of electronic intrusion in this age of openness and connectivity.

The Higgins Psychiatric Hospital was located in a beautiful, but small and obscure town in western Vermont. Among the rolling hills and verdant pastures one could find a discrete edifice which housed some of the finest medical professionals in the entire world. One could also find numerous wealthy and famous individuals among the many patients in this august hospital. Higgins was a haven for celebrities, and, as a result, it had developed over the years a security consciousness that permeated the hospital's decision and policy-making processes.

Like other administrators at Higgins, Fuller was a medical doctor by training. After working for several years as a specialist in the medical profession he decided to become a hospital administrator. He took a job as an associate director at a large teaching hospital in Boston. During his stay at this hospital he also earned an MBA degree at one of the local universities. When the job at Higgins opened several years ago, he saw an opportunity for advancement and sent his resume to the search committee. They were impressed with Fuller's background and experience and offered him the position. What especially impressed members of the committee was Fuller's background in technology and his vision of how technology could make the hospital's operations more efficient. Consequently, when he took the job he was charged with bringing Higgins's antiquated computer technology "into the twentieth century."

Fuller was convinced that he had made great strides toward achieving this challenging goal. He had carefully developed the hospital's information technology architecture and established guidelines and policies for the use of IT resources. He threw out the hospital's outdated computer system and replaced it with a more contemporary and versatile infrastructure: client/server technology using an IBM minicomputer as the host linked together with IBM PCs and other compatible machines.

Once this new system was installed, Fuller began working with the hospital's small MIS staff to work out plans for the development and enhancement of some critical applications. These included a patient tracking and billing system and also a scheduling system for the physicians who dealt with outpatients. At the heart of this system was the patient data base, including personal data and medical histories.

Most of the physicians at Higgins had never laid hands on a computer before Fuller's arrival. However, in an effort to make computing technologies pervade the hospital environment, Fuller required every physician to schedule his or her appointments using the automated scheduling system. As more and more doctors became comfortable with using their IBM personal computers they began using the e-mail facility, wordprocessing programs, and other packages that were available on the host system.

Overall Fuller and the hospital administration were quite pleased and even astonished at the progress that had been made in this critical area. But progress has a price and Fuller now faced a thorny decision about the future direction of the IT system at Higgins. During several recent meetings of the hospital's operations committee, which was chaired by Fuller, some of the more technically sophisticated doctors voiced their opinion that it was time that Higgins took the next step and connected to the Internet. One or two doctors admitted that they were using modems to connect to the Internet in order to communicate with colleagues in other hospitals. They felt that the time had come for Higgins to provide for greater Internet access. As one of the staff physicians put it, "As I see it, connecting to the Internet is inevitable. There are just too many benefits that we are foregoing by not being on the network. For one thing it's becoming increasingly difficult to stay in touch with our counterparts in other hospitals, since this is the way they communicate and share valuable information." The head of the research division echoed this sentiment: "The Internet is vital for sharing our research with other institutions all over the world. There's no doubt in my mind that this connectivity will greatly increase our productivity." Other physicians on the committee, though still novice computer users, agreed with this assessment and encouraged the hospital administration to expand its vision and connect to the Internet.

Fuller was certainly sympathetic with these persuasive arguments. There were many advantages to the worldwide access that the Internet provided so easily and inexpensively. However, this was not a simple decision. He was deeply worried that making this connection would just be too risky. His biggest concern, reflected in the news articles he had been reading recently, was that hackers could penetrate the hospital's private network to steal or tamper with confidential patient data. Or they could possibly eavesdrop on information being exchanged with those outside the hospital. What if a Higgins physician was communicating with another physician about a particular patient's problems and the communication was intercepted by an unscrupulous hacker?

Thus, his major concern was the extraordinarily sensitive nature of the information stored on the host system: private medical records. Also, since Higgins continually had many celebrities in its midst, it was imperative not to put their privacy in jeopardy in any way. What if an intrusive hacker were able to penetrate one of the hospital's patient data bases and tap into individual medical records? The potential ramifications were chilling.

Fuller and several others voiced these concerns at the committee meeting but for the most part they fell on deaf ears. Many were skeptical about his arguments that the system could not be made secure. They also felt that to a great extent the tremendous benefits of greater connectivity far outweighed the small risks of intrusion. They seemed to believe that the administration was just being overly cautious and conservative. In their view, this was the way of the future—a simple and convenient method of communicating with colleagues and fellow researchers all over the world.

After several other meetings and extended debate on this proposal, Fuller realized that he faced a difficult decision. Sometimes the debate became heated and at one meeting Fuller was called a "paranoid alarmist." He had been considering the alternatives for several weeks but was no closer to a resolution of the conflicting issues. He was still worried that the hospital might be liable for a security breach. Also, would others look upon this decision as irresponsible and short-sighted if hackers were able to intrude the hospital's network and retrieve sensitive information about one or more of its patients?

As he reflected once again on this difficult problem, he recalled the advice from one of his counterparts at a nearby medical hospital: "The Internet is wonderful, but let's face it, it provides no security and no measures to protect privacy or data integrity." There were certain security measures that could be taken such as the construction of a "firewall" but even this was not foolproof and it was also fairly expensive.[5] Given the hospital's budgetary constraints, there might not be adequate funding at the present time to provide this level of security.

Fuller wondered whether he *was* being too conservative and apprehensive; perhaps he should be a bit more permissive and recommend the connection. Or should he continue with the strategy many in the hospital had now dubbed as "Internet abstinence?"

Internet Abstinence (B)

Fuller concluded that he needed more information in order to make a more informed decision. He arranged to hire a security consultant to review the hospital's present security and offer some advice on the feasibility of connecting to the Internet. After studying the hospital's situation for several days the consultant submitted a detailed review to Fuller. The following are the main points of his extensive report:

- Present security is quite adequate but connecting to the Internet brings a whole new level of risk to the organization for which it may not be fully prepared, technically or culturally.
- The Computer Emergency Response Team (CERT), a federally funded organization that keeps watch over the Internet, has recently issued an advisory describing a rash of recent break-ins at several major hospitals; these have allegedly been orchestrated by a group of hackers who want to demonstrate the poor security systems of the medical establishment.

- If the hospital decides to connect to the Internet it must implement state of the art security such as a well-configured application-level firewall, which will create a subnet or separate zone between the internal network and the Internet. It includes a router (or gateway) between the internal network and this zone and between the zone and the Internet. These routers, configured according to internal security policy, are designed to filter out unauthorized entry into the network. Estimated cost (including installation and configuration): $60,000.
- This firewall will harden the system against potential damage from an intruder but it is not foolproof. No system can be made absolutely secure, but with a robust, high-level security system the risk of intrusion can be minimized.

Fuller pondered this report during his brief lunchbreak. It was Friday afternoon and he was determined to bring this matter to closure sometime next week. It had already consumed too much of his energy and attention and he was anxious to move on. The consultant's analysis and security review were certainly helpful but he still had many substantive questions.

He was also deeply concerned about the *process* of making this decision. He knew where many of the hospital staff stood on this matter but what about the patients whose personal data was at stake and who were most at risk from security breaches? Should they play some role in this decision and, for that matter, in other security decisions? Should he consult the hospital's advisory board which included several patient representatives, or would the discussion of this matter cause unnecessary anxiety and alarm?

Fuller began to reread the consultant's report as he thought about how to respond to these questions.

Case 7.3   A Programmer's Dilemma

Charles Darnton was not looking forward to the weekly Monday morning meeting at D&M Consulting. It was just about 9:00 AM when he entered the third floor conference room and the meeting was just about to get underway. He poured some coffee and took one of the few remaining seats around the walnut conference table. He gazed at the usual managers and support staff seated at the table and pulled out some notes that he had quickly prepared the night before. Darnton was scheduled to give a presentation on a key project that he had been working on for several months. This was the first project which he had managed and he was somewhat apprehensive about giving this particular status report.

Darnton had been working at the D&M Consulting firm in various capacities for over 4 years. He accepted a job here as a junior consultant after working for several years as an education specialist and product support representative at a major software firm. He was quite content at D&M until Brian Gillin took over as the Director of his division. He sometimes clashed with Gillin whose style was rather abrupt and even abrasive. However, Gillin rose to power because of his particular expertise as a project manager. He had a reputation for bringing in projects on time and under budget, a difficult accomplishment in the world of computer programming. Some said that Gillin was occasionally ruthless, but in the view of upper management his decisions seemed to be sound since they always helped the bottom line.

D&M was founded in 1979 by several ex–employees of IBM in order to provide "complete computer consulting services" to a wide variety of businesses. In other words, D&M would design, program, and test the systems which it built; a company that hired out D&M would only have to administer a system once it took it over from the D&M consultants. Moreover, for an annual fee D&M did offer the option of providing ongoing support for its larger and more complex projects that required some maintenance and occasional updating.

The firm enjoyed an excellent reputation in this nascent industry and grew quite rapidly through the 1980s. It benefited greatly from the trend toward outsourcing and eventually its revenues approached $500 million. It usually hired computer science and management graduates from the top schools, who were eager to work at such a prestigious organization, and sometimes raided other consulting firms when it needed talented individuals with special skills. D&M was the envy of the industry and for many years it had no problem charging a premium for its much sought after services.

However, in the early 1990s, partly on account of the many new entrants in the consulting industry, the company experienced some competitive pressures and its growth slowed considerably. In addition, managers underbid on two large projects and the company barely broke even on both of them. As a consequence, there was widespread pressure within D&M to stay on schedule and impose stringent financial controls to ensure a consistent level of profitability. Also, the company recently began hiring project managers who had less technical skills but were more adept at managing and controlling costs. As a result, the firm's financial performance began to improve, and in 1995 its profits were on the rise for the first time in 3 years.

It was in this context that Gillin was hired away from a rival firm where he had developed a reputation as a "hard charger" and an aggressive, results-oriented manager. During Gillin's first year at D&M his department had the best record of completing its projects on schedule. They also rarely exceeded their projected budgets. Beyond any doubt, Gillin was a "rising star" at D&M and many felt that they were fortunate to be in his department.

Darnton, however, never considered himself as "fortunate" to be working for Gillin. He found Gillin impolitic, intransigent, and sometimes myopic, willing to cut corners and take some unnecessary risks to get projects completed on their tight schedules. Thus, Darnton, recently promoted to Senior Consultant, was rather nervous about his current project.

D&M had recently taken on a new client, a distinguished furniture retailer, called Hamilton Furniture, Inc. Hamilton had 93 stores located throughout the west and midwest with projected 1996 sales of $374 million. Despite their success and profitability, their corporate offices were in some disarray and this included their information systems function.

Recently, the retailer had attempted to develop a store level sales and inventory system. With the help of this system corporate executives would be able to get a comprehensive overview of the previous day's sales performances at Hamilton's various stores. But its Information Systems (IS) department was not up to the task and the system never got off the ground. As a result, Hamilton turned to D&M for some assistance.

A D&M consulting team headed by Darnton assessed the inchoate system built by the Hamilton IS staff and concluded that it should be scrapped and that a new system should be built from scratch. It presented Hamilton with some design specs based on a careful needs assessment. The new system recommended by D&M would include a credit feature that would do on-line credit checks while the customer waited. Hamilton executives were impressed and they handed the project to D&M. After some negotiations both companies agreed on a fixed fee and a schedule for the project's completion.

Darnton's group had been in on the ground floor of this project and it played a major role in working on the architecture and the requirements for this system. The hardware would consist of Hamilton's IBM mainframe as a host computer connected by a LAN to a network server; the network server would be connected to workstations in different Hamilton stores by means of a WAN (or wide area network). These stores could access the host system for credit and inventory information. They would also transmit sales data to the server on a daily basis. The software consisted of a Structured Query Language (SQL) data base and a computational "engine" that would aggregate the disparate sales data. D&M would build a front end graphical user interface that would insulate the users from the need to learn a query language such as SQL. The front end was completely menu-driven and end users could simply key in a choice off the menu to retrieve, enter, or update information.

The contract with Hamilton called for D&M to design, code, and test this sophisticated system. Once the programming was completed and the system had been adequately tested, it would be "turned over" to Hamilton's IS manager and her small staff. They would bear the responsibility for administering and maintaining the system.

After Hamilton's aborted attempt to build this system with their own staff, the company hired a new IS manager. She was involved to a limited extent in the design stage of the project, but she virtually always deferred to D&M's "expert judgment." Darnton suspected that she was somewhat naive and did not really have the experience and technical acumen to appreciate the implications and nuances of the decisions and choices that had to be made. Although the corporate staff was generally capable, there were clearly still some vulnerabilities in the area of information systems.

The entire team for this project consisted of three other programmers. Darnton as Senior Consultant was the team leader, and he was responsible for ensuring that the project was completed within the 11-month time frame determined by Gillin and approved by a D&M executive vice president. Charles resisted this deadline but after several futile conversations with Gillin he had to demur to Gillin's judgment. Gillin felt that an 11-month time limit was quite appropriate for designing and implementing a system of this scope. He reminded Darnton that if the project could be wrapped up in the scheduled 11-month time frame D&M would make a pretty healthy profit from this job which would certainly enhance the year end bonus picture for him and his staff.

But 8 months later Darnton was feeling enormous pressure since the team had fallen behind largely because of forces beyond his control: an illness that felled one of the programmers for three and a half weeks, some unusually nasty software bugs, and some other unanticipated setbacks. Darnton was quite skeptical that he could finish the project on time, but he had not yet said anything to Gillin. He realized, however, that he had to do so at this meeting, even though he dreaded communicating this "bad news" to Gillin.

Gillin began the weekly meeting in the usual way by reviewing D&M's revenues and project updates for the past week. He then conveyed some general news about the comings and goings of various people at the company. When he finished, he turned to Darnton for his progress report on the Hamilton project.

Darnton talked for 10 minutes about some of the different challenges and features of the project. He explained that several modules had already been coded and were currently being tested. There were more bugs than expected, he noted, and taking time to fix them properly was slowing down the team's progress. Gillin seemed rather disinterested in these details. Finally, after several more minutes he interrupted Darnton.

"Let's cut to the chase, Charles. Will you make the October 15th deadline?"

"Well, I'm not so sure," replied Darnton. "Right now I would have to say no. I think that the bug fixes are really slowing us down. Also I don't feel that the security is robust enough at this point."

Gillin was clearly perturbed and became more animated and annoyed as the awkward conversation continued.

"When *will* you have this thing completed? Give me a date!"

"As I said," responded Darnton, "I'm not exactly certain but my best guess is around December 1st."

"December 1st!!!", bellowed Gillin, "you've got to be kidding! I need your engineers for two other major projects, and you're scheduled to team up with Joan in Frankfurt in mid-November to take a look at that Army Corps application. No, December 1st is totally unacceptable."

Gillin could see that this confrontation was escalating and in order to avoid a scene he told Darnton that they should discuss this in his office right after the meeting. A tense atmosphere prevailed as the meeting continued, but the other managers gave their reports without incident.

Later in Gillin's office the emotional exchange continued. Gillin was clearly upset that this project had fallen so far behind schedule and that he had not been informed of this at an earlier date. Darnton was quite defensive but he was also cautious not to further upset his volatile boss. Gillin pressed Darnton on what could be done to get back on schedule, and the conversation turned once again to the contentious issue of security.

"The only way to stay close to the schedule," Darnton remarked, "is to cut back on some of the security features, but I don't think that would be such a good idea."

"Why not?" queried Gillin. "Security should not be a big deal for a project like this. Just make sure that the application is restricted to authorized users and that the network is reasonably secure. Nothing fancy, Charles, because we just don't have the damn time!"

But Darnton was insistent that more needed to be done.

"I'm afraid that I can't agree with you, Brian. I have a comprehensive security plan with a good deal of emphasis on network security and detection measures. It's especially critical to build in audit trails identifying invalid access attempts. I also want to make sure that those sites using modems have call back authentication. And I'm convinced that we have to have terminal controls that prevent display of passwords on the screen and provide for an automated logoff capability."

"Ah, screw that," Gillin angrily responded.

He picked up the specs for this project from a pile of folders on his desk. He studied them for a few minutes while Darnton stared blankly out the window.

"I've just been looking over these specs, and I think that the level of security which you are proposing is preposterous," commented Gillin.

"It's overkill. I do *not* believe that the Hamilton system needs all those features. After all, this is not highly sensitive data that we are talking about. If we were protecting corporate secrets, then it might be a different story. Also, let me point out that nobody at Hamilton is pushing for this kind of security. It doesn't seem to be a big thing to them either."

"But look at all the publicity in the computer journals about security," Darnton replied. "Everyone is talking about the need to enhance the basic security of our information systems. I think that we have an obligation to make this system as secure as possible, regardless of whether the client explicitly asks for it or not."

Gillin responded coolly to Darnton's rather impassioned arguments:

"On this project, Charles, security is simply a luxury we can't afford. Besides my philosophy is that if the customer is not asking for all that security then they don't really need it."

The discussion continued for a while longer and Darnton continued to implore for a more secure system. But Gillin's position was unyielding: There was no time or money to build "robust security" into this sales tracking and inventory control application. Hamilton would have to settle for the usual user verification controls.[6] There would be minimal network security and no detection measures or audit trails except those that were already provided in the software that was purchased. His obstinancy was characteristic, and Darnton recognized the futility of pursuing the matter further.

When Darnton left Gillin's office he was in a state of some consternation. He did not feel that it was fair to the client to shortchange them on vital security features. But Hamilton's managers were not cognizant of these issues, and the security specifications in the design document were not too specific. Hence, he was fairly sure that they wouldn't balk at the security level being proposed by Gillin. Security was on the agenda for the next milestone meeting with Hamilton's IS manager. Darnton could outline the specific security features of this system and clearly give the impression that the security was comprehensive.

Nonetheless Darnton still felt that he was obliged to provide Hamilton with a truly viable system, and this meant one with adequate security, not one with a lot of security holes. Also, he worried about D&M's accountability if there were a security breach. At the very least this could reflect badly on the firm's reputation as well as his own.

On the other hand, as he mulled over these concerns he wondered about what recourse he had. Gillin was adamant that the project be completed on time even if this meant compromising the application's security. Darnton was convinced that he was right but he was perplexed about exactly what to do at this point.

Case 7.4   A Harmless Prank

Steven Mackey was a junior and a computer science major at Riverview State College, a moderate size 4-year college located in the midwest. He had worked with computers since the days of his childhood and he chose to attend Riverview because of its excellent computer science department. He consistently received good grades and he was highly regarded by the department and its faculty. During this second semester of his junior year he was learning two new computer languages, C and PL/1, and he was taking a difficult course on compilers.

Mackey was also known among his friends and fellow computer science students as a typical "hacker." He enjoyed traversing through the Internet especially at night, and he sometimes boasted about his ability to crack codes and break into computer systems that he had not been authorized to use. Some of the other students in the computer science department admired Mackey's antics; in their eyes these transgressions merely confirmed his technical expertise. Mackey's exploits were also well known around other circles of the campus, but since he had not tampered with any university systems he was never reprimanded by faculty or administrators.

One late evening in April just 3 weeks before Riverview's final exams Mackey and his girlfriend decided to see if they could tap into the administrative network at Riverview. This network included the files of the administrators at Chauncey Hall who were responsible for managing the financial affairs of the university. Many of these files contained confidential data about university finances or personnel matters. Mackey was most interested in the payroll file which included the salaries of all Riverview employees, including the faculty. He was not interested so much in looking at those salaries but in demonstrating his exceptional ability by cracking the passwords to this file. His interest in doing this was stimulated by one of his professors who mentioned that he had helped to design the security system for this file and that he considered it "virtually impregnable." Mackey construed this boasting as a challenge to the class, while others seemed to pay little attention to this remark.

But Mackey was intrigued and excited about this challenge. He worked for four and a half hours to achieve this objective. It was relatively easy to tap into the university network since its security was rather weak. But the payroll file did prove to be another matter. Mackey ran algorithms used to crack passwords but they kept failing. Eventually, however, through sheer ingenuity and persistence he broke the code and gained access to the file. He was so elated that he didn't even bother to look at any of the salaries or the other information maintained there. By now he was so exhausted that he simply logged off the computer and went to sleep.

The next day the system administrator found evidence that there had been an unauthorized entry into the IBM mainframe's CICS system at 2:36 AM. She also detected that the payroll file had been accessed but that no individual records had been read. University officials and campus police were notified immediately, and they were eventually able to trace this intrusion to Mackey's computer. No one was surprised that Mackey was the culprit, given his penchant for this sort of activity.

Several days after the incident Mackey was summoned before the Dean of Students, Dr. Lillian Green, who confronted him with the overwhelming evidence. In his defense Mackey sheepishly claimed that this was a harmless incident, "just a prank," which merely disproved his professor's contention that the payroll file was supposedly unassailable. He claimed that gaining entry to such a tightly secured system was both a hobby and a challenge. Indeed, Mackey argued, he had done the university a favor by exposing the vulnerability of this file, which was hitherto thought to be so secure. Furthemore, he pointed out that he did not look at any of the payroll data, and finally, he gave to the Dean some specific instructions on how to buttress security for the administrative network. He said he had been formulating these recommendations since the morning after his break-in.

Dean Green became less hostile as the meeting proceeded since she saw that Mackey was not a mean or especially devious person. Moreover, she appreciated his candor and sincerity. Prior to the meeting with Mackey she reviewed his academic record and ascertained that he had a 3.4 grade point average and that he had not been subject to any disciplinary actions during his enrollment at Riverview. Given this and Mackey's contriteness she was inclined to be somewhat lenient with him.

Nevertheless, this unfortunate incident was not viewed so benignly by college administrators who were furious over the break-in. Also, whatever sanctions were imposed on Mackey would be construed as an important signal from the Dean's office. There was some apprehension that others might try to mimic Mackey's exploits.

After Mackey completed this explanation of his actions he apologized and promised not to try this again. Dean Green thanked him for his cooperation and honesty, but she also pointed out that this was a serious offense that the university could not take lightly. She told him that her assistant would call him tomorrow to set up a second appointment. At that time she would discuss the university's decision regarding an appropriate penalty for his actions.

Later that day in the faculty dining room she discussed the young man's plight with a small group of administrators and faculty members. Some of her colleagues felt that a stern lecture and a warning to Mackey were sufficient. But others felt that a more stringent punishment was in order, perhaps even suspension for a semester. One person said that he would have no qualms with expelling a student for doing this. Such a bold action would send a clear message to other "hackers" on campus that this sort of antisocial and deviant behavior would not be tolerated. The Dean listened carefully to this advice as she tried to decide how the university should deal with "on-line offenders" such as Mackey.

Case 7.5   Interview with a Hacker

> hacker n. . . . [deprecated] A malicious meddler who tries to discover sensitive information by poking around[7]

In February 1995 the author interviewed Ed Jones (fictitious name), a professional computer programmer who also describes himself as a "hacker." Jones is a 28-year-old college graduate who was often described as a computer "genius" as far back as the eighth grade. During his high school and college days he worked with computers incessantly. In the following interview he is asked some pointed and specific questions about his experiences and his overall philosophy of computers, the Internet, and many other topics.

The interview has been edited and condensed by the author.

Question: Mr. Jones, how would you describe a hacker today?

When most of us on the net use the term "hacker" we're simply referring to a person who enjoys programming, a person who enjoys solving computer problems and puzzles. Hackers love to focus intently on a problem—it's called being in hack mode and it's almost a mystical experience for some of us. For most hackers their lives revolve around a computer and their community is the electronic network.

Question: But the term now has a negative connotation, doesn't it?

Yes, it seems to. But this is the way the media has come to use the term. They have clearly distorted its original meaning. We like to refer to malicious hackers as "crackers." They're the ones with the outlaw sensibility who cause big problems by undermining security or stealing someone's files.

Question: We hear a lot these days about the hacker ethic. Is there a simple definition of this?

I've always liked the way that Steven Levy described this in his book about hackers. Some of the main tenets of this "ethic" are that access to computer systems should be unlimited and unrestricted. I think he called it the "Hands-On Imperative." Also all information should be freely accessible in order to help others learn and develop their skills. Most hackers deeply mistrust authority and bureaucracy, which they see as impediments to learning and progress.[8]

Question: In other words, the hacker credo is that access to information should be free and not monopolized by big corporations?

Sure—that's exactly what we're saying.

Question: Is this sort of activity common? Are there a lot of hackers or crackers around today who engage in devious behavior?

I still have many friends that you would describe as "hackers," though I have outgrown it myself. Yes, I would have to say that it's still common.

For many computer cyberpunks and others, slogging around on the Internet and breaking into computer systems is really exciting and enticing because it's so challenging. There will always be hackers who deviate from the rules of society. It's also too tempting, especially since so many system administrators don't have a clue about security. And as systems become more open the threats posed by these individuals will continue to grow.

Question: It seems that hackers are lionized by the press and that the hacker subculture is admired, particularly by impressionable young people.

A lot of this hacker coverage is just hype, if you ask me. It doesn't mean very much. They're not big heroes, just a bunch of people fighting for freedom, you know, freedom of expression on the Internet and freedom to explore this new frontier.

Question: Most of us think that if "freedom" manifests itself in exploiting security weaknesses and logging on to someone else's system, there's a problem. We regard such activity as a form of trespassing and a violation of property rights. Do you agree with this?

I'm not sure what I think about that, but let me say that most hackers I know believe that this network is a public place and that anyone connected to the network is part of that public place. After all, companies, schools, and government agencies choose to get on there knowing full well the possible consequences. In our estimation, information on the net is in the public domain and we have every right to access it if we can find a way to get at it.

Question: But break-ins are a security manager's worst nightmare. Don't you think that they cause considerable damage and disruption?

In some respects these break-ins can provide a helpful service to organizations by identifying security weaknesses and vulnerabilities. Otherwise these individuals would not pay any attention to these problems, and a real thief or someone into corporate espionage might cause bigger headaches. I think that our intrusions have actually led to many enhancements in system security. Hackers believe that they keep organizations on their toes and that otherwise they wouldn't pay any attention to security issues. In other words, we keep them one step ahead of the real bad guys.

Question: In other words, hackers are performing a great service to their country by engaging in these activities?

Well, that's a pretty sarcastic way to put it, but right! It sounds strange but there is something to be said for this point of view. Also, study after study shows that the big problem is not with hackers but with ex–employees and other insiders.

Question: There's another issue that people bring up about this and that's the fact that hackers tie up computer resources through their unauthorized forays into different systems.

I've heard this complaint a few times, but it's a real bogus argument. For one thing most hackers work during the late night or early morning hours when no one else is usually on the system. It's a perfect time to do some exploring and probing of some system. Hence, contrary to popular opinion, we are not wasting computer resources.

Question: But let's be frank about this, aren't you trespassing on someone's property?

Ahh, yes and no. But either way, I really don't see the problem here. What's wrong with snooping around especially if I do not alter any data or screw up some commands or programs? Also, we're not interested in copying anything; most of the stuff we see is really boring and it's of no interest. So where's the damage? It's the same as walking across Farmer Brown's field—as long as I leave the animals and the crops alone what harm have I done. People do that all the time in this country and everyone leaves them alone.

Question: What's your motivation for this? What's the big thrill? I have to admit that I don't get it.

Yeah, no offense, but people like you will never "get it." My friends and I grew up with computers and we love working with them. And doing this stuff on the Internet is like pushing forward into new frontiers. I suppose that we do it because it's a terrific challenge. It's a way of testing our computer acumen and ingenuity. It sharpens our skills and wits. And, I repeat, it doesn't do any real harm to anyone.

Question: But can you do *anything* on the Internet? Is there a line that one shouldn't cross?

The line, I think, is between snooping around and outright theft. For most respectable hackers it's OK to look around some corporate or government system but you shouldn't steal data and try to profit from it.

Question: What do you think of those people who get their kicks out of propagating a virus or WORM through a web of computer systems? Isn't *this* going a bit too far? Does it cross the line that we're talking about?

The prevailing wisdom is that viruses and WORMS are intellectual curiosities. However, I do admit that this is pushing it, especially if one unleashes a virus that destroys property and ends up costing somebody a lot of money.

But let me make a few remarks about those who do work with these viruses and other strange programs. Some of these guys get a little carried away, but creating a virus is a real learning experience; they just have to keep these things under control and not let them wreak havoc on some mission critical application. Viruses that propagate themselves but allow programs to run normally are no big deal. They might include nice display hacks that are sort of fun. On the other hand, nasty viruses that nuke someone's data are definitely a problem.

Question: Well, we've covered a lot of ground here. Thanks very much.

Don't mention it.

Case 7.6   The Case of Craig Neidorf

A SUMMARY OF EVENTS

Craig Neidorf was a young pre-Law student at the University of Missouri when he found himself at the center of an investigation by the U.S. Secret Service and Southwestern Bell. He was being accused of serious crimes including fraud and the theft of proprietary information. The "crimes" were allegedly perpetrated while Neidorf was a young teenager.

Several years before entering the University of Missouri he began an electronic newsletter known as *Phrack*. According to one account of this story, "*Phrack* provided information that could be useful for someone trying to gain access to a system or free use of telecommunications lines."[9] In other words, *Phrack* disseminated information that sometimes facilitated the illicit intrusion of certain computer systems. It liked to publish articles that revealed a system's vulnerabilities and its security holes. In this respect, according to Dorothy Denning, "it is not unlike some professional publications such as those issued by the ACM."[10] Of course, such publications do not encourage users to exploit those vulnerabilities, and sometimes *Phrack* would encourage such exploitation. Neidorf was the publisher of this journal and in that role he solicited and edited articles for publication. In many ways he saw himself as a pioneer in the struggle to share information as widely and openly as possible.

In January 1990, Neidorf was confronted by Secret Service agents along with representatives of Southwestern Bell. The subject of their inquiry was a document about the Enhanced 911 (E911) emergency telephone system that was published in a recent issue of *Phrack*. These officials claimed that this E911 text file was a proprietary document that belonged exclusively to BellSouth. They estimated its worth at approximately $23,900. They further maintained that the document functioned as a guide to the workings of the 911 computer system and that in the hands of some clever hacker it could allow for the manipulation of that system. In short, the illegal publication of portions of this document could be a serious hazard for public safety. Finally, it was alleged that the document was pilfered by Robert Riggs "as part of a fraudulent scheme . . . to break into computer systems in order to obtain sensitive documents" that would be made available to the hacker community through the medium of *Phrack*.[11]

Shortly after the investigation was initiated, a federal grand jury in Chicago indicted Neidorf on ten counts of wire fraud and interstate transportation of stolen property. The federal wire-fraud statute which was being applied in this case required the government to prove that the defendant's objective was to take "money or property" from its legitimate owner. The maximum penalty for these crimes was a 65-year prison term.

In his defense, Neidorf's attorney, Sheldon Zenner, argued that *Phrack* was not a subversive sort of publication but simply one that allowed for the distribution and free exchange of information. With the help of Dorothy Denning, a computer science professor at Georgetown University, he set out to prove that the E911 document published in

Phrack did not contain any trade secrets. Professor Denning's investigative work attempted to prove that there was an abundance of other material in the public domain that also provided ample information about breaking into a system. Thus, it was unfair to single out this document's publication in *Phrack* as a subversive act.

The case did go to trial but half way through the trial the government decided to drop the charges. Neidorf was vindicated and the government was embarrassed by its apparent overzealousness. It is important to note that during the trial Riggs gave testimony about his role in this incident. He described how he downloaded the file from a Bell-South computer system and sent it to Neidorf via e-mail for publication in *Phrack.* It was also revealed during the trial that pamphlets made available by BellSouth contained just as much information about the E911 as did this document. Most of what was in this document, then, was already in the public domain. Presumably, as these revelations were made public, the government realized the superficiality of its case and so made the decision to drop the charges just 4 days after the trial had begun. The government's lawyers apparently realized the dubious nature of their claim that Neidorf had deprived BellSouth of "money or property."

SOCIAL AND ETHICAL ISSUES

Aside from the possibility of government harrassment there are many other issues triggered by the case of Craig Neidorf. The most obvious issue concerns First Amendment rights. Does the right of free expression extend to the publication of proprietary documents such as the E911 file? According to Johnson, "What is at stake here is freedom of expression on-line and how much power the government, or anyone, should have to patrol and control on-line activities."[12] Perhaps a larger and more important question is whether or not our First Amendment rights extend to electronic communications without qualification. Should publications in on-line newsletters or pronouncements on Internet bulletin boards enjoy precisely the same level of protection as articles in newspapers or speeches given in a city square? For example, in the 1960s the Supreme Court invoked the First Amendment in its ruling that allowed *The New York Times* to publish the *Pentagon Papers,* a proprietary document misappropriated from the Defense Department. Should the same protection be afforded to electronic newsletters or on-line publications such as *Phrack?*

Another point about this case that deserves some discussion is the apparent overreaction exhibited by the U.S. government and BellSouth.

Were the actions of these constituencies warranted by the publication of the E911 text document or was this blown out of proportion? Was this another manifestation of "hacker hysteria" among law enforcement officials? Or were Neidorf and his colleagues culpable of a real crime and hence a legitimate target of these officials? Should the offense of publishing proprietary information be considered a felony?

To some extent, the answer to this question depends upon whether or not information should be characterized as property. According to Samuelson, "The traditional rule of the criminal law was that someone could not be prosecuted for theft of information alone."[13] The reason for this seems clear enough: when one takes information instead of physical property the owner still has use of that information. Thus the Neidorf case and several others like it raise the question of whether information should be treated by our legal system as property. If so, its misappropriation would be considered as a clear case of theft. Many argue that in an information economy the protection provided by such laws is essential. But, as Samuelson cautions, "A world in which all information is a discoverer's property under all circumstances is unthinkable."[14]

Clearly, the Neidorf case generates many other questions but these are certainly the most dominant and controversial ones. It is worth noting that although this incident happened in 1990 these complex matters have still not been resolved or even adequately addressed by computer professionals and law enforcement authorities.

NOTES

1. Elaine Appleton, "Network Security: Is Your LAN a Sieve," *Datamation*, September 1, 1993, p. 79.
2. John Markoff, "Data Network Is Found Open to New Threat," The New York Times, January 23, 1995, p. A1. Copyright © 1995 by The New York Times Company. Reprinted by permission.
3. See, for example, Eugene Spafford, "Are Computer Hacker Break-ins Ethical?" *Journal of Systems Software*, January 1992, pp. 41–47.
4. This case originally appeared in *Ethical Aspects of Information Technology*. Englewood Cliffs, NJ: Prentice Hall, 1995.
5. A firewall is a router or dedicated computer that is located between the Internet and internal networks and computer systems; it includes software that protects from outside intrusions.
6. These included user authentication, system forced password changes, the ID and password verified at the sign on time and the storage of passwords encrypted in the system.

7. Eric Raymond (ed.) *The New Hacker's Dictionary.* Cambridge, MA: MIT Press, 1991, pp. 191–192.

8. Cf. Steven Levy, *Hackers.* New York: Doubleday, 1984, pp. 26–36.

9. Dorothy Denning, "The U.S. vs. Craig Neidorf," *Communications of the ACM,* March 1991, p. 25.

10. Ibid., p. 28.

11. Ibid., p. 26.

12. Deborah Johnson, *Computer Ethics,* 2nd Ed. Englewood Cliffs, NJ: Prentice Hall, 1994, p. 107.

13. Pamela Samuelson, "Is Information Property," *Communications of the ACM,* March 1991, p. 16.

14. Ibid., p. 18.

8

Liability, Safety and Reliability

INTRODUCTION

This chapter will focus on the safety and reliability of computer products, including both hardware and software. It will also consider the liability and obligations of vendors who provide these products. They have a great deal of power over their customers because of the growing dependence on information technology in most homes and offices, and with this power comes certain duties and responsibilities. In addition, new forms of liability engage our attention in this chapter such as the liability of on-line service providers for the content of messages posted on their bulletin boards. This issue too must be addressed along with the more traditional question about the scope of liability for software vendors.

One moral, but arguable, premise is that vendors which supply software have a minimal obligation to ensure that their products are as reliable and as bug-free as possible so that they will function as intended. A company that rushed its product to market without adequate testing would certainly be negligent both from a legal and moral perspective.

However, what are other obligations of companies that manufacture and supply computer technology products? Are software companies, for instance, also obliged to provide products with some guarantee of ongoing utility? Is it fair to consumers when products are abruptly discontinued or become incompatible with a piece of hardware that suddenly has a new operating system? One must bear in mind that the price of software is rather inconsequential when compared to the other costs for installation, ongoing maintenance, and training. Learning a complicated software system can consume many hours of productive work time and this makes many companies hesitant about adopting new products and technologies.

These questions, then, seem more difficult to address. At a minimum vendors should be candid and forthright about their future prospects and their plans for various products. Also, for the sake of their customers they must make product support a critical issue in the event of a takeover or buyout.

An especially serious problem has been the software industry's reliance on vaporware. As we have pointed out elsewhere, "vaporware can take many forms, on a wide spectrum from misleading and exaggerated advertising to the introduction of products that are not ready for the marketplace, but perhaps the most common problem is preannouncing."[1] In other words, products are announced "as ready" and sometimes they are even sold before coding and testing have been completed. This is usually done in order to freeze the market and impede the sale of a competitor's products while consumers await the new offering. More commonly, companies announce release dates that reflect the most optimistic scenarios for product completion, but such dates are almost always unrealistic, since they do not factor in contingencies and unexpected events.

Another important topic covered by the cases in this chapter is safety, particularly the use of software programs to control the safety of sophisticated devices and machines. Consider that software products are now used for a wide range of applications that can directly affect people's lives. These programs control airplanes and air traffic control systems along with telephone and financial systems. They are also at the heart of advanced medical technology products. Moreover, as programs become more complex, the likelihood of undetected bugs is bound to increase exponentially. What if a bug lurking in these millions of lines of code causes a plane crash or the loss of life on a hospital table? What is the vendor's moral and legal liability for such catastrophes, especially when the problem is virtually unforseeable?

In the U.S. and many other countries the seller is held to a standard of *strict liability*; this means that the vendor is liable for any injury regardless of whether it was at fault. Thus, according to this demanding standard one is liable to compensate for a harm even though one is not strictly speaking responsible or blameworthy for that harm. Strict liability, however, is normally not applied if the damages are purely economic. The strict liability standard certainly encourages software vendors to produce safe and reliable systems.

The first case, *Prodigy Services Co. and Bulletin Board Liability*, raises some novel liability issues. It serves as a fitting transition from the last case in Chapter 7 ("Craig Neidorf") where the notion of bulletin board liability was clearly intimated. Should on-line service providers such as Prodigy and CompuServe be held liable and accountable for the content of their subscribers' electronic messages? Should a strict liability standard prevail in this context or is this too harsh? The case also challenges us to ponder what is a responsible policy for these companies. Should they adopt a hands off approach or seek to establish some ethical rules for bulletin board users? The basic question in this case is what is the appropriate analogy for these companies: Are they like telephone companies who are not responsible for what is said over their wires or like publishers who are responsible for content?

The next case, *The Therac-25*, dwells on a different aspect of liability. It considers the issue of product safety from the viewpoint of the users and the so-called software penumbra, that is, those affected by the software.[2] The case chronicles the lethal problems associated with this radiotherapy machine. The primary issues are the company's apparent failure to test this product adequately and its reactive response to the crisis which it precipitated.

We then turn to the more common, but not inconsequential, problem of product reliability, the theme of the *NCR's Warehouse Manager* case. NCR unknowingly marketed a bug-ridden application that caused damage to the financial and inventory records of several companies, seriously disrupting their businesses. How should NCR respond and what is a fitting compensation for the victims of this faulty software?

A second case study on reliability is *Intel's Pentium Chip Product Controversy*, dealing with the once infamous, but now commercially successful Pentium chip. This case raises some interesting questions about true product reliability and consumer perception of reliability. What are the management and ethical lessons that high-tech companies can learn from this public relations debacle?

In the last two case studies we focus on the problem of vaporware. *The Product Manager* case provides a compelling description of a company apparently promoting vaporware to its customer base. But there is some ambiguity about the release date and this creates a true quandary for the product manager. The second case on this topic is entitled *Chicago,* the code name for Microsoft's new version of Windows, a product that has been subjected to many significant delays. One can discern some similarity between Microsoft's actions and IBM's strategy for its 360 mainframe computer which was also introduced to the market well behind schedule despite IBM's deliberate efforts to keep expectations high. Like its predecessor, this case considers some of the moral implications of vaporware.

Case 8.1   Prodigy Services Co. and Bulletin Board Liability

In May 1995 a New York state judge sent shock waves through the legal community and the on-line industry when he issued an opinion stating that Prodigy Services Co. was responsible for the content of its subscribers' electronic messages. The opinion was written as a response to a $200 million lawsuit filed by the investment banking firm, Stratton Oakmont Inc. which claimed that Prodigy should be held liable for slanderous messages left on a popular Prodigy bulletin board. Those messages accused the firm of fraudulent behavior and criminal conduct. Prodigy responded by maintaining that it could not and should not be held responsible for what its subscribers posted on its bulletin boards.

Because of this and similar cases the explosive issue of bulletin board liability is emerging as a challenging and potentially expensive problem for on-line vendors. In the wake of this ruling executives at Prodigy must reexamine the company's current policies and mechanisms for screening electronic messages. As the company's top executives reviewed the May decision and subsequent events, they knew that the road ahead would be filled with many pitfalls and perils.

COMPANY BACKGROUND

Prodigy Services Company was formed in 1988 as a joint venture of International Business Machines Corp. (IBM) and Sears, Roebuck & Company. The company operated a proprietary electronic information and communications service which could be accessed over telephone lines with a modem and a personal computer. The service was known simply as Prodigy. It made available to users a wide array of on-line activities from shopping to travel arrangements to stock trades.

Subscribers also had access to e-mail facilities which enabled them to transmit private messages to other members. In addition, they were provided access to Prodigy's public bulletin board service which enabled members to post electronic messages that could be read by other subscribers. The bulletin boards were divided into 114 broad topics and subdivided by subjects. Thus, bulletin boards might be devoted to various hobbies, political and social issues, health concerns, investment advice, and so forth.

Prodigy's subscriber base grew steadily and by 1993 it had signed on just over one million subscribers with revenues estimated at $250 million. Its market share was about 25%, second only to CompuServe which led the industry with 35% of the market. By 1995 the number of subscribers had doubled to 2 million. The nascent on-line industry had solid growth prospects but Prodigy had to contend with established competitors such as CompuServe, America Online and GEnie. In more recent years it also had to contend with new entrants such as Microsoft Network along with Internet software firms such as Netscape and Spyglass, which were designed to help people browse and communicate on the Internet.

Prodigy stood out among its competitors as the most family-oriented service because of its user friendliness and its publicized efforts to promote wholesome interactions on its bulletin boards. CompuServe, on the other hand, which is owned by H&R Block Inc., is more geared toward computer hobbyists. It offers users on-line chat services with software companies and Internet connections.

FREE SPEECH CONTROVERSIES

From its inception the Prodigy bulletin board service triggered controversies about free speech and censorship. For example, in 1989 Prodigy closed a bulletin board that involved a debate between gays and fundamentalist Christians. The reason given was the low volume of interaction and a lack of interest among the user base, but users who did participate charged Prodigy with censoring their messages. In another case the company put a stop to an on-line protest about its rate increase, cancelling the subscription of about a dozen members.

In 1991 the company became embroiled in a more serious controversy when it came under attack by the Anti-Defamation League (ADL) for failing to prevent the posting of anti-Semitic messages. The ADL complained that these notes contained remarks such as the following: "The holocaust is really an edifice . . . to the naive gullibility of the world in which even the most outrageous survivor's tales and the falsest testimonies are totally believed without the slightest doubt of criticism"; "Did it ever occur to you that Israel might be the cause of most of the trouble in the Middle East?"[3]

In the midst of a firestorm of protests over these and similar messages Prodigy responded by announcing that it would revise its guidelines in an effort to thwart the posting of such offensive and insulting messages in the future. The offensive category would now include expressions of bigotry such as those manifested in the messages cited by the ADL. The ADL was criticized by both *The Washington Post* and *The New York Times* for its efforts to censor free speech on the network.

SCREENING POLICY

Prodigy provided its members with ample warning that their messages would be subjected to scrutiny and possible censorship. Users had to indicate their acceptance of the membership agreement before being allowed on to one of its bulletin boards. This Agreement included the following terms:

> Members agree not to submit, publish or display on the prodigy service any defamatory, inaccurate, abusive, obscene, profane, sexually explicit, threatening, ethnically offensive, or illegal material. . . . Prodigy reserves the right to review and edit any material submitted for display or placed on the Prodigy service, excluding private electronic messages, and may refuse to display or remove from the service material that it in its sole discretion believes violates this Agreement or is otherwise objectionable.[4]

When the company first went on line it developed a three step process for reviewing bulletin board messages. In the first step, "all notes were screened by a computer program that searched for key words deemed obscene or indicating solicitations or blatant expressions of hate."[5] If notes were rejected for this reason they were returned to the sender with a brief explanation. Prodigy had another set of key words that was used to flag messages that *might* be a problem; these messages were then subject to further review by Prodigy staff members. Finally, if other Prodigy subscribers called attention to problem messages they would be scrutinized and removed if necessary. In general, then, the company's philosophy was to exercise limited editorial control in order to provide its users with a reasonable level of protection from offensive messages. Obviously this became increasingly difficult as the volume of messages continued to grow. In 1995 company officials estimated that about 60,000 messages were posted to its bulletin boards each day.

Prodigy continually reasserted its commitment to the ideal of free speech but recognized that some limits on free expression were necessary. It sought to provide a balance between respect for the right of free expression and the preservation of family and conservative cultural values which mattered a great deal to the majority of its subscribers.

It is worth noting that CompuServe and others in the on-line industry have adopted a strict hands-off approach to the content of electronic messages which are not monitored in any way. In recent years Prodigy has moved closer to this model. For example in late 1995 it began providing users the opportunity to set up their own Web pages, but there were no plans to screen the content of those pages.

THE LIBEL LAWSUIT

Despite its vigilance, problems continued for Prodigy when it found itself the subject of a $200 million lawsuit filed by Stratton Oakmont Inc., an investment banking firm on Long Island, New York. The company's president claimed that he had been libeled on Prodigy's most popular electronic bulletin board known as "Money Talk." The messages, which were anonymously posted in October, 1994, said that the president and others at Stratton had committed criminal and fraudulent acts in connection with the public offering of stock for a company known as Solomon-Page Ltd. According to *The New York Times*, the messages said the offering "was a major criminal fraud," and that Stratton was a "cult of brokers who either lie for a living or get fired."[6] Stratton had been investigated by the SEC for "boilerroom brokerage activities" and in 1994 the company was fined $500,000 and asked to pay $2 million in restitution to its clients.

The New York Supreme Court took up the Prodigy case in order to determine whether it was appropriate to sue an on-line subscriber service for libelous messages posted on a bulletin board by one of its subscribers. Prodigy maintained that it should not be held liable for the actions of its subscribers', but a New York state judge, Justice Stuart Ain, issued a contrary ruling stating that Prodigy *is* responsible for the content of its subscribers electronic messages. Prodigy and others in the on-line industry had consistently claimed that they should be treated like bookstores or lending libraries. On-line service companies, they argued, are similar to these entities since they function as passive conduits of information with no control over content. The judge's ruling did not dispute this analogy, but it pointed out that Prodigy had marketed its on-line services by emphasizing its editorial control, and this put it into a different category from other on-line providers: "Prodigy's conscious choice to gain the benefits of editorial control, has opened it up to a greater liability than CompuServe and other computer networks that make no such choice."[7] The judge cited the software screening program and its "content guidelines" as unequivocal evidence of Prodigy's editorial control.

The lawsuit was eventually dropped by Stratton Oakmont, Inc. after Prodigy issued a formal apology for the libelous remarks. However, Prodigy's appeal to reargue the case was turned down, and hence Justice Ain's ruling still stands. The judge cited "a real need for some precedent in laws of cyberspace" as the primary reason for refusing to reverse his ruling.[8] This means that in future cases Prodigy can be held liable for comments posted on its bulletin boards.

OTHER INDUSTRY LAWSUITS

The on-line service liability issue is not limited to libel cases. The question of liability has also been raised when subscribers infringe a copyright. In another recent lawsuit a federal judge ruled that Netcom On-Line Communication Services Inc. may be liable for copyright infringement for failing to remove postings of religious material copyrighted by the Church of Scientology. The ruling stated, however, that Netcom would be liable only if it knew that the material posted was unauthorized. Netcom refused to remove the texts even after they received a request from the church's lawyers. The company defended itself by arguing that it was a "passive transmitter" of Internet messages and that it could not possibly control the content of those messages. It used the analogy of a landlord who should not be held accountable for the actions of his/her tenants.

Under current court precedent on-line service providers would also be liable for financial damages if a user posted a pirated copy of software even if they had no knowledge of such a posting. Industry representatives maintain that this *de facto* strict liability standard is much too onerous and will ultimately chill the transmission of communications in cyberspace.

PRESSURES CONTINUE IN 1996

In the midst of these legal disputes Prodigy executives contemplated their next steps. They realized that they were caught in an untenable and awkward position. Prodigy sought to occupy a middle ground between functioning as a publisher and adopting a laissez-faire, "anything goes" approach to content. If it chose to exercise editorial control over offensive messages it would be held liable for whatever its users posted on bulletin boards according to the standard set forth by Justice Ain. Unfortunately, this included messages of libel or slander that could not be easily detected by means of key word searches looking for offensive language or other hot-button words. Thus, by exercising any discretionary, editorial control over the elements of content (such as offensive language) that it could control, it would be held liable for content that in all likelihood it could *not* control.

Moreover, to further complicate matters some respectable political groups were calling for on-line service providers to exercise even more editorial control. In January 1996 The Simon Wiesenthal Center sent a letter to Prodigy (along with America Online, CompuServe, and Microsoft Network) requesting that the company block access to Internet sites set up by white supremacists and neo-Nazis. The letter also called on these companies to enforce "ethical rules of engagement" for on-line communications. It urged Prodigy not to provide a platform for the destructive propaganda of hate groups such as the Aryan Nations.

As Prodigy executives reflected on this letter Judge Ain's ruling was clearly on their mind. If they chose to continue and perhaps strengthen their policy of enforcing some ethical rules of engagement in cyberspace, they would also have to take responsibility for the content of all messages posted on their bulletin boards. They would be liable, therefore, for libelous or slanderous remarks and even for inaccuracies that might cause some damage to subscribers.

The top management of Prodigy had to determine how they could best deal with these conflicting demands and how they should respond to the Simon Wiesenthal Center. They also had to decide what actions, if any, to take next.

Case 8.2   The Therac-25

As software products begin to pervade our environment, the risk that they will cause a great calamity increases significantly. One such calamity happened in the late 1980s when a product known as Therac-25, a radiotherapy machine, was allegedly responsible for several deaths because of a flaw in the machine's software. How could this happen and who is to blame? Moreover, how can this terrible tragedy be prevented in the future? There are no easy answers to these and other questions raised by this troubling case.

COMPANY AND PRODUCT BACKGROUND

The Therac-25 was manufactured by Atomic Energy of Canada, Ltd. (AECL) located in Ottawa, Canada. AECL was not a private corporation but a "crown corporation" of the Canadian government. It entered the field of medical linear accelerators or radiation therapy machinery during the early 1970s when it joined forces with a French company called CGR. These companies first produced the Therac-6 which was then followed by the Therac-20. Shortly before AECL introduced the Therac-25 this business relationship was terminated. The division of AECL involved in radiation machines has recently been privatized and separated from AECL. It is now called Theratronics International Limited.

The Therac product line of medical linear accelerators was highly regarded and included some of the most sophisticated radiation therapy machines available. The price of these products was typically in excess of $1 million. Medical linear accelerators are used to treat cancerous tumors or skin lesions with radiation. The machine is capable of providing two types of radiation therapy, X ray and electron, depending on the type of cancer that is being treated. When delivering X ray therapy a high intensity electron beam is deflected by a tungsten target interposed between the patient and the beam, and then yields the proper level of therapeutic X rays. When the machine functions in this fashion it is operating in "X ray mode." But in its so-called "electron mode" the Therac's built-in computer system, Digital Equipment Corp. (DEC) PDP-11 minicomputer, removes the tungsten target from the beam's path and reduces the intensity of the electron beam by a factor of 100. This electron mode was used to treat superficial skin lesions while the more powerful X ray mode was used to treat malignant cancer tumors.

The Therac-25 was introduced to the marketplace in the latter part of 1982. This product was different from its predecessor, the Therac-20, in several important ways. Like the Therac-20, the Therac-25 was controlled by the DEC PDP-11, but unlike that machine the Therac-25 relied much more heavily on the system's software, especially for controlling safety. Whereas, the Therac-20 included mechanical interlocking devices to prevent accidental overdoses, the Therac-25 contained no such hardware interlocks. The elimination of these devices helped keep costs under control. The machine's safety precautions were completely controlled by the sophisticated software. Other advantages of this machine were its higher energy level along with its improved user-friendliness.

It is important to highlight that the Therac-25 software was not designed from scratch. Rather, Therac-6 design features and modules along with Therac-20 routines were utilized in Therac-25 software programs.

A FLAWED PRODUCT

According to company records, a total of 11 Therac-25s were sold and installed prior to the product's recall for safety problems. Shortly after the machine's introduction there were several fatal accidents. Apparently, in some circumstances the Therac-25 malfunctioned by delivering a fatal dose of radiation to an unsuspecting patient. Moreover, there was no clear indication that this had happened, no warning or intelligible error message.

During the malfunction "the Therac scrambled the two modes, retracting the target as it should for electron mode but leaving the beam intensity set on high for X rays; the unobstructed high-intensity beam traveled through the accelerator guide destroying any human tissue in its path."[9] In other words, when the two modes were scrambled, the tungsten target would be removed but without any reduction in the beam power. The beam struck the patient with the same force as a bolt of lightening, and, although built in error checking mechanisms abruptly stopped the dose, much of the damage had already been done. Of course, an overdose of radiation can be fatal.

THE VICTIMS

The first reported incident happened at the Kennestone Regional Oncology Center located in Marietta, Georgia. On June 3, 1985 a woman with malignant breast cancer was at the Center to receive radiation therapy and accidentally received an overdose of radiation. The cause was not clear at the time, but it appears as if the modes were scrambled and the machine operated in the electron mode without deflecting the electron beam. AECL was immediately informed of the incident though they were not given specific information. They did not conduct a full investigation of the incident. The woman filed suit in November 1985. Although a severe radiation burn was verified, AECL denied that it was caused by their machine, and eventually the lawsuit was settled out of court.

One month later in a clinic in Ontario, Canada, another patient received an overdose. In this case AECL dispatched an engineer to investigate the incident. In addition, the FDA and its Canadian counterpart, the Bureau of Radiation and Medical Devices, were informed that there might be a safety problem with the Therac-25. The patient died in November but the cause of death was cancer and not the radiation overdose. AECL's investigation determined that there was probably a "transient failure in the microswitch used to determine the turntable position."[10] The company made some adjustments and declared that "the new solution indicates an improvement over the old system by at least five orders of magnitude."[11] It should be underscored, however, that at this point the company only suspected the cause of the accidents. It had not yet determined a definitive cause.

Other users were informed of a possible problem by way of a Class II recall. Users were given a list of things to check on their machines. In addition, users were informed that once AECL's software modifications were installed, they could put the machines back in full, normal service. Users were never told by AECL, however, that there were any patient injuries.

Meanwhile two far more serious incidents occurred at the East Texas Cancer Center in Galveston, Texas. On March 21, 1986 Voyne Cox received a lethal dose of radiation during a routine radiation therapy session at the Center. Cox felt a shock go through his whole body when the first dose was administered, but there was no indication of an overdose on the machine's computer terminal. Instead it appeared that he had actually received an underdose (according to the dose monitor display), so the operator repeated the procedure and ended up giving Cox a second overdose. Cox tried to get help but was unable to communicate with the operator because of disconnected or broken audio and visual monitors that completely isolated the patient from the operator. The technicians instead observed an error message that read "Malfunction 54." The machine's error list explained that this was a "dose input 2 error" but there was no further explanation of what this meant. It was later verified that "dose input 2 error" meant that there was some kind of discrepancy between the prescribed dose of radiation and the real dose. Within days, however, Cox became quite ill: he felt excruciating pain, vomited frequently, and eventually lapsed into a coma. In September 1986, just 5 months after receiving the fatal dose of radiation, he passed away in a Dallas hospital.[12]

Officials at the East Texas Cancer Center initially denied that there had been any radiation overdose. The radiological physicist at the hospital contacted AECL about Cox's unusual reaction. The company instructed the hospital to conduct a series of diagnostic tests; they uncovered no problems so the hospital continued to use the machine. AECL did not inform the East Texas Cancer Center about the other incidents in Ontario and Georgia. One month later the same thing happened to another patient, Verdon Kidd, at the cancer center. He too died shortly after the fatal treatment. Right after the lethal dose was administered to Kidd, the hospital discontinued using the machine.

At this point AECL also suspected that there was a more serious problem with their machine, and so initiated an investigation of these disturbing incidents. These investigations uncovered the core problem: when operators erroneously selected the X ray mode and then quickly corrected their mistake with a series of rapid keystrokes, the machine would get confused. For example, in the case of Cox the operator entered a full screen of prescription data and then keyed in "x" (X ray mode) instead of "e" (electron mode). To fix this error she used a cursor to move up the screen and changed the "x" to an "e." However, unbeknown to the operator this editing maneuver led the Therac-25 to scramble the two modes by removing the tungsten target while not reducing the high-powered electron beam. The esoteric "Malfunction 54" message was displayed but there was no explanation of what this meant in the user manuals.

With the help of the resident physicist in East Texas, AECL was able to duplicate the problem and to verify its cause. According to one report, "they determined that data-entry speed during editing was the key factor in producing the error-condition: if the prescription data was edited at a fast pace . . . the overdose occurred."[13] AECL quickly developed a "fix" for this problem that forced the operators to start at the beginning and re-enter all treatment data when a mistake had been made. They also disabled the "cursor up" key on the terminal keyboard. The same problem was found in the Therac-20 but it had never led to a fatality since this machine is equipped with an interlocking safety device that automatically prevents an accidental overdose.

POSTSCRIPT

The East Texas fatalities were obviously brought to the attention of the FDA which immediately required a CAP or Corrective Action Plan. After two more incidents in Yakima, on February 10, 1987 the FDA ordered a recall and took the Therac-25 out of use. Despite the software fix implemented after the overdoses in East Texas, the FDA concluded that "software alone cannot be relied upon to assure safe operation of the machine."[14]

After extensive negotiations with the FDA an agreement was finally reached about an acceptable CAP. This included (among other things) hardware interlocking devices to prevent an overdose in the case of a software malfunction along with many software adjustments including the elimination of the problematic editing keys.

There have been many postmortems on how such a dangerous problem could go undetected. According to one perceptive report on the Therac-25 machine in *Forbes* magazine, the fundamental difficulty with this product was not software bugs but poor design and a "failure to model reality." Unfortunately, according to *Forbes*, "no one had thought to test the machine's reaction to quick resets; the automatic safety check should have been done *before* the dose was administered."[15] Moreover, despite AECL's claims to the contrary, the machine's user-friendliness was still a problem since it did not generate clear and unambiguous error messages. A more intelligible error message might have led the company to solve this fatal problem much sooner. Finally, in the opinion of software safety experts, the company's biggest problem was its lack of commitment to make "its safety protocols fail-safe."[16]

Lawyers for the two Texas victims, Cox and Kidd, filed lawsuits against the vendor, AECL, the East Texas Cancer Center, and even the radiation technicians at the hospital. The suit alleged that the product was seriously defective and that the hospital was negligent in its use of this product. A key issue in these legal cases was whether this was a case of both product liability *and* medical malpractice as the lawsuits contended. The hospital vigorously disputed that they were at all to blame for what had happened. In their view, this was simply an open and shut case of product liability.

Case 8.3   NCR'S *Warehouse Manager*

In the relatively short history of software there have already been several notoriously flawed products that have fallen far short of the expectations of unsuspecting customers. One such product is undoubtedly the ill-fated *Warehouse Manager*. This program was marketed by NCR Corp. (now known as AT&T Global Information Solutions or AT&TGIS) in the late 1980s. It ran on the company's proprietary ITX operating system and cost approximately $180,000 (exclusive of installation, training, and set-up expenses).

According to a report in the *Wall Street Journal*, one "victim" of this product was Hopper Specialty Co. located in New Mexico. Hopper was a profitable distributor of industrial hardware for oil and gas drillers. The company purchased the *Warehouse Manager* in 1988 in order to keep track of the quantity and prices of the many items in its vast inventory. The product also generated invoices and produced itemized monthly reports showing the revenues for each of Hopper's many products.

Hopper purchased this software program partly because of the convincing sales pitch of NCR. The company's sales staff claimed that the product had been effectively deployed at over 200 locations. They did not mention, however, that at those myriad sites *Warehouse Manager* was working on a different operating system that was made by Burroughs Corp. NCR had licensed this software from Burroughs and converted it to run on its own proprietary ITX hardware system. Thus, what was sold to Hopper was a product that had been substantially revamped and recoded.

It appears, however, that this version of the product was not adequately tested since it caused tremendous problems for its small customer base. Difficulties occurred with even the most standard computer operations. One problem was the system's response time—basic commands that should have taken no more than a second or two ended up taking minutes. Also, according to the *Wall Street Journal*, "operators at different terminals would find that when they tried to get simultaneous access to the central computer, both their terminals would lock up; NCR engineers referred to this as the 'deadly embrace.'"[17] When this so-called "deadly embrace" occurred users had to log off the computer and then log back on, and sometimes during this process data would be lost or destroyed. In other words, *Warehouse Manager* was not a genuine multiuser software system which would automatically prevent any such problems. These and other equally serious flaws made it manifest to NCR that there were compatibility problems of serious magnitude— *Warehouse Manager* simply did not function effectively in the ITX operating environment. This disappointing discovery prompted NCR to stop selling the product in the middle of January 1988, just about 9 months after the product's official release.

Hopper did *purchase* the system well before this date, but NCR's salespersons had not been forthcoming about *Warehouse's* well-documented flaws. Also, Hopper had not yet received the product when NCR announced its sales moratorium in January. Despite that announced moratorium NCR began the installation process in February 1988, and Hopper began using the system in September of that same year. However, the end result was sheer chaos for Hopper's business operations. The slow response times and terminal lock-ups often left frustrated Hopper customers waiting in long lines. The system allegedly mixed up the prices of various items causing clerks to sell them to unsuspecting customers at the wrong price. Finally, "the most damaging problem stemmed from huge gaps between what the computer told Hopper Specialty was in stock and what was actually there. The *Warehouse Manager* might show 50 parts in stock, for instance, when in fact Hopper needed to order 50. Other times, it would show that items were on order when they were sitting on the shelf."[18]

Throughout this entire period of time Hopper was never informed that such problems had been documented at other sites and that *Warehouse Manager* sales had been suspended. Rather, customer support analysts at NCR consistently gave Hopper the impression that they were the only ones experiencing any sort of malfunctioning.

Obviously, this bug-ridden software seriously disrupted Hopper's entire business structure. The company consistently lost revenues since it couldn't keep track of what it had in stock. Clients couldn't rely on Hopper to get parts or equipment in a hurry and this put Hopper at a tremendous disadvantage. Many loyal customers went to Hopper's competitors where they could get more reliable service.

Indeed, Hopper is claiming that this system devastated the small company and cost it millions in lost revenues and profits. According to a report in *Computerworld*, "After purchasing the system in 1988, Hopper watched his then $4 million business dwindle to $1 million in annual sales today."[19] In addition, employees have been laid off and benefits have been reduced for those employees who still remain at the company. Hopper has filed a lawsuit against NCR in which it seeks $4.2 million in lost profits in addition to the total cost of the software which is about $300,000.[20] In its lawsuit Hopper accuses NCR of fraud, negligence, and unfair trade practices.

Hopper, of course, was not the only customer to have experienced severe problems with *Warehouse Manager*. There are 30 other cases pending against AT&TGIS; the company claims that all but eight of these cases are in the process of being settled. However, there has been some criticism about the nature of those settlements. According to published reports, AT&T relies on its standard Universal Agreement to settle all such software product liability cases. This agreement "limits payments to the original cost of the products and services acquired, minus depreciation for use of the equipment."[21] The company has been criticized for such modest compensation given the heavy losses that have been incurred by many of its clients because of this malfunctioning software.

AT&TGIS has refused, however, to pay the $4.2 million in damages demanded in the Hopper lawsuit and continues to insist on its limited software liability. Moreover, the NCR Universal Agreement signed by Hopper requires that all disputes be arbitrated instead of litigated in the courts and so far the courts have refused to hear the case. According to the *Wall Street Journal*, "in legal papers drafted in Hopper's case, NCR contends it 'had every reason to believe' that Taylor Management's software worked on NCR equipment, despite NCR's own internal communications to the contrary."[22]

As of this writing, the lawsuit is still unresolved. It is currently scheduled for arbitration some time in 1996. AT&TGIS has completely discontinued the system and has publicly acknowledged that the product was a failure. It continues to claim, however, that its liability is limited only to the purchase price of the software.

Case 8.4   Intel's Pentium Chip Product Controversy

This celebrated case began in the summer of 1994 when the Intel Corporation began marketing a new computer chip for personal computers know as Pentium. In an unusual strategy for a semiconductor company it heavily advertised this chip with the "Intel Inside" campaign. Problems began for Intel in October when a mathematician uncovered a division error. Intel admitted that it too had discovered the error over the summer but chose not to say anything because of the obscurity of this flaw. There was tremendous negative publicity, and while the press berated Intel for its insouciance and arrogance, IBM decided to halt sales of PCs with the Pentium chip. Eventually, the beleaguered company agreed to replace the chip for anyone requesting such a replacement.

THE INTEL CORPORATION

The Intel Corporation was founded in 1968 by Robert Noyce, Gordon Moore, and a group of scientists including the present CEO, Andy Grove. Its initial objective was to replace magnetic-core computer memories with semiconductor memories. The company's first product was a bipolar static random access memory (SRAM). This was immediately followed by a dynamic random access memory (DRAM) chip with more memory capacity than the SRAM; this product was known as the 1103 DRAM which soon became an industry standard.

In 1974 Intel developed the 8080, the first commercially successful microprocessor, and it too became the industry standard for 8-bit microprocessors. Although this product was quite successful, competitive products from Motorola and Zilog were challenging Intel's pre-eminent position in the microprocessor business. Intel's next offering was a 16-bit microprocessor known as the 8086 which was introduced in 1978. Sales volume for the 8086 started slowly and did not gain much momentum until 1980. This was the result of several factors including the success of Motorola's 16-bit microprocessor.

But Intel did not sit idley by in the face of this competitive threat. According to one analysis, "When Motorola's competitive 16-bit microprocessor began gaining momentum, Intel responded by initiating Operation Crush—an 'all out combat plan,' complete with war rooms and SWAT teams, to make the 8086 architecture the industry standard."[23] Intel succeeded in its efforts. In 1980 IBM adopted the 8086 chip for its personal computer.

Because of the success of the 8086 and Intel's other offerings, the company's sales increased to $885 million by 1980. The company expanded from 12 employees in 1968 to 15,000 in 1980. Thus, in a little over a decade Intel had established itself as a major player in the semiconductor industry.

Intel's rapid growth and profitability continued throughout the 1980s. Its most popular semiconductor products introduced during that period were the 386 and 486 chips, both 32-bit microprocessors. The 386 microprocessor is still one of the most widely used chips on the market today and chugs away on PCs made by vendors such as IBM, Compaq Computer, and Dell Computer Corporation. Its successor, the 486, was developed in 1989 and became known as the "mainframe on a chip" because of its superior processing power.

The Pentium chip is a much faster successor to the 486 and despite the setback caused by this controversy, the Pentium generation of chips is still expected to be a highly successful and profitable product line.

Intel's recent success and current dominance of this industry is indisputable. Since 1991 Intel has been the largest U.S. semiconductor supplier. In 1994 the company earned a net profit of $2.3 billion on sales of $11.5 billion.

CORPORATE CULTURE AT INTEL

Intel began as a functional organization but over time a matrixlike management structure began to evolve. The company explicitly encouraged substantial interactions between its divisions. Matrix relationships were cultivated by team projects and other programs that transcended departmental boundaries. Many innovative ideas originated from these teams, and for the most part these ideas "rode on the backs of 'product champions,' middle managers within Intel who became fanatically wedded to these ideas."[24] Many of the successful product champions became cultural heroes. Further, this entire tradition seemed to enhance the company's identity as a technologically superior organization capable of extraordinary accomplishments. It is no surprise then that Intel valued its competencies in engineering and manufacturing over other functions in the organization.

Some of Intel's extraordinary success can be attributed to its aggressive behavior and an attitude of confidence bordering on righteousness. This aggressiveness was clearly manifest in the company's well-known Orange Crush campaign. Intel employees were generally known for being extremely intelligent but opinionated and somewhat arrogant. Company meetings were typified by heated debates and sharp confrontations.

In addition, the Intel culture became quite insular over time. Andy Grove fostered a corporate paranoia that kept Intel quite vigilant about its environment and protective of its turf. Thus, according to John Markoff, "Inward looking and wary of competitors, [Intel] developed a bunker mentality, a go-for-the-jugular attitude and a reputation for arrogance."[25] In the mid-1980s this reputation for arrogance dogged Intel which was perceived by customers as aloof and unresponsive.

One reason for Intel's belligerent and defensive management style was its experience with Japanese competitors in the early 1980s. Several of those companies nearly drove Intel from its computer memory chip business. The company survived this ordeal because of the generosity of IBM which invested $250 million in Intel at this critical time in exchange for 12 percent of the company. Thus, Intel's difficult experiences with the Japanese intensified its paranoia and have helped to shape the unique Intel culture. That closed and performance-oriented culture seems based on the core values of employee discipline, product quality, risk-taking, and engineering excellence.

OVERVIEW OF EVENTS

The Pentium chip, successor to the 386 and 486 line of chips, is the most powerful and fastest line of chips produced by Intel. This high performance chip reached the market in May 1993 and was an immediate success. Approximately five million computers using the Pentium chip were sold prior to the controversy in the fall of 1994. Some of the reason for this success was Intel's decision to market the Pentium chip directly to consumers. As a result, the company spent $150 million on an aggressive advertising campaign centered around a logo that read "Intel Inside." Most consumers are unaware of the chip contained within their PCs but because of the success of this campaign Intel became well known beyond the community of "techies" and computer professionals.

The ads for the Pentium processor stressed that the powerful chip will increase the life span of a computer, "since it will still have plenty of horsepower when tomorrow's applications come along." These print ads saturated many popular publications such as *Business Week, Time,* and so forth. The end result was an unusually high profile for an engineering company that specialized in making computer chips.

However, during October of 1994 a mathematician disclosed a flaw with the Pentium chip that could lead to erroneous results in some mathematical calculations. This flaw in the chip's floating-point unit is obscure, but with certain numbers the Pentium cannot divide correctly. Consider, for example, the following calculation:

$$4{,}195{,}835 - ((4{,}195{,}835/3{,}145{,}727) \times 3{,}145{,}727)$$

The correct answer is quite obviousy 0 but the Pentium chip yields a solution of 256! Apparently Intel failed to perform a basic test that would have detected the error before the product was shipped.

The *Electrical Engineering Times* published the first article on the chip's flaw. The company quickly admitted that it had become aware of the problem during the summer of 1994 but chose not to say anything because it felt that this was such an obscure flaw that would affect very few users. Intel corrected the problem but admits that it continued to sell the flawed chip to computer makers until its production change-over to the new chips was completed. The company offered to replace the flawed chips but only to those users who qualified because they were doing sophisticated calculations. On November 22, 1994 CNN broadcast a report about the Pentium chip, and two days later articles about the problem appeared in the *New York Times* and the *Boston Globe*.

Despite the increasing negative publicity, however, Intel maintained its defensive posture. The company was beseiged with complaints and questions from concerned customers who had purchased a computer with a Pentium chip or were contemplating such a purchase. On the Internet Intel was the subject of ridicule and fierce criticism for its lack of concern about the problem and especially for not having disclosed the problem when they first encountered it over the summer.

Insiders at Intel admit that the company once again adopted a "bunker mentality" as it tried to cope with this growing crisis. A committee was formed to deal with the problem which met once in the morning and once in the evening. In the end these company officials concluded that they were on the right track in resolving the problem; at the center of their deliberations was a careful assessment of the very low probabilities of this problem's occurrence. In short, the company focused primarily on technical arguments and issues. Moreover, according to one report, "Throughout the next two weeks, the company continued to believe that its customers were listening to its explanation that the Pentium's computational errors were so infrequent that ordinary users did not have to worry."[26]

The company's beseiged CEO, Andrew Grove, felt that the situation was under control as some of the negative publicity began to subside. Many consumers, however, balked at the need to "explain" exactly why they needed a new chip. Customers who called the company's help line were asked a sequence of questions about how they are using the machines. They were offered a replacement chip only if they "passed" this qualification process. During the interview Intel reps asked users about their occupations and their computer applications and software. Some users bristled at being forced to justify their need for an unflawed chip; some pointed out that even if they were not now doing sophisticated calculations this did not mean they would not be doing these calculations in the future or using software packages that were doing such calculations.

Further, in an effort to placate its angry and bemused consumers Grove posted an apology on the Internet on November 27. In his apology, Grove pointed out that "no chip is ever perfect." He also reiterated the company's replacement policy that restricted such replacements to those doing intensive mathematical calculations.

Just as these positive public relations efforts were beginning to have some effect, IBM unexpectedly announced on December 12 that it would immediately cease shipping computers with the flawed chip. Intel had claimed that the flaw was so obscure that it might occur once every 27,000 years for the average consumer. But IBM's researchers concluded that this flaw could surface once every 24 days for the average user. For a corporate user with 1000 machines this might mean one or two errors a day! Some analysts criticized IBM's bold move as self-serving, since IBM was developing the PowerPC chip in conjunction with Motorola that competes directly against the Pentium. Perhaps this was IBM's way of undermining sales of the celebrated Pentium chip?

Regardless of the purity of IBM's motives, its announcement caused major problems for Intel. The flawed chip was now back in the limelight and Intel found itself once again defending its actions to a skeptical public. Intel responded angrily to IBM's announcement intimating that IBM had manipulated the test conditions in order to get these prejudicial results. However, the damage had already been done. IBM's announcement was a serious blow to Intel's efforts to suppress this controversy. Consumers felt more confused than ever as they wondered whom to believe, Intel or IBM. Indeed, the credibility of the entire industry seemed to be at stake here.

RESOLUTION

Despite the IBM announcement Intel steadfastly refused to modify its much criticized replacement policy. To a certain extent, Intel's intransigence could be attributed to its cultural traits which emphasized a rational and calculated approach to the solution of problems. Thus, it continued to defend its policy of replacing chips only on an as needed basis and only if the consumers would respond to interviews on how they were using the product. Meanwhile reports kept appearing that described fresh, new encounters with the flawed chip. A major New York City Bank discovered serious calculation errors, while "scientists at Brookhaven National Laboratory on Long Island got wrong answers in calculating the impact of colliding subatomic particles. . . ."[27] Similar reports of problems with fairly routine calculations surfaced on the Internet and in various trade journals. Also, concern over Intel's handling of this crisis continued to effect adversely the company's stock. During the week of the IBM announcement the stock was down $3.25 and closed at $59.50.

As Christmas approached Intel had had enough. On December 20 the company finally announced that it would reverse its policy and that it would now offer all customers a free replacement on request with no questions asked. Also, the company agreed to cover the replacement expense for anyone who requested it. Unfortunately, the company also indicated that it would be several months before new chips would be available on a widespread basis. Intel also initiated an advertising campaign apologizing for the flawed chip *and* its inept management of this problem.

Analysts provided various estimates of what Intel would need to spend in order to replace the defective chip. By the end of December 1994, roughly four million chips had been shipped, but Intel projected that 30–70 percent of those chips would need to be replaced. If this were true, the cost of the replacement would be a $200–$500 million charge before taxes. This seemed to be a small price to pay for the positive publicity that accompanied the announcement of this decision. Implementing this decision, however, was a formidable challenge for Intel. It took several months to ramp up its production of the corrected chip and the replacement process was continued through the fall of 1995. But with its decision this public relations debacle for Intel finally appeared to be at an end.

AFTERMATH

Analysts now estimate that only about 20% of the flawed chips were returned. There has been no significant financial impact on Intel. The company did set aside a $475 million charge in 1994 to cover the costs associated with the chip replacement project. More importantly, Pentium sales continue to grow quite rapidly.

Case 8.5   The Product Manager[28]

A MEETING IN BOSTON

It was late Friday afternoon and Richard Martin was rushing to Boston's Logan airport to catch the last flight back to San Francisco. As the cab traversed through the busy, confusing streets of downtown Boston, Martin gazed at the surrounding urban landscape. He felt truly elated over the speech he had just given. He had come to Boston for Jupiter Software's east coast user group meeting. Martin was the product manager for the company's popular relational data base product, INFORM-2. In his speech he unequivocally announced that the long awaited release of INFORM-3 would be available on May 1, 1989. In this speech and in private meetings with Jupiter's major clients he exhorted Jupiter's nervous customer base to wait for this timely new release and not to jump ship to more advanced competitive products. Because of the work of Jupiter's talented engineering staff, he was able to present a demo of this new product despite the fact that some pieces of the product were still not even coded or designed. But the "demo" was a great success and added significant credibility to Martin's confidence and insistence that the product would be ready for distribution by May 1.

But as Martin settled into his first-class plane seat and peered at the changing scenery below, his mood began to change rather dramatically. His speech and visit to Boston was assuredly a great success on one level, but he began to wonder about the ethical propriety of announcing a release date in such unequivocal terms, especially when no one at the company was really confident about this date. Martin's confident and dogmatic style at the meeting masked feelings of insecurity and concern about the May 1 target that pervaded the entire company. Unfortunately, this was the first of many such user group meetings and Martin was scheduled to make the same speech and exude the same level of confidence in several other cities across the United States, Canada, and Europe. However, as the plane reached its cruising altitude he wondered about his future at Jupiter and whether he was the right man to continue this tour of the company's user group meetings.

THE COMPANY

Jupiter Software was founded in the late 1970s by three California entrepreneurs. One of these individuals, Larry Connors, was an engineer with undergraduate and graduate degrees from Stanford. After completing his studies at Stanford, Connors went to work for the data processing department of one of California's largest banks. Shortly after his arrival Connors developed a sophisticated input screen to facilitate data entry for the bank's clerks. This input screen allowed clerks to enter data more quickly into the firm's hierarchical IBM data base. This tool was quite successful and Connors was sure that he could sell it to other companies with similar data input requirements. He promptly resigned from the bank and formed his own company, Jupiter Software. Connors needed additional capital to get this company off the ground so he invited two friends to invest $25,000 in return for a major stake in

Jupiter. These individuals were "silent" partners who were not involved in the day-to-day operations of Jupiter. The company earned a small profit on first-year revenues of around $100,000.

During this time much was being written about the potential and promise of relational data-base technology. Hierarchical and network data bases prevailed among large commercial users, but they were often criticized for their complexity and inflexibility. Both of these data-base models arrange records in a hierarchical manner with a master record and its subordinates. However, despite their speed and efficiency these data bases did not adapt well to a company's changing information requirements.

The relational model was developed by Edgar F. Codd of IBM in 1970. It immediately showed great promise because of its simplicity and flexibility. According to this model, each record in the file is conceived as a row in a two dimensional table and each field becomes a column in that table. The table could be augmented with new fields if necessary and tables could be joined to each other if they had an item in common through a simple "join" or "relate" command (see Exhibit 1 on p. 223). The relational data-base management system (or RDBMS) was organized for maximum flexibility, ease of use, and quick retrieval of information. The only drawback with the relational model at this time was its slow performance compared to the network and hierarchical models.

Connors astutely realized that the benefits of relational technology far outweighed its liabilities. Consequently, he hired a small group of engineers to expand his simple data input form into a full scale relational data base. By 1981 INFORM-1 was born. It was initially designed for the IBM mainframe but as the product grew in popularity it was ported to DEC, Hewlett Packard, and Data General minicomputers. Sales quickly took off on all of these platforms as relational technology found great favor with many companies looking for an alternative to the more primitive data-base technologies of the 1960s and 1970s.

By 1984 revenues reached $12 million and the company was growing very rapidly. Connors moved the company from a small building in San Mateo and leased the second and third floors of a major office building in Burlingame, a city close to San Francisco and just on the periphery of the famous Silicon Valley. The engineering staff had expanded to 25 and new sales offices were opened in Boston, Washington, DC, Atlanta, Dallas, and Toronto. The company also signed on distributors to sell INFORM throughout Europe. In 1985 Jupiter's sales almost doubled to $21 million as the company released a new version of the product, INFORM-2. This new release included more sophisticated functionality than the first release, such as a better report writer, additional security features, and an input screen or data entry form that provided more substantial validation of data as it was being entered into the data base by end users.

Jupiter's niche in the data-base market place was the departmental DBMS which normally resided on a departmental processor such as a minicomputer. Departmental computing systems were considered a high-growth segment of the market. International Data Corporation (IDC), a leading consulting firm, estimated that shipments of departmental DBMS software would increase at a compound annual growth rate of 31 percent through 1991. IDC also projected that the installed base of departmental DBMSs would increase from 139,000 in 1986 to 531,000 in 1991. Surveys of current customers and prospective buyers revealed the salient minimum requirements of an acceptable departmental DBMS:

- **SQL** compatibility (The Structured Query Language was the standard method of querying the data base to retrieve the appropriate records)
- Performance-oriented systems
- Distributed processing capability
- Multivendor interfaces (i.e., to IBM mainframes and various PC platforms)
- Transaction processing
- Easy-to-use end user interface

As the RDBMS market evolved, commercial systems without these important features would be at a serious competitive disadvantage.

JUPITER'S MANAGEMENT TEAM

As the company continued to expand Connors realized the need to make the sometimes difficult transition from an entrepreneurial environment to a management environment. Hence, in the 1983–1984 time frame he brought to Jupiter a skilled team of professional managers. Jeff Bennet became the vice president of Marketing; he was lured away from a competitor with a hefty salary and stock options. During this time Martin was promoted to a newly created job, Associate Product Manager for INFORM. Martin had joined Jupiter in 1983 after receiving his MBA from a prominent east coast university. His good friend from college, Joe Casey, had joined Jupiter a year earlier as manager of the Marketing Services Department. He persuaded Martin that this was an opportunity that he shouldn't pass up. Martin agreed. He moved to California after he was hired by Jupiter as a consultant and marketing support specialist. He provided training to INFORM-1's new customers in addition to consulting services on how to design and utilize this system efficiently. Martin was highly effective in this role as he quickly mastered the intricacies and nuances of this sophisticated and complex software. Thus, when Mary Hastings, INFORM's young product manager, sought an associate, Martin was her first choice for this position.

The product manager reported to the vice president of Marketing and was responsible for shepherding new releases of the product through various stages from coding to beta testing. Hence, this individual occupied a critical position in Jupiter's management hierarchy. He or she was the key interface person between Jupiter's marketing departments and its engineering staff. Perhaps more than anyone else, the product manager must make sure that a new product or release was what the market wanted, that is, what the customer valued and considered important. To be successful at this difficult job the product manager had to have both technical skills and marketing acumen. Both Hastings and Martin fit the bill and worked very well together for over a year.

The management team was rounded out by Sales Manager, Dennis Johnson, and the vice president of Product Development, Jeffrey Coleman. Coleman had an engineering degree from Stanford and was responsible for managing Jupiter's engineering staff, the QA (quality assurance) teams, and the documentation workers. Finally, during these growth years, the company was pressured to elevate its phone support for its rapidly expanding customer base. As a result, a separate customer support department was established and was initially headed by Louise Cassidy from the Marketing Services Department. With this management team securely in place Connors hoped to take Jupiter to new heights.

1986–1988

Sales for Jupiter's INFORM-2 product peaked in 1986 at $26 million. By now there were sales offices all over the United States as well as in London, Paris, and Singapore. However, as competition among relational data-base vendors intensified and the market began to mature, it became increasingly difficult for Jupiter's seasoned sales staff to close new business. Although revenues had increased by about 15 percent in 1986, Jupiter had actually lost some of its market share during the last year as other companies grew at an even faster rate. Thus, its overall market share fell from a high of 9.2 percent in 1984 to about 8.5 percent in 1986. As a result, despite the revenue growth and continued profitability there was cause for alarm and incipient concern among Jupiter's executives.

The reasons for Jupiter's emerging problems were manifold, but for the most part they could be attributed to its failure to keep up with technology. The latest release of the product, INFORM-2, was revised in the early 1980s to include some minor enhancements to the data entry screens and the report writer along with some query optimizers to speed up the retrieval process. But INFORM-2 was being eclipsed by competitive products in both performance and functionality. For example, INFORM-2 did not provide for on-line transaction processing (OLTP) which was becoming a required feature of relational data base systems. OLTP allowed multiple users to work on the same data file by locking a record that was retrieved by a particular user until that user completed his or her update. In addition, INFORM-2 used a proprietary query language instead of the industry standard language, SQL. Finally, the product sorely lacked a robust report writer, and its performance deteriorated significantly when the number of records in the data base exceeded 100,000 records.

Competitors such as Oracle and Ingress became highly adept at exploiting these vulnerabilities and consequently prevailed repeatedly in head-to-head competition with Jupiter. The word in the marketplace was that INFORM-2 was a fine tool for small- to medium-size applications but was not well suited for large scale departmental applications where 100,000+ records and transaction processing were the norm. For these applications, products like Oracle and Ingress were seen as far superior.

The company's managers worked hard to counter this negative image but to no avail. As a result, for the first time in Jupiter's history sales dropped precipitously in 1987 to about $19.5 million and the company posted its first loss of $2.1 million. To get its costs under control Connors quickly implemented a layoff of 10 percent of the staff at the Burlingame headquarters and closed three of the company's eight sales offices.

Of course, Connors knew all too well that the company's dim prospects could not be reversed unless INFORM-2 could be revised to include considerable new functionality such as support for SQL, transaction processing, a better report writer, and so on. A team of engineers had been working feverishly on this project throughout the past year but made little progress. Much of the blame for this lack of progress could be laid at the feet of Coleman, the vice president of Product Development. Unfortunately, he was not an effective leader. For example, he had difficulty resolving disputes among his engineers regarding many design issues for the new product which was to be called INFORM-3. In early 1988, Connors, still perturbed by the company's first unprofitable year, met with his Board to discuss the fate of Cole-man. After this brief meeting it was decided that Coleman had to go; no one had confidence in his ability to accelerate the progress of INFORM-3's development. On February 11, 1988 Coleman was asked to resign. Several days later Connors announced that Coleman's replacement would be Warren Clemens, a 33-year-old engineering graduate of MIT. Clemens had worked briefly for Coleman after he first moved to California, but the two men rarely saw eye-to-eye, so Clemens went to work for another data-base company in Silicon Valley.

Shortly before Coleman and several loyalists among the engineering staff were fired, Connors arranged a clandestine meeting with Clemens to discuss his possible future at Jupiter. Connors wanted a virtual guarantee from Clemens that he would "get the new product out the door in a big hurry." As a result of this meeting and the prospect of a substantial bonus Clemens publicly committed to getting this product to the marketplace within 14 months. This would mean that the new product would be ready for sale by May 1989.

On February 21, a company meeting was called in Burlingame. Connors enthusiastically announced the appointment of Clemens as the new Director of Engineering. With Clemens by his side, he also announced the release date for the revitalized INFORM data base of May 1, 1989. Connors exhorted all Jupiter employees to wholeheartedly support this effort, and he encouraged skeptics to seek employment elsewhere:

> Jupiter will succeed in getting INFORM-3 to market by next May. Our whole future depends on this. But we need 110 percent effort from everyone in the company. If you're not committed to this or you think this is impossible, maybe you shouldn't be here!

Although most of Jupiter's employees were still skeptical they decided that remaining at Jupiter was probably worth the risk. Many had substantial stock options so Jupiter's success could pay off handsomely for them. Also, shortly after the meeting, Connors distributed more stock options as an additional incentive for employees to remain with the company. But the task ahead was truly Herculean. Clemens believed that all of Coleman's work was virtually worthless so he decided to start from "ground zero." Also, because of the radical nature of the changes, it would be necessary to design and code the product from scratch. According to Clemens, it would not be expedient to modify the "spaghetti-like code" written by some of his inept predecessors. Clemens hired six new engineers to complement the staff of those who remained after Coleman was fired. Thus, he had a total staff of 24 engineers. Most of them were quite competent and had experience with other companies in the Valley. Nonetheless, experts estimated that to construct a viable relational data-base product for the minicomputer environment would require at least 3 years and 35 to 40 engineers. Could Jupiter beat these impossible odds and construct INFORM-3 in 15 months with only 24 engineers? Connors was convinced that this was possible and that this project would become legendary in the software industry.

As sales plummeted further in 1988 there was even greater urgency in getting this new product to market. Jupiter continued to lose sales to its competitors and to lose money because INFORM-2 didn't measure up to more sophisticated competitive products. Its main source of revenue at this point was from the existing customer base. In 1988 there were approximately 2800 installations of INFORM-2. As is customary in the software industry, each site was required to pay an annual maintenance fee which entitled the customer to product upgrades, bug fixes, compatibility adjustments, and customer support. The fee ranged from $1200 to $4100 depending on the size and memory capacity of the hardware. Since the average fee was about $2600, maintenance fees generated about $7.3 million in revenues for Jupiter.

The customer base, however, was becoming increasingly disenchanted and disillusioned with Jupiter. Many clients had purchased the product in its infancy in the early 1980s but their needs had outgrown INFORM's limited capabilities. They had been promised a major upgrade for several years but nothing happened. The company and its managers were often ridiculed at user group meetings for failing to deliver. Some customers started to jump ship and purchased a new RDBMS. As one disgruntled user said: "I'm tired of Larry Connors' empty promises. I can't wait any longer for this mythical INFORM-3."

The summer of 1988 represented a crucial juncture in Jupiter's troubled history. There was tremendous discontent among the user base; many customers were quite skeptical that they would ever see INFORM-3 after Coleman's abrupt termination. The company was rife with rumors that many clients would not renew their maintenance agreement when the fall billing was issued (Jupiter billed its client base every fall for the maintenace renewals of all customers). The loss of this revenue would obviously be devastating to Jupiter. Hence, to rescue his floundering company, Connors knew that decisive action was essential.

A NEW PRODUCT MANAGER

By the summer of 1988 the development effort for INFORM-3 was in high gear. Tensions began to mount in the company, however, especially over Clemens's dogmatic and uncooperative management style. As product manager it was Hastings's responsibility to assure that INFORM-3 addressed the needs of the market. However, Clemens often did not involve her in the design of key modules such as the input screen and the report writer. When she confronted him about this he would complain: "I just don't have the time to be consulting *you* about this stuff! You'll just have to trust my instincts."

A marketing team was assembled in June and met every week with the lead engineers. The purpose of these meetings was to provide key departments with knowledge of the new product so that they could begin to prepare training manuals, brochures, and other promotional material. It was essential that these groups work together to plan and develop a product that balances market requirements with technical feasibility. But the meetings between the marketing and engineering personnel were usually volatile and unproductive. Clemens and Hastings argued vociferously at times. She continued to demand more involvement in the design of INFORM-3 but Clemens steadfastly resisted. Connors tried to mediate this hostile dispute but usually ended up siding with Clemens. On one occasion he excoriated Hastings for not being a "team player." By mid-July Hastings was completely frustrated, and she handed in her resignation.

Martin was the logical choice to succeed Hastings as Product Manager. He had performed admirably as Associate Product Manager, and he was intimately involved in the development effort of INFORM-3. He was often more conciliatory to Clemens and frequently made valiant efforts to bridge the widening gap between the engineering and marketing groups. Hence, on July 15, 1988 he was promoted to Product Manager. At the same time Connors put pressure on Clemens "to get Martin more involved." Clemens responded by inviting Martin to the Monday morning meetings of the engineering and quality assurance staff under his control. At this meeting the lead engineers discussed their progress on the modules under their responsibility.

After attending several of these meetings and familiarizing himself with the work that had already been accomplished, it became increasingly clear to Martin that the May 1, 1989 release date was highly improbable. He estimated that the design and coding of a functional system could be completed by May 1, but only under extremely optimal conditions. This assumed that the individual engineers kept to their demanding schedules and that there were no resignations or long spells of absenteeism. However, even under these conditions the product would most likely be ready for quality assurance testing sometime in late March or April. This would mean that there would be about 1 month available for the QA process, and most would agree that this was not adequate time to thoroughly test the product and fix all its bugs. Also, there would be no time to ship the product to beta sites for testing by customers with real-life applications; this was normally done after the QAD Department had exhausted its search for the product's elusive bugs and flaws. Thus, beyond any doubt May 1 was a *very* optimistic date. In Martin's estimation, the odds were strongly against the product's availability for shipping by May 1. As the summer turned to fall several other managers at Jupiter were equally troubled about this ambitious release date.

FALL USER GROUP MEETINGS

One of the rituals at Jupiter was its series of regional user groups meetings each fall. These meetings were usually spread out in the months of October and November. The regional Jupiter user groups were divided as follows: West Coast, Mid-West, East Coast, Washington, DC (this group catered to Jupiter's many government clients), Canada, and Europe. Thus, there were always six key regional meetings in addition to the international meeting which was held in the spring. It was customary for the product manager and other middle managers to speak at these meetings. This year the focus of the entire user group was on the soon to be released INFORM-3. Attendance would be high since the users had many pressing questions about this new product. Besides technical concerns two questions were uppermost in their minds: Was the development team on schedule and would they get their copies on May 1 or shortly thereafter?

Despite assurances from Connors, Bennet, and others, some of the company's most loyal customers joked openly about the May 1 date ("We'll be fooled again by Jupiter!"); many others were skeptical about INFORM-3. Hence, Connors knew that these user group meetings were pivotal for Jupiter's survival. He could not afford to lose a substantial portion of his customer base, since he depended so heavily on the maintenance fee revenues. These customers also continued to purchase training, consulting services, and so forth, which were also a major source of revenues for Jupiter. In addition, the company's reputation would be further damaged by more defections to other products. At this point INFORM-2's sales were almost nonexistent except for an occasional sale in Europe or the Far East. The fall maintenance money would give Jupiter enough resources to hang on until May when the sales staff could begin selling a state-of-the-art data-base product, INFORM-3. Thus, it was critically important to instill confidence in the users regarding the May 1 release date.

In September, as Jupiter prepared for the user group meetings, Connors called a meeting of the management committee including Jeff Bennet, Warren Clemens, Joe Casey, Richard Martin, and Louise Cassidy. He told them it would be vital to assure Jupiter's customers that May 1 was INFORM-3's release date and that there had been no slippage in the schedule. He emphasized the importance of being definitive and exuding confidence. The future of Jupiter depended on their ability to convince customers that they could have a new product in their hands by May 1989. If they could convince most customers to hold on, Jupiter could count on a high maintenance renewal rate.

The meeting grew tense as Martin and others protested Connors's injunction. Martin said: "Well, Larry, I realize how important it is to keep our customers but we don't have a lot of confidence in the release date. At the Monday meeting yesterday I learned of delays and serious setbacks with two key modules. Also, the input screens haven't even been designed yet. It's already mid-September, how can we possibly have a saleable product by May 1?" Cassidy concurred, "I'm hesitant about sounding so confident. My group has very little knowledge about INFORM-3. Even if we shipped in May could we support 2500 customers with a new product? I just don't think so!" Bennet, Jupiter's Marketing vice president, voiced a mild protest but wasn't nearly as strident as the other managers at the meeting. Bennet had a reputation for being politically savvy and resisted what he regarded as a challenge to Connors's authority.

Connors listened soberly and carefully to his managers but then responded: "We have no choice. There are *no* other sources of cash besides this maintenance revenue—if we lose a big piece of it we're finished as a company. I know there are some problems with INFORM-3, but we can fix them even if I have to do it by myself! We'll get that product out the door by May! This is no time to lose faith. We all just have to work harder to make it happen. Clemens and the other engineers are committed to making it happen, and I need your commitment too. As a company we have to be in lock step on this issue and sing from the same hymnal: INFORM-3 will be available May 1! If you don't think so, maybe I should look for some new managers who have the commitment we need to get the job done."

Martin and his colleagues were duly chastened by Connors's speech. They reluctantly agreed to do everything in their power to convince the user group community that May 1 was a realistic release date. Later that evening at the local bar they talked about what they would be doing. "Maybe INFORM-3 will be ready?" said Casey. "It's a long shot, but it's not impossible."

"Well," responded Martin, "I would say there's about a 10 percent chance that it will be finished. Those aren't very good odds."

"Look," injected Cassidy, "other software companies around here do this all the time. You guys have heard of vaporware, haven't you! Companies are always announcing products even when they're unsure about the release date. We're no better or worse than they are."

"Yeah," pondered Martin, "if the product is a few months late who will be hurt. I don't see the harm. On the other hand, if we're ambivalent and lose customers there might be no Jupiter Software next May. Then the customers will really be hurt—no bug fixes, no new product releases, no customer support."

"None of us like it," remarked Casey, "but what choice do we have? If we don't go along with this our jobs will certainly be at stake."

THE DILEMMA

As Martin flew back to Burlingame he recalled that conversation. He also took from his briefcase and re-read Connors's recent memo to the whole company exhorting everyone to cooperate for the common good (see Exhibit 2 on p. 223). On the surface, things were beginning to improve. As Connors's memo indicated, the product was beginning to shape up, and there was a tentative plan to get a beta release by March 15. Nonetheless, despite the positive tone of Connors's memo, Martin still thought that this was a real long shot. He had, however, concealed his doubts and won over many "doubting Thomases" among the east coast users. Martin's speech and the product demo was quite convincing. The slick product demo had been prepared by several of Jupiter's engineers who were able to simulate pieces of the product which had not even been coded yet; these were interspersed with modules that were completed and to the audience the new product came across as a seamless whole. It undoubtedly left the impression that the product was on the brink of completion.

Martin also went out of his way to talk with all the major customers at the meeting to assure them that they would have the new product in May. He had known many of these clients for several years since he had been to many of the key sites on the east coast as a trainer and consultant. Most customers liked Martin and felt he was a man of his word. If he made them a promise or a commitment, he always delivered. Thus, as Martin meandered through the user group meeting, greeting and encouraging Jupiter's various customers, he relied heavily on his credibility to dispel any doubts about INFORM-3 and Jupiter's future. And judging from the reactions to his speech and the product demonstration Martin felt quite sure that he succeeded. As he left the meeting he got a pat on the back from Bennet who told him that "Larry would be very pleased."

But now as Martin's plane approached the San Francisco airport he considered future meetings. There were several more coming up in the next few weeks. Was he willing to give the same speech and the phony product demonstration to these other groups? Was he prepared to put his credibility on the line once again? Shouldn't he at least qualify the statements about the May 1 release date—let unsuspecting clients know that it's possible but not a sure thing? Martin realized, however, that any sort of ambivalence would be interpreted by Connors as treason and that his job would surely be at risk. He wondered too about the ethical questions involved here. After all, there was a slim chance Jupiter would make the May 1 release date. Technically, then, his statements were not lies. But did he have a moral obligation to reveal the whole truth? Software developers were *always* wrong when they announced release dates so most customers would be forgiving and understanding even if the product was late. Wasn't vaporware standard industry practice—why should Jupiter set new ethical standards?

As Martin's plane prepared to land he gazed at the bright lights of the San Francisco airport. He could find no easy answers to these perplexing questions. Nor was he sure what he should do at the Canadian User Group meeting the week after next. If he gave the same speech which was such a hit in Boston, it would be another long flight home.

Exhibit 1   Sample Data-Base

Customer File: Cust-No, Cust-Name, Cust-Address
Order File: Cust-No, Order-No, Order-Date

Exhibit 2

Jupiter Software
Office of the President

Memorandum

To: Jupiter Employees
From: Larry Connors
Subject: INFORM-3

> I spent the day yesterday reviewing Product Development's progress on INFORM-3 with Warren and Richard. We reviewed the symbol table handler, the low levels, the standard file interface, the screen handler, the data dictionary, the data file editor, the report writer, the output screens and the commands. The progress to date is really outstanding, and the whole engineering staff deserves a great deal of credit. We also discussed upcoming efforts on the transaction processing facility and the data input screens along with the conversion utility. We reached tentative agreement on a schedule to bring us to the March 15th Beta release date.
>
> As each of you are aware, in every position, you are now being called on to overcome and rise above your personal limitations. In the next six months, with limited staff, we have to continue to operate our daily business and maintain our current products, while at the same time producing all of the elements required for a successful launch of what is substantially a new product. We can only do this with an all-out effort on the part of each individual and 100% team work. We have a great opportunity to turn things around and make this work, but success will require everyone's total commitment and dedication.

Case 8.6   Chicago

Vaporware: A term used sarcastically for promised software that misses its announced release date, usually by a considerable length of time[29]

OVERVIEW

"Chicago" was the code name for a new version of Microsoft's Windows operating system. The company announced in 1993 that this new operating system would be available to its users by the end of 1994. It then postponed the product introduction to the first half of 1995. And in December 1994 the company postponed the product launch once again stating that it would not be available until August 1995, about 9 months after the initial due date. Were these delays unavoidable or was Microsoft deliberately much too optimistic about its delivery date?

In a recent antitrust case Federal Judge Stanley Sporkin criticized Microsoft for its past practices of promoting vaporware. He cited Microsoft's announcement of Quick Basic 3.0 (QB3), a programming tool for Windows developers. It was alleged that Microsoft preannounced this product in order to impede the sales of a competing product of Borland known as Turbo Basic. The judge cited an internal memo from CEO Gates saying, "the best way to stick it to Philippe is preannounce . . . to hold off Turbo buyers."[30] Microsoft has vehemently denied these allegations, and they will not be further pursued by the Justice Department as Judge Sporkin had requested.

Now Windows 95 can be added to the list of well-known vaporware products. But how do we assess Microsoft's latest intentions in preannouncing this product? Is it a strategic ploy to avoid losing customers to companies such as IBM and Apple or is this practice more benign, a way of dealing with customer demand for more information?

THE MICROSOFT CORPORATION

The Microsoft Corporation was founded in 1979 in Seattle, Washington as a small upstart software computer company. Its founder and president, William Gates, was convinced that the personal computer market had enormous potential which could be easily exploited by Microsoft.

Gates proceeded to make a deal with IBM to supply the giant computer company with an operating system for its new personal computer. Gates purchased for $50,000 an outdated operating system known as 86-DOS from a small company called Seattle Computer Products. He revised the 86-DOS program and called it MS-DOS. He licensed this product to IBM in 1981 but wisely retained ownership. As a result when other vendors (such as Compaq and Dell) decided to clone the IBM PC they had to license their operating systems from Microsoft. Presently, MS-DOS is used in over 70 million IBM and IBM-compatible computers, and, as a result, Microsoft has over 90 percent of the world market for operating system software. The company also generates significant revenues from its applications software products such as its spreadsheet (*Excel*) and its word-processing package (*Microsoft Word*), which were initially written for Apple's proprietary operating system.

In just 15 years Microsoft has grown into a $5 billion company with a 25 percent net profit margin and a market value of over $40 billion. It now employs 16,400 people who work in forty-nine countries. Although its revenues are not as substantial as other high-tech companies such as IBM and Apple, no one can doubt Microsoft's clout in the marketplace. As a recent *Time* magazine article observed, "In some respects, the power Microsoft wields over the computer industry may exceed IBM in its heyday."[31]

A BRIEF HISTORY OF WINDOWS

Windows is the name for the operating system created by Microsoft to succeed its very popular MS-DOS system. An operating system is essentially the heart of the computer, allowing it to communicate with peripheral devices such as printers and disk drives. It also controls the movement of data within a computer. Despite its popularity and widespread use, MS-DOS had many problems such as its lack of user-friendliness. It was frequently unfavorably contrasted with Apple Computer's proprietary operating system which was much more intuitive and easier to use. Hence, Microsoft decided to construct a new, state-of-the-art operating system that would provide a graphical user interface similar to the one used by Apple. Windows is still a DOS-based operating system but, unlike DOS, it is not command driven, relying instead on icons, pull down menus, and simpler instructions.

The first version of this product was known as Windows 1.0, and it was announced in November 1983 for availability in June 1984. But Microsoft ran into development problems and pushed out the release date to June, 1985. It finally began shipping this product in November, 1985. But despite this long gestation period Windows 1.0 had many deficiencies and drawbacks such as memory barriers, and hence it did not receive a warm welcome in the marketplace. But in May 1990 Microsoft introduced an improved version known as Windows 3.0. which did a much better job of overcoming the limitations of DOS. Since the launch of Windows 3.0, Microsoft has sold over 40 million copies. It should be pointed out that Windows 3.0 was shipped before it was a stable product. The numerous bugs were fixed in version 3.1, but the company's reputation was unquestionably damaged by this hasty release of Windows 3.0.

A subsequent version of the product, known as Windows NT (which stands for "new technology") incorporates networking technology and allows users to link together PCs. In effect, it is a server operating system. Although Gates estimated that sales of Windows NT would exceed one million copies in its first full year (1994), actual sales have been much more modest.

MICROSOFT'S STRATEGY

Part of the reason for Microsoft's stunning success with Windows and other products has been a consistent reliance on its core competence. The company has been extremely well focused and has adroitly leveraged its technologies. For the most part it has eschewed the strategy of bigger computer firms such as IBM and DEC which offered a full range of products and service to their clients including hardware, software, consulting services, service contracts, and so forth. But up to this point in its history Microsoft has concentrated on operating systems and applications software. It also encourages developers to invest in these technologies and this has led to the wide spectrum of software that runs on its systems.

In short, the company has avoided the perils of spreading itself too thin and thereby losing the edge in its core technologies. Observers note

of its competitors, has developed a notorious reputation for failing to meet its production schedules. Hence, most users and developers have become weary of the company's promises and skeptical of its commitments. Many trade journals took the company to task for this latest example of vaporware, but most noted that they really did not expect Chicago to ship on time anyway.

But did Microsoft make a good faith effort to announce a realistic delivery date for Windows? Were these delays unavoidable, attributable to the unpredictable nature of software development? Or is this another example of vaporware, a practice of announcing a product too far in advance of its availability in order to lock out competitive products? Was Microsoft seeking to freeze the market to keep users from migrating to IBM's OS/2 system?

Many in the computer industry press seemed to think so. At least one editor suggested that the Chicago preannouncement strategy was similar to the tactics used by IBM in its heyday.[39] IBM's overriding goal in the 1960s and 1970s was to maintain market share at all cost. During the early 1960s IBM dominated the mainframe market with its 1400 system. But despite IBM's dominance its technology was vulnerable. Also, it charged exorbitant prices and made huge profits, and this attracted considerable competition. Honeywell, for example, assailed the 1400 line with its H-200 system that processed data faster than the IBM and sold for much less.

Honeywell was initially successful with this machine as its sales began to erode IBM's market share. But IBM's way of dealing with the popular H-200 was to prematurely announce its competitive system known as System/360 in order to freeze the market and avoid losing customers. According to Richard DeLamarter,

> IBM rushed its System/360 in to the breach to stop Honeywell, Control Data, and other competitors. It was the mere promise of that family of computers, as much as their actual installation, that saved the day for IBM. IBM's telling customers about the System/360 helped it corner an overwhelming share of the fast-expanding market for computer systems, even though several models of it did not make it into customer's hands until almost two years after their April 1964 introduction. . . .[40]

Was Microsoft to some extent mimicking the strategy of IBM in order to avoid losing customers to competitors (ironically one of whom is IBM) with better operating systems? Microsoft too is obsessed with market share and what better way to retain one's users than to lock them in with expectations about the imminence of a new and more powerful operating system?

Microsoft has directly responded to these innuendos and accusations by writing an industry white paper entitled "Vaporware in the Software Industry." In this paper the company claims that preannouncing products well before their official release date is nothing more than "predisclosure" and not vaporware. Furthermore, it serves an important purpose of engaging "customers and the industry in a useful dialogue about products that help customers make better decisions and developers make better products."[41] Microsoft's argument, then, is that the public benefits immensely from early information and so-called preannouncements about products since it helps users to make long-term decisions. In addition, if product announcements are too tightly controlled, isn't there a risk that the distribution of legitimate information could be impeded?

AFTERMATH

Windows 95 was finally released on August 24, 1995 to much publicity and fanfare. Microsoft's advertising budget for the product was estimated to be $220 million. Sales were brisk during the first few weeks after the launch, and the product appeared to be stable. Microsoft announced that in addition to strong retail sales it had commitments for over 300,000 Windows 95 units from a number of major corporations. Finally, in the midst of the hype the company revealed the scope of this project: 11 million lines of code and 293 person years of development time!

NOTES

1. Richard A. Spinello, *Ethical Aspects of Information Technology,* Englewood Cliffs, NJ: Prentice Hall, 1995, p. 82.
2. W. Robert Collins et al., "How Good Is Good Enough?" *Communications of the ACM,* January 1994, p. 85.
3. Lynn Sharp Paine, "Prodigy Services Company (A)," Cambridge, MA: *Harvard Business School Publications,* 1993, p. 13.
4. Quoted in Peter Lewis, "On Electronic Bulletin Boards, What Rights Are at Stake?" *The New York Times,* December 23, 1990, section 3, p. 8. Copyright © 1990 by The New York Times Company. Reprinted by permission.
5. Paine, p. 13.
6. Peter Lewis, "For an Apology, Firm Drops Suit Against Prodigy," *The New York Times,* October 25, 1995, p. D5. Copyright 1995 by The New York Times Company. Reprinted by permission.

7. Stratton Oakmont Inc. v. Prodigy Services Co., New York Supreme Court, Mineola Case No 31063/94.

8. Peter Lewis, "Judge Stands by Ruling on Prodigy's Liability," *The New York Times,* December 14, 1995, p. D1. Copyright © 1995 by The New York Times Company. Reprinted by permission.

9. Ed Joyce, "Software Bugs: A Matter of Life and Liability," *Datamation,* May 15, 1987, p. 90.

10. Nancy Leveson and Clark S. Turner, "An Investigation of the Therac-25 Accidents," *Computer,* July 1993, p. 23.

11. Ibid.

12. The details of Vayne Cox's ordeal are provided in the Joyce article on "Software Bugs."

13. Leveson and Turner, p. 28.

14. Ibid., p. 35.

15. Philip E. Ross, "The Day the Software Crashed," *Forbes,* April 25, 1994, p. 154.

16. Ibid.

17. Milo Geyelin, "Doomsday Device: How an NCR System for Inventory Turned into a Virtual Saboteur," *The Wall Street Journal,* August 8, 1994, p. A6. Reprinted by permission of *The Wall Street Journal,* © 1994 Dow Jones & Company, Inc. All rights reserved worldwide.

18. Ibid.

19. Mary Brandel and Thomas Hoffman, "User Lawsuits Drag on for NCR," *Computerworld,* August 15, 1994, p. 125.

20. Ibid.

21. Ibid.

22. "Doomsday Device," p. A6.

23. Christopher Bartlett and Ashish Nanda, "Intel Corporation—Leveraging Capabilities for Strategic Renewal," Cambridge, MA: *Harvard Business School Publications,* 1994, p. 3.

24. Ibid., p. 5.

25. John Markoff, "The Chip on Intel's Shoulder," *The New York Times,* December 18, 1994, Focus Section, p. 6. Copyright © 1994 by The New York Times Company. Reprinted by permission.

26. John Markoff, "Intel's Crash Course on Consumers," *The New York Times,* December 21, 1994, p. D6. Copyright © by The New York Times Company. Reprinted by permission.

27. Laurie Flynn, "A New York Banker Sees Pentium Problems," *The New York Times,* December 19, 1994, p. D1. Copyright © 1994 by The New York Times Company. Reprinted by permission.

28. This case originally appeared in *Ethical Aspects of Information Technology,* Englewood Cliffs, NJ: Prentice Hall, 1995.

29. Entry in the *Microsoft Press Computer Dictionary,* Seattle: Microsoft Press, 1991.

30. The reference is to Phillipe Kahn, the CEO of Borland.

31. Philip Elmer-Dewitt, "Master of the Universe," *TIME,* June 5, 1995, p. 50.

32. Gates has recently invested in one alliance to make interactive entertainment products and another to make interactive TV systems.

33. "The Future of Microsoft," *The Economist,* May 22, 1993, p. 27.

34. This means that the computer can process 32 pieces of data at one time.

35. Plug-and-play refers to the capacity to handle various peripheral devices produced by different manufacturers.

36. Doug Barney, "Microsoft Cuts Chicago Beta Cycle 10 Months," *INFOWORLD*, vol. 16, issue 26, p. 1.

37. Stuart Johnston and Ed Scannell, "Microsoft Bets Big on Beta Test of Chicago," *Computerworld*, February 28, 1994.

38. Lawrence Fisher, "Another Delay at Microsoft," *The New York Times*, December 21, 1994, p. D6. Copyright © 1994 by The New York Times Company. Reprinted by permission.

39. See Paul Gillin's comments in, "Halftime Report," *Computerworld*, July 11, 1994, p. 36.

40. Richard DeLamarter, *Big Blue*. New York: Dodd Mead & Co., 1986, p. 58.

41. White Paper, "Vaporware in the Software Industry," Seattle: The Microsoft Corporation, 1995.

9

The Social Impact of Computer Technology

In this final chapter we focus on how computer technology is insinuating itself into the social fabric. There are many pressing social concerns that must be confronted by users, executives, and policy makers because of the rapid expansion of the information revolution. In the case studies of this chapter several issues emerge that transcend the topics of information or computer ethics.

Some of these issues are dauntingly complex and will probably need to be resolved by carefully crafted legislation and innovative public policies. As computers reshape our society bold new policies may sometimes be called for to ensure that social costs are minimized and inequities are kept in check. For example, as the entire world becomes networked what will happen to those families and individuals who cannot afford computers and hence access to that network? Will there be a greater division in society between the information "haves" and "have nots?" Should the United States encourage the same policy of universal service that has been supported by the telephone companies for many years? That policy has virtually guaranteed inexpensive phone service to anyone who wants it. Or, on the contrary, is the provision of universal network access a luxury we simply cannot afford?

Further, as technology becomes a greater presence in the home and the office, we are witnessing its profound but paradoxical effects. On the one hand, technology can greatly expedite routine tasks and thereby make our work and home environments more efficient. On the other hand, technology can bring about greater isolation and impersonalization. Also, the revolution in digital media has the potential to transform the way we work and play. For example, the old boundaries between home and the office, between our public and private lives, are disappearing as more and more workers telecommute. Clearly, we need to carefully ponder the social ramifications of this intensifying trend.

These and other concerns are discussed in the first case study of the chapter, *Ethics, Technology, and the Workplace*. This case addresses the impact of technology on the work environment and describes how technology has made it possible for firms to constantly reorganize and reinvent themselves. One consequence of this has been that job losses seem to be a fixture of the U.S. economy. Although most economists agree that in the long run technology will create more jobs than it destroys, there is no doubt that it will have a more lasting impact "on the composition of jobs and the pattern of wages."[1] This case briefly examines the topic of technology and unemployment, but concentrates more thoroughly on the changes in the work environment wrought by networking and on the gradual emergence of the virtual corporation. It assesses what could happen when and if organizations are constituted by a dispersed group of individuals and teams who work and collaborate over a network. In these situations the organization will probably no longer function like a capsule or community concerned with the welfare and rights of its employees. This is the obvious downside to virtuality that needs more careful and deliberate consideration.

The second case, *Social Questions and the Internet*, reflects on some of the social and moral problems that have resulted from more extensive usage of the borderless global technology known as the Internet. These include the capacity to send messages and conduct business anonymously along with the issue of free speech in cyberspace. It also examines the contentious question of universal access, presenting an overview of the various options available to policy makers.

The next case is *Censorship at New England University*, and the alignment here is intentional since this case follows up on the free speech issue in the *Social Questions* case. In this actual scenario university officials must make a decision about censoring sexually explicit user groups on the University's Internet connection. How does the University balance protection of free speech rights with the need to preserve and honor its cultural and moral values?

The next case on the *Crypto Wars* is also closely related. It discusses the pros and cons of allowing the government to have the key to a commonly used encryption scheme. This question takes on greater significance as more and more users around the world engage in electronic communication and transactions by means of the Internet.

The chapter concludes with a topic that has received too little attention: the extraordinary influence of technology on the burgeoning gambling industry. The revolutionary developments in connectivity have the potential to make gambling truly ubiquitous, but how are we prepared to deal with the potentially high social costs of this development? The case, *High-Tech Gambling*, provides an opportunity to probe this and several related questions.

Case 9.1   Ethics, Technology, and the Workplace

Although recent technological developments have been embraced by most workers and executives alike, there is a widespread apprehension among many rank and file employees that technology is destroying millions of their jobs. In numerous industries technology has greatly enhanced productivity since it has allowed opportunistic companies to produce much more with fewer employees. But the downside to higher productivity is usually the loss of jobs. For example, AT&T's productivity gains have been about 10 percent a year since the mid-1980s and one consequence has been an unabated string of job cuts and layoffs.

This fear that technology is destroying the job market has yielded many pessimistic forecasts about humanity's future. The evidence seems indisputable that automation and information technology along with weakened unions and foreign competition have led to contraction in many old industries. Lockheed Martin, for instance, has cut its job force from 32,000 to 13,000 since 1990. As a result, job security, periodic salary increments, and other workplace verities have vanished for many employees. But how bad will things get? Will there be a large permanent contingent of the unemployed? Will computers and robots eliminate more jobs than they create?

While some economists answer those questions in the affirmative, others believe that this apocalyptic vision of the future work world is exaggerated. They steadfastly maintain that technology will ultimately create more jobs than it destroys. This is because "technology creates new demand, either by increasing productivity and hence real incomes, or by creating new goods; for example, as demand for black-and-white televisions was becoming satiated in most rich industrial countries, color televisions were introduced, and then video-cassette recorders."[2] As the output of these new goods expands, productivity growth will be accompanied by rising employment. Moreover, history strongly suggests that while technology does destroy old industries it will also generate new ones such as those that merge biology and technology. Some of those industries will undoubtedly create many new job opportunities.

Even if this economic theory is true, there will still be considerable upheaval in the workplace. Old jobs will become obsolete, and workers will be forced to migrate to companies and industries where the new jobs have been created. There will sometimes be long lags between job losses and the evolution of new job opportunities. In some cases displaced workers will need to acquire new skills to qualify themselves for these new jobs. In many other cases, it will be too difficult for individuals to transform themselves into the "knowledge workers," who will be most in demand in this new economy.

All of this compels us to come to terms with some difficult social questions. How does society deal with these shifts in employment patterns? What sort of safety net could and should it offer? What are the implications of work that is more portable because of advances in networking and information technology? The remainder of this case will dwell primarily on this final question concerning the social impact of knowledge workers doing business in a networked environment.

BACKGROUND ISSUES—WHAT IS A CORPORATION?

From a legal and moral point of view the corporation has long been viewed as an autonomous entity or an artificial person, responsible for its actions and subject to criminal sanctions. Thus, the corporation can be personified and regarded as a moral agent with its own set of values and standards. The corporation can also be regarded as a moral environment, a microcosm of society to be managed with careful attention paid to the welfare and well-being of its members.[3] The corporation then is a sociopolitical, semipermanent community that exercises significant influence over the careers and lives of its employees.

Moreover, individuals as social beings need human fellowship and community membership for their own flourishing and self-fulfillment. For decades, the office or the factory has served this role for millions of workers. According to Solomon, "We find our identities and our meanings only within communities, and for most of us that means at work in a company or an institution."[4]

This implies that employees have certain rights and privileges as members of a corporate community. Also, those who manage these organizations inherit a complex range of obligations which includes taking some responsibility for the well-being of their workers. Some would argue that this means creating a caring and humane culture in which employees are treated fairly and even compassionately, when necessary. Membership in an organization, then, should provide for a certain degree of security, respect for one's rights, and even some expectation of assistance in time of need. This tradition of corporate paternalism has been especially strong among large, well-established institutions such as IBM, Dayton-Hudson, Procter & Gamble, and AT&T.

Membership in a corporate community, of course, also entails some loyalty and commitment on the part of employees. They are obliged to do their jobs conscientiously and efficiently while following the procedures and policies of their employer. They must provide a level of work that is consistent with their compensation. Moreover, they have several other obligations including "being on time and avoiding absenteeism; acting legally and morally in the workplace and while on work assignments; and respecting the intellectual and private property rights of the employer."[5] Thus, there is a clear quid pro quo or social contract between the employer and the employees.

However, the current wisdom is that within our increasingly competitive global economy this paternalistic model of the corporation is becoming outmoded. Organizations with a substantial permanent investment in labor resources do not appear to be nimble enough in a business environment that demands constant change and adaptation. What will take its place as an effective substitute? Will the new corporate structure still function as a political, social, and economic community where concern is manifest for the welfare and rights of its many members?

To a certain extent this question regarding the new face of corporate America will be answered by technology. The new global economy demands a relentless pace of change, and evolving technologies make that change possible. Furthermore, the role of information and knowledge as the key assets of the organization should not be underestimated. Obviously, this shift toward knowledge work is enabled by information technology. We turn then to a cursory treatment of the evolution of technology in the workplace and the emergence of the networked organization which is ushering in such radical changes.

THE COMPUTERIZATION OF THE WORKPLACE

Computer technology in the office environment can be traced back to the 1960s when banks and insurance companies first began to use automated information systems. These primitive systems worked in batch mode, that is, data was entered into the system by way of cardboard cards typed by key punch operators. These cards were taken to data processors for a weekly "run" in which new records were input, existing records were updated, and reports were produced. However, during the late 1970s and the 1980s corporations began to replace these cumbersome office systems. More compact and powerful minicomputers took the place of bulky mainframe systems. In more recent years powerful microcomputers have emerged as substitutes for mainframe and minicomputer systems. In addition, the development of data-base technology has permitted the evolution of more flexible computer-based information systems. The relational data base, for example, allows users to input, update, and retrieve records quickly and efficiently. As a result, because of these advances, computer technology has now permeated the workplace.

The technology that is currently having the greatest impact on the organizational infrastructure and new forms of work organization is the computer network, which links office computers through phone lines or cables. Also, through wide area networks (WAN) organizations can link up with other computer systems throughout the world. Communication is facilitated through servers that function as a central repository of data and software systems such as groupware. Groupware software, for example, can allow many conversations to occur across the network simultaneously. Consequently, computer networks are rapidly altering the way companies and their employees engage in business, as information now flows more freely throughout the organization. Also, external networks have enabled many companies to have a more dispersed workforce while at the same time allowing more remote divisions to remain in closer contact with the main office.

Thus, networks are clearly bringing about notable changes in the way people work and interact. While some of these changes have improved the work environment, others appear to be producing some significant externalities such as the demise of physical community.

On the one hand, a major advantage of this technology is its effect of making the entire organization more transparent to its workers as information and the input going into decisions becomes more available across the network.[6] If technology is used effectively the underlying business and organization processes will become more evident to a broader spectrum of workers. On the other hand, greater reliance on electronic communications via the network diminishes human interaction and could impair workplace relationships. The proliferation of e-mail communications is one example. Many workers communicate more and more by e-mail instead of by phone or face-to-face meetings. E-mail is a more impersonal mode of communication and some fear that its more extensive use may begin to undermine the communal nature of the work environment.

In addition, some organizations now routinely have meetings or brainstorming sessions about certain issues over the network. These so-called cyberspace meetings in which the participants key ideas and suggestions into their PCs has the distinct advantage of anonymity—no one knows where the idea has originated; perhaps it has come from an executive or a worker much lower in the corporate hierarchy. The benefit is that the ideas will be judged more objectively and on their own merit. The disadvantage is once again the lack of direct human contact. Can electronic communications be enough to sustain organizational loyalty and maintain morale? Or do workers need more human interaction, more physical contact with co-workers, in order to feel part of a team or a real member of the corporate capsule? Is the sense of community and commitment to shared goals lost or awakened by this growing use of networks?

Another potential disadvantage of connectivity is that it often allows managers to exert even greater control over their staff, however dispersed it may be. If all workers are linked together by means of a network, a manager can easily check on the status of reports or examine other work of his or her subordinates in great detail. Consider the Mexican cement maker, Cementos Mexicanos, which has installed "an information system that allows it to monitor every component of its multinational empire . . . [including] how much energy an oven in its Spain operation is consuming."[7] It uses this same system to track the activities and whereabouts of its employees. Connectivity facilitates computerized monitoring and this could lead to the creation of a Big Brother atmosphere that threatens a worker's autonomy, privacy, and basic human dignity.

It is no surprise then that the literature and opinion on the social effects of computerization is so divided. One school of thought seems to embrace a "technological utopianism" that "portrays information-age office work in utopian terms—flexible, efficient, cooperative, and interesting."[8] Many others are more pessimistic about the impact of technology and hence emphasize antiutopian themes. Thus, they dwell on "a darker social vision in which computerization only serves to amplify human misery—people dependent on complex technologies which they do not understand, or doomed to routine work, because computers have usurped interesting intellectual tasks."[9] It is difficult to imagine that either of these extreme positions captures the essence of technology's impact which cannot be simply formulated or reduced to a single pithy expression. While the technology of networking has produced many benefits for employees, these gains have not come without certain costs which might include reduced job satisfaction or diminished organizational commitment.

THE VIRTUAL CORPORATION

This greater reliance on network technology is certainly hastening the trend toward the prevalence of a new paradigm known as the "virtual organization." A formal definition of the virtual organization is the "management of goal-oriented activity in a way that is independent of the means of its realization."[10] In other words, it implies a logical distinction between the conception and planning of activities or projects and their implementation. The key element of the virtual organization is "its dynamic switching capability,"[11] that is, its ability to switch to the most cost effective and efficient means of achieving its objectives. Such switching capability of course gives the virtual organization extraordinary flexibility and enhanced responsiveness to a changing environment since it can rely on many different suppliers, groups, or individuals to meet its diverse needs. Instead of hiring a large workforce, managers can simply subcontract. Companies will coordinate their activities in the free marketplace where they will bid for the services of workers and experts needed to develop and market their products.

In one manifestation, the virtual organization could be nothing more than a group of collaborators who work together in order to take advantage of a particular opportunity such as creating and marketing a new product. One group may contribute its marketing skills, another serve as the accountants for the project, and so forth. Thus, in the world of the virtual corporation "teams of people . . . would routinely work together, concurrently rather than sequentially, via computer networks in real time."[12]

There is, however, no simple description or comprehensive definition of the virtual corporation. According to one analysis, to those outside the organization "it will appear almost edgeless, with permeable and continuously changing interfaces between company, supplier, and customers; from inside the firm the view will be no less amorphous, with traditional offices, departments, and operating divisions constantly reforming according to need."[13] In most cases this new corporate entity will provide a virtual product, that is, one that is customized and adaptable to the customer's changing needs.

This virtual enterprise that we are describing is far from being the norm in corporate America, in part because of organizational and cultural challenges. Indeed, envisioning the concept of a truly virtual arrangement is impeded by our tendency to think of organizations in well defined, functional terms. But these impediments to change are gradually being surpassed as more and more companies are adopting some form of virtuality in their organizational structure, pooling resources from many different sources in order to exploit a market opportunity as swiftly as possible. Moreover, global competitive pressures will likely force corporations in this direction whether they like it or not.

By 1996 almost 10 million American workers will be "telecommuters." Experts estimate that by the end of this century the first Fortune 500 "virtual corporations" will emerge. These companies will not have a traditional central headquarters, but instead "will maintain multi-use hubs combining meeting and communication centers, employee lounges, and classroom space for teaching new skills to a geographically dispersed work force."[14]

VIRTUALITY AND SOCIAL CONSIDERATIONS

As employees move forward into this uncertain new world of virtuality they are apt to find the nature and quality of the relationship to their employer vastly different. In the past many corporations held out the promise of life time employment, a plethora of benefits, and clear-cut career and promotion paths. However, in the virtual environment the employee's connection to the corporation will become more contingent. Instead of permanent staff there will be a revolving door of personnel. The new contract between employer and employee will emphasize mutual independence and self-reliance instead of loyalty and job security. In addition, corporations will be far less paternalistic than they have been in the past, since the relationship with their employees will be much less substantial. Companies may feel less obligated to provide benefits or other workplace amenities. Many "virtual" enterprises will rely increasingly on this interim workforce that is called upon to work on projects as needed. Hence the fear that virtuality will soon erode "subjective notions of loyalty, either to persons or to countries."[15] Perhaps, some argue, even the notion of a job will become obsolete as greater numbers of workers become independent contractors.

As a result, there are legitimate concerns that the new workplace will not foster a true sense of community or provide the intangible benefits that employees now derive from work such as collegiality and friendship. Employees may begin to feel increasingly insecure and isolated in such an environment, and this could attenuate their commitment to this loosely structured virtual organization. As Pfeffer points out, "the biggest disadvantage of contingent employment arrangements is the difficulty in obtaining loyalty, dedication, or willingness to expend extra effort on behalf of the organization."[16] Hence an atomized, mobile, contingent workforce may not be the best way to conduct business.

Thus, there are many unanswered questions about the impact of this transition to a radically new work environment. For example, what will be the consequences of a new breed of corporation which is not paternalistic and does not provide any real security to its workforce? Also, what will be the effects of workers who are more isolated and less intimately involved with their colleagues? We cannot forget the crucial role that personal relationships now play in the business environment. As Solomon observes, "Too much emphasis on the *results* of business life—profits for the company, a salary plus perks for oneself and our family—leads us to ignore the actual content of business life, which consists largely of work relationships, friendships, and more."[17] As the virtual corporation becomes closer to reality and as contract employment and self-employment continue to grow, this personal side of the corporation may quickly begin to evanesce.

On the other hand, this impending transformation of the workplace could have many advantages and benefits for workers. As employees are extricated from bureaucracies they will enjoy greater self-direction and control over what they do. The present realities of supervision and management will give way to team-based structures and much more decentralization. This could lead to a higher degree of job satisfaction and greater personal fulfillment. Further, in most situations employees will have more opportunities to re-educate themselves in order to keep up with evolving technologies. Finally, they could benefit from a greater mobility, a freedom to move to virtual entities and projects with the highest rewards and the most satisfying and challenging work assignments.

Thus, the fundamental question remains—will the new workplace be more liberating or more menacing? Will it offer more promises or perils? Will it really empower workers or require them to relinquish the little control and power they now have in the face of computerized monitoring, more abstract work requirements, and diminished opportunities for social interaction and physical contact? This controversy will only be settled when and if virtuality becomes a more predominant paradigm throughout corporate America.

Case 9.2   Social Questions and the Internet

> the Net is being buffeted by forces that threaten to destroy the very qualities that fueled its growth. It's being pulled from all sides: by commercial interests eager to make money on it, by veteran users who want to protect it, by governments that want to control it, by pornographers who want to exploit its freedoms, by parents and teachers who want to make it a safe and useful place for kids.[18]

BRIEF HISTORY

The Internet, the world's largest computer network, is rapidly altering the nature of communication in America and throughout the world. The genesis of the Internet can be traced back to the ARPANET project of the Advanced Research Projects Agency of the Defense Department. This agency provided generous grants to universities and corporations in order to develop a digital communications network. The purpose was to link researchers at remote sites and thereby enable them to share their research results by means of electronic mail or file transfers from one site to another. The ARPANET became operational in 1969 with only four computers, but by 1978 over 100 computer systems were "on line."

Since ARPANET access was restricted, other networks were developed by the academic community. The most prominent of these were CSNET and BITNET. Initially, these networks used different protocols and hence were isolated from each other. However, in the mid-1980s the National Science Foundation intervened by supporting a network structure called NSFNET which became the common backbone of all the networks that constitute the Internet.

The development of the NSFNET, which eliminated the problem of isolated networks, laid the groundwork for the rapid growth of the Internet. This vast global web now links almost two million computers in fifty countries. It allows millions of individuals to access scientific and government research archives and conduct other forms of business. Universities, high tech corporations, and government agencies still represent the core constituencies of the Internet. But the employees at many other organizations such as schools, libraries, and manufacturing corporations are now signing on to this network in record numbers. In addition, the Internet has become readily available to home computer users through on-line information services such as CompuServe and Netscape. The latest estimate is that about 30 million users worldwide are now connected to the Internet.

The result of this influx of new users is that the communication that takes place on the Internet is heavily commercial. Its diverse users also rely on this global network to send private messages (via e-mail) and to post news items and other types of information on electronic bulletin boards (known as Usenet newsgroups). Finally, the Internet has become a favorite medium for the hacker subculture which enjoys exploring its many weblike paths.

Despite its swift expansion and growing popularity, there are still no central controls or central index of available services such as its bulletin boards and list servers. Hence, it is fairly difficult for many users to navigate their way through this maze of data and on-line services. Also, since no one group or entity controls the Internet there is no centralized authority to formulate and enforce rules that might prohibit or restrict use for miscreants and other troublemakers.

Other inadequacies of the Internet include insufficient mechanisms to guarantee privacy and security. Many users also suffer from "information overload" due to the overwhelming volume of information that can be found across the network. Others argue that Internet connectivity is still too expensive for the average person. Despite these shortcomings, however, the Internet is the most likely candidate to become the foundation of the nation's emerging "information superhighway."

However, as the previously mentioned citation indicates, this growing reliance on cyberspace has had some unintended consequences and has provoked some especially troublesome problems. At this point the full social impact of electronic communication is far from evident. In the remainder of this discussion we will present an overview of several of the most pressing and vexing social and moral issues that are connected to usage of the Internet. These include the ability to remain anonymous while communicating in cyberspace, the civil liberties question, and the problem of universal access.

ANONYMITY IN CYBERSPACE

One of the apparent benefits of communicating in cyberspace is the option to remain anonymous. Such anonymity can sometimes promote free expression and enable more inhibited users to express candidly their feelings and thoughts about various issues. It can also allow users who have been stigmatized because of certain ailments or social diseases to communicate openly and freely about their plight without the risk of negative repercussions. Thus, many cyberspace dwellers argue that they can really be themselves only in the confines of this ethereal realm. Usually this anonymity is achieved and sustained by the use of pseudonyms and other forms of false identity.

Unfortunately, this sort of disguised communicaton can also lead to strange excesses. A user can pretend, for instance, that he or she is really a member of the opposite sex, or a child can pretend to be a mature adult. In other words, one can take on a whole different *digital persona* in the realm of cyberspace. Many psychologists are justifiably concerned about the ill-effects of such aberrant behavior. As Hays eloquently observes, "How do you react when you discover that your best on-line friend is just a figment of another user's imagination? And what are the psychological implications for a high-school student who spends his evenings inhabiting the persona of a 28-year-old woman?"[19] These cases may be extreme but they are becoming more common as many more individuals discover and inhabit this bewitching world of cyberspace. Also there is concern that occupying a digital persona will lead to a greater rootlessness, accelerating the marginalization of certain groups in American society.

There are other problems with the scale of anonymity made possible on the Internet, since it diminishes accountability and responsibility for one's actions. It's possible to engage in slanderous or inflammatory dialogue without fear of retribution. Hence the anonymity made possible in cyberspace has led to flamming and other forms of antisocial behavior that have sometimes eroded the normal civility prevailing in this environment.

Some of these problems are accentuated by the growing phenomenon of anonymous servers or "remailers." Users can send messages to these servers which then strip away the original sender's name and any traces of his or her identity before "remailing" them on the Internet. The message could be sent to one electronic address or to thousands, and can even be sent through other anonymous servers. Although some of these anonymous servers or remailers are used for legitimate purposes (e.g., allowing AIDS patients to communicate with other individuals while preserving their anonymity), others will send any type of anonymous communication anywhere on the Internet. Thus, an individual could use one of these servers to distribute pornographic or slanderous material and his or her identity would never be revealed.

The largest remailer site is the one in Helsinki, Finland with the address [anon.penet.fi]. It processes 6000 messages a day from users throughout the world. The Finland site and other remailers justify their operations as a necessary antidote against the erosion of privacy. They underscore the right of Internet users to communicate behind a cloak of total privacy. Further, American civil libertarians remind critics of remailers that in the United States anonymity in cyberspace is protected by the constitutional right to free speech.

Some commercial network operators (such as Netcom) block all anonymous messages from their network servers. Another countermeasure to anonymity is the use of a digital signature. These signatures require both the sender and the recipient to know the electronic code that is transmitted along with the message. This enables the recipient always to verify the true identity of the sender.

Civil rights advocates are often critical of these efforts to restrict or suppress electronic anonymity. They point out that these efforts violate a user's right to privacy and free expression, and they argue that this mode of communication has considerable social utility since it can protect political and moral dissidents, whistleblowers, and others who are engaging in perilous forms of self expression for the sake of the common good.

Anonymous electronic communication does pose certain problems; however, issues of freedom and privacy are at stake. Thus, public policy makers must prudently consider how to prevent abuses without imposing oppressive and counterproductive restrictions.

FREE SPEECH IN CYBERSPACE

Another controversial area of concern for users and regulators of the Internet is the emergence of newsgroups carrying pornographic material. Among the more prominent newsgroups that propagate this obscene material we find [alt.sex], [alt.binaries.pictures.erotica], and [alt.sex. bondage]. The proliferation of such salacious pictures and text in cyberspace raises many problems since much of this could now be more easily available to young children who have mastered their way through the maze of Internet newsgroups. While it is relatively easy to restrict the sale of pornographic material to minors in stores or other physical locations, restrictions on pornography in cyberspace are much more difficult to implement. This material can be downloaded in homes or schools at any time of the day or night. Such unrestricted access and immediate gratification could be problematic for vulnerable segments of the population. According to one report, "the great fear of parents and teachers, of course, is not that college students will find this stuff but that it will fall into the hands of those much younger—including some, perhaps, who are not emotionally prepared to make sense of what they see."[20]

But, how does society deal with this problem? What is the most acceptable method of setting reasonable limits for electronic free speech? And should the initiative to curtail free speech when necessary come from the government or from the users of the Internet?

As one might expect, the battle lines in this debate are well drawn. Many libertarian groups (such as the ACLU) are ardently opposed to any form of censorship, since they believe that the value of free speech should always take priority. Some civil rights advocates argue for an unconditional right to electronic free speech, while others come quite close to absolutism, admitting exceptions only under the most extreme conditions or as a last resort. They chastise users who curtail certain forms of free speech as "censors" and hold them responsible for undermining First Amendment rights. They argue that any form of censorship stifles the climate for free expression and sends the wrong message to users. Thus, the position of many civil libertarians is that the extreme solution of censorship should be eschewed in order to avoid creating a repressive atmosphere in cyberspace.

Another school of thought on this issue proposes a solution of prior restraint of this material by the government. The Telecommunications bill recently passed by Congress levels fines of as high as $100,000 and jail terms up to 2 years for any organization or individual that transmits "indecent" material to minors. This model of proscribing expression in cyberspace is based on the so-called "broadcast model" which applies to radio and television and subjects these media to strict government censorship. The "pervasive presence" of television and radio has induced the government to exercise censorship in order to protect viewers and listeners from obscenities and other perverted forms of expression. Consequently, the FCC imposes fines on those who broadcast indecency. But should the broadcast model apply to communications in cyberspace?

Critics of government censorship point out numerous philosophical and practical problems with this solution. They contend that such prior restraint is a clear violation of the First Amendment. In addition, they cite the difficulty of enforcing this legislation because of the global nature of the Internet. What can be done, for example, about newsgroups dispensing obscene material from countries such as Sweden or Denmark?

Still, a different school of thought would maintain that offensive material should be restricted and suppressed not by government but by users, organizations, and local communities. According to this viewpoint, parents should have the authority and the means to protect their children from unwanted pornographic material. Similarly, universities or other organizations should ban sexually oriented newsgroups from their Internet servers if they believe that it is within the best interest of the community to do so. Underlying this approach is the belief that the First Amendment right of free speech is *not* absolute but subject to certain limits. Obscenity, slander, libel, and false advertising are just some of the forms of expression that are not protected by the First Amendment even if one uses the medium of the written or spoken word. Moreover, in 1973 when the Supreme Court reaffirmed that obscenity was not protected by the First Amendment, it also emphasized "the right of the nations and the states to maintain a decent society."[21]

In some situations these pornographic images are not just viewed from the privacy of one's terminal but instead are downloaded and then publicly displayed. Some social critics would undoubtedly argue that even under these circumstances no suppression of these newsgroups should be put into effect. Rosenberg, for example, does admit that the display of hard core pornography in public places poses a grave problem, since it might offend the sensibility of some women. But, according to Rosenberg, "women who find it offensive and whose feelings are ignored in attempts to improve unpleasant situations can initiate sexual harassment procedures."[22] Thus, while sympathetic to the plight of women in these situations he and others contend that any sort of censorship would "chill the climate for free speech beyond the immediate issue of pornography on networks."[23]

The issue of free speech in cyberspace also entails the use of electronic hate speech whose purpose is to incite animosity towards individuals or groups because of their racial background or ethnic origin. Here again difficult questions must be addressed as institutions seek to balance the right of free speech against the need to protect groups from the lethal and humiliating effects of this form of expression.

The First Amendment right of free speech is obviously a fundamental principle of American democracy that should not be unnecessarily compromised. Some civil libertarians see the potential erosion of this right if censorship in the realm of cyberspace becomes more prevalent. Thus, they generally adopt the position recently articulated by Fogelman that "the right to send even the most unpopular and unsavory communications should not be suppressed—over any medium—so long as less constricting alternatives are available."[24]

UNIVERSAL ACCESS

The Internet will most probably be the prototype of the information superhighway or national information infrastructure (NII). Once this NII is more fully developed, it can have great social and economic benefits for the future. It can help stimulate economic growth in our global economy and can also help promote more equal opportunites by relieving the constraints of geography. For instance, in the future many companies will be able to conduct a considerable amount of business on the NII. According to a Presidential report on the economic potential of this network:

> An advanced information infrastructure will enable U.S. firms to compete and win in the global economy, generating good jobs for the American people and economic growth for the nation.[25]

This network can also become a vehicle to promote democracy by allowing people, especially those in more remote locales, to participate in decision-making processes on line. Further, there is a growing belief that technology will give ordinary people more of a voice in politics by making it possible to share their ideas and policy suggestions by communicating over the Internet through electronic mail or other means. One could certainly envision a time in the not too distant future when citizens will even be voting electronically.

Given the potential and importance of the NII, it could be plausibly argued that electronic access to this network will soon be as important as having a telephone. In the 1930s Congress passed legislation that required AT&T to provide universal service, that is, affordable telephone service to anyone in the country who wanted it. The telephone was deemed an essential service that citizens required for their basic well-being. But the notion of essential phone service is quite simple to understand and fairly inexpensive to provide. On the other hand, how do we define the essential elements of a connection to the Internet? Is there some basic configuration that everyone should have that would ensure them participation in the NII? Does it include the necessary equipment such as a computer, a modem, and software? Does it include access to certain information services that might be considered "essential?" Also, should all users have a direct connection to the network "backbone" or is a more indirect connection acceptable for residential customers? Answering these questions and determining a workable definition of "universal service" will clearly be a formidable challenge.

Nonetheless, despite this difficulty, a recent report on the NII published by the Computer Professionals for Social Responsibility (CPSR) took the position that providing some level of "universal service" is both economically feasible and morally responsible. The report argued that such service "is required to ensure that society does not become divided into the information-poor and the information-rich."[26] The CPSR is justifiably concerned that the NII not become another source of division in society and that everyone be able to share in its benefits. This will be especially critical if electronic communication begins to alter this country's political habits. Thus, the report strongly recommends that the U.S. Government find a way to provide equitable and universal access to the network. But, the report makes it clear that its prescription for overcoming inequities goes beyond access requirements to *universal service*, which includes providing some assistance to marginal users. The report realizes that in order to make universal service a reality, computers and modems will need a much wider distribution:

> Access will require not merely a connection to the NII, but the hardware to use that connection. A telephone wire to one's house is useless if one cannot afford a telephone. What the user's equipment will look like remains to be determined: it may be a computer terminal or some completely new device, but we must find a way to offer access to everyone at an affordable, perhaps subsidized, price.[27]

The report goes on to point out that all will benefit, both politically and economically, by universal service.

An alternative, of course, is to provide only *universal access* to the network instead of universal service. Under this scenario, government regulators would control the access to the NII by making sure that there was no discrimination based on geography or other factors. It would also make sure that information standards are established so that users will have the *means* to access important information services. The goal is to provide users with the opportunity to link up with the NII but not with the resources or equipment to do so. According to some models, however, this provision of universal access may include subsidizing marginal users so that they will be able to purchase certain "essential" information services.

To be sure, there is a notable gap between universal access and universal service, and this issue will continue to be the focus of intense debate among public policy makers and concerned citizens. The larger question in all of this is the government's role in eliminating the fissure in society between the information "haves" and "have nots." Should the government explicitly seek to close this gap or should it be left in the hands of free market forces?

CONCLUSIONS

Anonymity, free speech, and universal access are just some of the challenges that public policy makers must confront as they get involved in designing and regulating the NII. Other issues concern the protection of individual privacy, the need for security,[28] and perhaps the importance of ensuring that public interest goals are not displaced by purely commercial considerations. None of these issues can be dealt with simply, but it is vital that they be given due attention before the NII becomes a reality and communicating in cyberspace becomes the normal routine for larger segments of the population.

Case 9.3   Censorship at New England University

Dean Jenkins glanced out his second story window at the antique clock on the tower building across the quad. It was already 6:00 PM. It had been another long day for the Dean of Administration. Several student and faculty groups had visited his office to protest the decision to censor some of the newsgroups received over the Internet at the University. On this day he had also received a long protest letter from the local chapter of the ACLU, and was pilloried in an editorial of the school newspaper for "selling out" on the First Amendment. His mind was sluggish but he decided to stay in the office a bit longer and catch up on some paperwork. Tomorrow he would be visiting the President's office to discuss the situation and determine a future course of action.

NEW ENGLAND UNIVERSITY

New England University (NEU), located in the greater Boston area, was founded in the late 1940s in order to provide an affordable private education to students in New England and its environs. Many of its students were veterans of World War II attending the college on the GI Bill. It was always seen as a respectable alternative to Harvard, MIT, Wellesley, and other more elitist and expensive private universities in this area. Its liberal arts undergraduate program enrolled about 1800 students and its school of management enrolled about 600 students. The university also enrolled over 1000 students in its continuing education and graduate programs. About 90 percent of the undergraduates were residential students while the remainder were commuters.

The school had been quite successful in recruiting students because of the outstanding reputation of its faculty. Its specialty areas included the sciences, especially biology, biochemistry, and geology, along with several of its management departments such as marketing and finance. In recent years, however, due to demographic pressures in the New England area, it had to contend with a precipitous drop in applications. The school was always able to fill the freshman class with quality students, but this objective was becoming more difficult to achieve.

For many years NEU had been in the forefront of technology. From the early 1980s the school was linked to the Internet so that its faculty could exchange research information with colleagues at other universities. As the Internet became more popular it attracted the attention of more and more faculty and university employees. Students were also encouraged to make use of the Internet's ample resources. While many students had their own computers, the university had established several computer labs where students could go to type their papers, conduct research, and so forth. Students were also allowed to use these computers to connect to the Internet in order to complete assignments. This was a common exercise for students taking certain computer science courses. In addition, computer science classes or group exercises were frequently held in these labs.

The entire student body had access to the computer labs which were monitored by student employees. These individuals would keep an eye on things while they were reading or doing homework. They were also responsible for certain maintenance tasks and for reporting any technical problems to the Information Technology department.

"A MINOR CRISIS"

University administrators were certainly cognizant of the pornographic material available on the Internet, but they had never heard of any overt problems or reports of abuse in their school. However, in October, during the middle of the first semester, the school had to contend with what NEU's president described as a "minor crisis." A group of male students downloaded some images from [alt.sex.erotica] and left them for display on the computers in one of the computer labs. They did this deliberately just before a freshman computer science class was to use the lab that day for several programming exercises. When the instructor and the students entered the room they noticed the pornographic material on several of the workstations. The pictures were quite graphic and degrading, and some of the young women in the class became quite distraught. The pictures were quickly deleted from the screens, but the damage had been done. The instructor reported the incident to the Dean of Students who set out to find the students who were responsible for this misbehavior. Since there were several witnesses, this would not be too difficult.

Several of the women students voiced their profound concerns to the Dean of Students who was investigating the incident. One woman said that the pictures were so disturbing that she had trouble sleeping for several nights and that she had "bombed" an exam in the class she took after the lab. She claimed that she was too distressed to concentrate on the material. Several other students maintained that they felt "harassed." The Dean apologized and assured them that whoever was responsible would be punished severely. He also promised that he would try to ensure that this would not happen again.

Several days later the Dean of Students, Dr. Shirley Pellegrisi, met with Dean Jenkins to discuss this complicated matter. She told him that the male students responsible for this "prank" had been apprehended and were being suspended for the remainder of the semester. They could return to school in the spring semester. Some of her colleagues felt that this punishment was too harsh, but Dr. Pellegrisi was convinced that this matter was quite serious, and she wanted to send a strong message to the other students. The purpose of this meeting with Jenkins was to discuss preventative measures. What could the school do to protect its students, especially females, from being subjected to unwanted pornographic images in public facilities?

After several long discussions with her and other key administrators, Jenkins decided to restrict the University's access to the Internet. NEU would block sexually oriented newsgroups from its Internet servers since some of these newsgroups are dedicated to the posting of explicit digitized pornographic images. The university was concerned with the moral ramifications of allowing such images to be displayed in public places on campus, and it was also worried about its organizational liability. If it did not take action was it legally liable for any future incidents involving the display of indecent material? The university's President shared Jenkins's concerns and he reluctantly concurred with his decision. The decision was put into effect immediately and was implemented by the university's system administrator.

THE AFTERMATH

Dean Jenkins and his colleagues, however, were not prepared for the aftermath of that decision. After its announcement in the school newspaper he received many e-mail messages and phone calls from angry faculty who protested that censorship and prior restraint was not the way to deal with this problem since it suppressed the right to free speech. They agreed, of course, that the culprits should be firmly punished and that such strong action would itself serve as a deterrent for those students who might be foolish enough to think of doing this again. Several of the female faculty members sent letters supporting the Dean's decision, but about 90 percent of the faculty feedback was negative. The students were less strident, but they too were clearly opposed to the university's censorship of the sex newsgroups.

The protests and criticisms culminated in today's meetings with two faculty committees which asked Dean Jenkins to reconsider his "unfortunate and untimely" decision. At the same time, the problem was beginning to escalate as a result of the mounting negative publicity. The press had picked up on the story and several articles had appeared on NEU in several computer papers along with the local newspapers. Also, Dean Jenkins's secretary had received a call earlier in the day from the producer of a local televison newsmagazine. They were interested in doing a story about this bold but controversial decision to filter out the sex newsgroups; the producer did indicate that the show would try to present both sides of this volatile issue.

Jenkins knew that at tomorrow's meeting with the President and the university's general counsel it would be necessary to reassess this course of action. Should NEU back down and reverse its decision or should it hold firm even in the face of this severe criticism and escalating turmoil?

Case 9.4   The Crypto Wars

In February 1994, the Clinton Administration announced the now infamous Clipper Chip as a government standard for cryptography. Under this standard, the government would hold in escrow a digital key that could be used to decipher any encrypted message in case of an emergency or for other situations approved by the courts. In the face of widespread opposition President Clinton withdrew this proposed standard, but many are apprehensive that the idea of the government holding the key to all electronic communications will be resurrected in the near future. As a result, the debate continues about whether such a technology is really necessary. For some, the Clipper Chip is a symbol of a fast-approaching Big Brother environment, a grave threat to personal privacy and basic civil liberties. To others, however, this key escrow plan is essential in order to safeguard national security and to help protect the safety of U.S. citizens.

After explaining the basic technology of cryptography, this case study will present both sides of this slippery problem. The objective is to let the reader assimilate the various ethical and technological arguments on each side of this question in order to formulate a more informed opinion about the need and advisability of the Clipper Chip or some analogous security system.

CRYPTOGRAPHY

The term "cryptography" generally refers to data encryption which is currently used to safeguard confidential electronic communications. Data encryption is nothing more than a secret code. These codes have been used by generals such as Julius Caesar for over 2000 years. Others who have worked extensively with cryptography include Francis Bacon who several centuries ago developed certain cryptographic algorithms that are still in use today.

Essentially, cryptography works by taking a message such as "we will invade tomorrow" and translating it into some sort of unintelligible gibberish. The only way that this gibberish can be translated into something intelligible is by means of a key. For example, the key used by Caesar was the replacement of a letter by the letter that was three places ahead of it in the alphabet (thus the letter "d" would be replaced by the letter "g"). With the aid of this key, presumably known only by one's troops or allies, messages could be easily decrypted and rendered meaningful.

Computer cryptography or encryption has been in widespread use since the 1960s and is recommended "when sensitive data, such as business, financial, or personnel information, are stored on line, archived to off-line media, or transported across a network. . . ."[29] It can be done in either hardware or software. Although numerous encryption algorithms have been developed, the most popular commercial one is the DES or Data Encryption Standard, which the government has utilized as its standard since 1977. The DES was originally created in the 1960s by IBM researchers but it was modified by the National Security Agency (NSA) before being adopted as a standard. In addition, there is the RSA or Rivest-Shamir-Adelman algorithm that was created by these three individuals at MIT. The DES is currently used in many e-mail and networking packages and was recently recertified by the government in 1993.

The DES is a symmetric private key cryptography system; this simply means that the same secret binary key is utilized for both encryption and decryption. In order for this to work properly, both parties, the sender and receiver of the data, must have access to this key. The key itself then must be communicated in a secure fashion or it could be intercepted by a third party and otherwise fall into the wrong hands. This is a serious disadvantage of the private key scheme.

The other popular encryption technique, RSA, is based on a public key cryptography. Public key cryptography works as follows: Each party gets a pair of keys, one public and one private; the public key is used to encrypt a message while a secretive private key is used to decrypt the message. The obvious advantage of public key cryptography is that the sender and receiver of the message do not have to exchange a secret private key before they begin to communicate.

THE CLIPPER CHIP SCHEME

The task of protecting sensitive military or government communications in the United States falls to the NSA. The NSA has been charged with the difficult challenge of implementing the Computer Security Act of 1987, which calls for a national standard for computer encryption. As the *New York Times* points out, "The goal of a national voice- and data-security standard is intended to provide privacy for Government, civilian, and corporate users of telephone and computer communications, while also assuring that law enforcement agencies can continue to eavesdrop on or wiretap voice and data conversations after obtaining warrants."[30]

The standard proposed by the Clinton Administration in conjunction with the NSA is the MYK-78 or, as it is most commonly called, the *Clipper Chip*. The Clipper Chip is a microprocessor with an encoded algorithm known as *Skipjack*. The Government maintains that the Skipjack algorithm, though not impregnable, would be strongly resistant to tampering or code breaking.

The Clipper Chip would permit users to deploy their "encryption devices" whenever they deemed necessary. These devices would exchange secret keys and then be used to encrypt data communications. The key would be used for purposes of decryption. In addition, the Government would maintain in escrow the master key to each Clipper Chip. The proposal was to have these unique numeric keys divided between two government agencies which would effectively act as custodial agents. In other words, one agency might hold one half of a key and the other agency would hold the other half. Whenever the FBI was granted a legal warrant to wiretap it could then extract the serial number from the Clipper Chip in usage and request the two portions of the unique key from the respective government agencies holding them in escrow. Once the two portions of the key were combined, the FBI would be able to use this key in order to decode the data transmission.

THE DEBATE

When the Clipper Chip technology was introduced it was met by fierce and vehement protests from many quarters. Cyberpunks, civil libertarians, hardware engineers, and many others voiced strong opposition to this project. Indeed opponents can be found at both ends of the political spectrum, from groups such as the ACLU concerned with infringements on free speech to hard-core conservatives who are suspicious of the government's meddling in the lives of its citizens. The Clipper Chip's supporters seemed to be primarily government and law enforcement officials. Most corporate leaders and managers seemed indifferent and stayed on the sidelines.

The key issue is how to balance the right to privacy with the requirements for protection of safety and national security. The debate is especially significant since to a certain extent it will force many to carefully deliberate about which important values should have priority. As Peter Lewis noted, "the outcome of the debate will, in large measure, illuminate the values of a society that is trying to cope with rapid change."[31]

It is unfortunate, however, that some of the debate has been fueled by an abiding mistrust of the federal government. Thus, one of the arguments advanced by opponents of the Clipper Chip is the excessive secrecy underlying this endeavor. The Clipper Chip's design is considered a classified secret and therefore would not be subject to any external review or testing by independent experts. But what if the NSA has incorporated some sort of "trapdoor" that would enable the government to engage in covert surveillance *without* the need to retrieve a key? Moreover, "civilian computer experts also say that their inability to test the inner workings of the technology gives them little certainty that the encryption system is secure enough to defeat efforts of the legion hackers who will surely try to break the code."[32]

The most basic arguments against the Clipper Chip, however, are not technical but philosophical. Opponents vigorously contend that this technology is a serious threat to civil liberties, especially the right to privacy, and that it gives the government too much control over the lives of ordinary citizens. They claim that this approach violates the Fourth Amendment which does allow law enforcement agencies to conduct "reasonable searches" (including wiretaps and electronic surveillance) whenever necessary. However, it is unreasonable, they say, to have the keys to every data transmission burrowed away in the files of two federal bureaucracies. Perhaps the critical issue is this: Is it a violation of privacy to give government the *means* or capability to monitor phone conversations or data transmissions? Should the government hold the key to all encrypted communications, including those of innocent and law-abiding citizens, even if that key will be used on rare occasions to thwart the schemes of criminals? For many the answer is a resounding "No," and they see the Clipper Chip as the beginning of a cyberspace police state, a way for government to increase its control of technology.

Finally, one must consider the potential for abuse and the possibility that the keys will fall into the wrong hands through negligence or sheer malevolence. After all, can everyone in government be completely trusted? What if corrupt officials leak these keys for a fee or there is some other sort of security breach? Can foolproof security really be guaranteed by the federal agencies that will function as custodians of these keys? The difficulty of answering these questions in the affirmative points to the vulnerability of the key escrow system wherein a supposed trusted third party holds the key.

However, there are surely cogent arguments on the other side of this intense debate. Those who support Clipper Chip technology contend that it is vital in order to undermine the plans of criminals and terrorists who may seek to use encrypted communication. It is even more important to help protect national security and to make sure that the Clipper Chip technology is not used *against* the Government. According to one account, "if the crypto revolution crippled NSA's ability to listen in on the world, the agency might miss out on something vital—for instance, portents of a major terrorist attack."[33] Clearly, the risks of not being able to decipher encoded information could be disproportionate to the costs and disadvantages of implementing the Clipper Chip scheme. Supporters of the Clipper Chip are counting on the public's fear of criminals roaming the net with impunity in the face of the government's impotence to intercept their communications. In other words, according to Steven Levy, the government is hoping that the "public will realize that allowing Government to hold the keys is a relatively safe price to pay for safety and national security."[34]

Supporters of the Clipper Chip also point out that there are safeguards to minimize the possibility of abuse or security breaches. The plan would require two people at each escrow agent to open the safe where the key is kept; in addition, one individual from each of the custodial agencies must be involved in assembling the key. This would make it quite difficult for anyone to extract the key without the proper authorization.

Also, as Denning observes, protection against abuse will be provided by extensive auditing of the system: "By examining detailed audit records, it will be possible to determine if keys are used only as authorized and to decrypt only communications intercepted during authorized surveillance."[35] Proponents of this technology, then, such as

Professor Denning, believe that there will be sufficient checks and balances to counter the potential for abuses or fraudulent behavior. Hence, they conclude that the Clipper Chip is a beneficial, low-risk deployment of technology.

To a certain extent the issue comes down to how much privacy and independence the political system can tolerate. Are privacy rights absolute or so critical that they are beyond the pale of social regulation? If so, how *do* we stop criminals or terrorists who may be using technology to perpetrate their malicious deeds? Should they too be entitled to full privacy rights? These decisions and tradeoffs are difficult and painful. However, society cannot have it both ways, and it must resolve the fundamental question of which value takes priority: privacy or security.

Case 9.5   High-Tech Gambling

> Even as I approach the gambling hall, as soon as I hear, still two rooms away,
> the jingle of money poured out on the table, I almost go into convulsions . . .
>
> *(Dostoyevsky)*[36]

Casinos, state lotteries, "calling for cash," off-track betting; and now video poker, lottofone, and numerous other "high-tech" approaches to gambling. Gambling has obviously become a tremendous growth industry. In 1993 Americans paid a total of 92 million visits to casinos. In addition, legalized gambling revenues in 1994 amounted to approximately $30 billion. The United States has become a nation of gamblers, and technology products are clearly feeding this frenzy by allowing wagers to gamble their money away more rapidly and efficiently.

This new genre of gambling made possible by high technology is often referred to as "techno-gambling." While some applaud this application of technology, others fear that various forms of techno-gambling such as cyberspace casinos will aggravate an already serious and costly social problem. All of this raises questions for state governments which must regulate this industry and for IT firms and professionals who produce and market a myriad of high-tech gambling products. Can they continue to produce electronic wagering products with impunity or do they bear some responsibility for the ill effects of the current gambling craze? Before considering this question in more depth we will first present a brief overview of the debate regarding the morality of gambling along with more thorough treatment of the increasing role of technology in the emergence of new gambling products.

GAMBLING: SIN OR RECREATION?

What is the ethical problem with gambling and why is it considered so problematic? According to philosopher Lisa Newton, the fundamental problem with gambling seems to be its violation of the duty of stewardship, that is, the duty to take care of whatever property has been entrusted to you. But if the gambler is only spending his or her own money on slot machines or horse races, where is the problem? Why not simply consider this an innocuous and socially acceptable form of recreation?

In Professor Newton's estimation, there are several lines of reasoning that illustrate why it is even wrong to squander or gamble away one's *own* property. According to one of these arguments, "there is a strong social interest in the care and conservation of all property in the commonwealth, that gives the public a justified and lively concern with the way people dispose of wealth that by law is their private property."[37] The problem is that squandering one's property could have many negative ramifications for one's family, the local community, and society at large; therefore, squandering one's valuable resources must be considered an offense against the common good.

Indeed the social costs of excessive gambling are quite well documented. The lottery, for instance, is to a certain extent a regressive tax on the poor and disadvantaged since they are most likely to gamble away whatever meager funds that they have. Also, the proliferation of various gambling activities compounds the temptations and problems for the compulsive or pathological gambler. One potential cost of gambling is that it could make addiction both more severe and more prevalent. Finally, crime seems to always accompany certain forms of gambling.

However, instead of trying to prevent gambling, state governments are endorsing and sponsoring this activity on a significant scale. Any impetus to make gambling activities illegal seems to be slowly dissipating. Many states have come to the conclusion that the criminalization of gambling leads to a waste of valuable law enforcement resources. Rather, they see gambling as a major source of new revenue, a way to fund public projects and ongoing needs without raising taxes. According to a recent analysis in the *New York Times Magazine:* "Thirty-seven states have lotteries; 23 have sanctioned casinos. More than 60 Indian tribes have gaming compacts with 19 states. As this century turns, it's expected that virtually all Americans will live within a 4-hour drive of a casino."[38] In effect, high principles of the past have given way to a more pragmatic and utilitarian view of gambling. But this sponsorship of gambling activities arguably impairs the integrity and credibility of state governments, particularly when those states prohibit private organizations from competing in this industry.

TECHNO-GAMBLING

Gambling can be made even more convenient and lucrative by technology. There is a multitude of new gaming technologies and many more are on the way. Here are just a few examples: LottoFone, Inc.'s lottery-by-phone system; Bell Atlantic's interactive video gambling system that will let users gamble from the comfort of their own living rooms; a new experimental game called "Triples" by NTN Communications allowing home parimutuel betting. Meanwhile computerized Keno and video-poker games have already had a notable impact on this industry.

Consider the popular method of video wagering which is often referred to as the "crack of gambling." Video-card gambling such as poker and blackjack is especially addictive since a gambler can play up to a dozen games a minute. Also, players get instantaneous feedback and do not have to wait for results as they would with other games such as craps or roulette. This combination of speed and instantaneous feedback can be dangerous for someone with a propensity for a gambling addiction. It is exactly this sort of instant gratification that most compulsive gamblers are looking for. Vendors which produce these games have enhanced them with all the "bells and whistles" necessary to keep the gambler engaged, including the enticing sound of coins clicking and the use of high-resolution screens. Finally, these machines do not have to be confined to casinos—in most states they can be located in bars, restaurants, and even grocery stores. Several states such as Montana, Oregon, and Louisiana have allowed widespread distribution of video-poker machines; many other states are still considering them. The pressures to use the machines in these and other states are enormous as a result of dwindling revenues from lotteries and the ever present need to raise new sources of capital. Thus, the use of video wagering may become even more widespread if many of these states have their way.

Probably the most significant problem looming on the horizon will undoubtedly be the development of interactive gambling channels that will become part and parcel of the information highway. This will enable individuals to gamble from the comforts of their own homes. Because of interactive technologies gamblers will be able to play the lottery, bet on the races, and engage in other forms of "telegambling" without setting foot out the door. It is also likely that they will be able to play video wagering games in this fashion such as Keno, blackjack, and poker. The bottom line is that interactive technology has the potential to make gambling activities easier and more accessible than ever before.

The interactive gambling system with the greatest revenue potential is the on-line casino, offering the full range of gambling activities which one would find in a regular casino. This includes digital blackjack, poker, and slot machines. These cyberspace casinos are being established in obscure, unregulated, tax-friendly countries such as the Caicos Islands or the Dutch side of St. Maarten. For example, the offshore Internet Casino, Inc. recently began operating its "Caribbean Casino" in the latter locale. Players can begin gambling in these virtual casinos once they transmit electronic cash to offshore bank accounts established by the casino's operators. Although gamblers are warned that they must be 21 years of age or older, it is virtually impossible to verify a user's age. It remains unclear how the law applies to these offshore casinos on the Internet. Gambling laws were certainly not drafted with this technology in mind. Also, the confusion of determining which jurisdiction's laws apply will make regulation and control of Internet casinos a formidable challenge.

ETHICAL AND PROFESSIONAL ISSUES

The role of information technology in the future of gambling is obviously quite pivotal. If gambling is at best a questionable activity and if it has the potential to cause harm to many individuals, then what can we say about the responsibility of IT vendors and professionals? In other words, are those IT professionals who work on such systems like cyberspace casinos somehow responsible for the deleterious effects caused by compulsive gamblers who abuse these systems? Or does this distort the meaning of responsibility? If they are responsible in some way is there an ethical imperative to refrain from working on these products that have the potential to be socially hazardous?

It is worth noting that the issue of gambling is not explicitly considered in the ACM code (see appendix) or in codes such as the one adopted by the IEEE. However, we do find some relevant injunctions in these codes which strongly suggest that "technology professionals have a clear responsibility to question whether any computer system has a harmful impact on society."[39] Specifically, the Code of Ethics for Engineers requires engineers and computer professionals to "hold paramount the safety, health, and welfare of the public . . ."[40] One could develop a persuasive argument that some of the present and future wagering systems do indeed jeopardize the public welfare because of the harm which they cause to millions of users who tend to abuse gambling. On the other hand, perhaps it is the role of government to monitor this industry more carefully in order to prevent abuses, but so far most state governments have simply been part of the problem not the solution. And finally, perhaps this is the price we must pay for a free market economy where consumers are free to choose how to spend their money. It is simply the inexorable forces of supply and demand that lead to technological developments such as interactive gambling, and people can either choose to play or refrain from playing.

NOTES

1. "Technology and Unemployment: A World without Jobs?" *The Economist*, February 11, 1995, p. 23.
2. Ibid.
3. For more discussion on this see Kenneth Goodpaster et al., *Policies and Persons*. 2nd Ed. New York: McGraw-Hill, 1991, pp. 618–619.
4. Robert C. Solomon, *Ethics and Excellence: Cooperation and Integrity in Business*. New York: Oxford University Press, 1992, p. 148.
5. Joseph W. Weiss, *Business Ethics: A Managerial, Stakeholder Approach*. Belmont, CA: Wadsworth Publishing Company, 1994, p. 187.
6. This point is made convincingly by Shosana Zuboff, "Informate the Enterprise: An Agenda for the Twenty-First Century," in Cash, Eccles et al., *Building the Information-Age Organization*. Homewood, IL: Irwin, 1994, pp. 226–233.
7. Paula Dwyer et al., "Tearing Up Today's Organization Chart," *Business Week*, Special Issue: 21st Century Capitalism, November 18, 1994, p. 86.
8. Rob Kling and Charles Dunlop, "Controversies about Computerization," *The Information Society*, vol. 9, p. 7.
9. Ibid., p. 6.
10. Abbe Mowshowitz, "Virtual Organization: A Vision of Management in the Information Age," *The Information Society*, vol. 10, p. 270.
11. Ibid., p. 272.
12. John A. Byrne et al., "The Virtual Corporation," *Business Week*, February 8, 1993, p. 99.
13. William H. Davidow and Michael S. Malone, *The Virtual Corporation*. New York: HarperBusiness, 1992, p. 5.
14. David Pescovitz, "The Future of Telecommuting." *WIRED*, October, 1995, p. 68.
15. Moshowitz, p. 287.
16. Jeffrey Pfeffer, *Competitive Advantage Through People*. Boston: Harvard Business School Press, 1994, p. 24.
17. Robert Solomon, *Above the Bottom Line*. 2nd Ed. Fort Worth, TX: Harcourt Brace, 1994, p. 462.
18. Philip Elmer-Dewitt, "Battle for the Soul of the Internet," *TIME*, July 25, 1994, pp. 50–51.

19. Laurie Hays, "A New World: Personal Effects," *The Wall Street Journal,* November 15, 1993, p. R. 16. Reprinted by permission of *The Wall Street Journal,* © 1993 Dow Jones & Company, Inc. All Rights Reserved Worldwide.
20. Philip Elmer-Dewitt, "Cyberporn," *TIME,* July 3, 1995, p. 40.
21. Patty McEntee, "Is Pornography a Matter of Free Expression," *America,* August 10, 1991, p. 66.
22. Richard S. Rosenberg, "Free Speech, Pornography, Sexual Harassment, and Electronic Networks," *The Information Society,* vol. 9, p. 288.
23. Ibid., p. 289.
24. Martin Fogelman, "Freedom and Censorship in the Emerging Electronic Environment," *The Information Society,* vol. 10, p. 302.
25. President William J. Clinton and Vice President Albert Gore, "Technology for America's Growth: A New Direction to Build Economic Strength," Washington, DC: White House, 1993.
26. Computer Professionals for Social Responsibility, "Serving the Community: A Public-Interest Vision of the National Information Infrastructure," sect. 3.2, Policy Recommendations.
27. Ibid.
28. See case 9.4 for a discussion of the clipper chip controversy.
29. Curtis L. Symes, "Cryptography and Computer Systems Security," *IBM Systems Journal,* vol. 30, no. 2, 1991, p. 133.
30. John Markoff, "U.S. as Big Brother of Computer Age," *The New York Times,* May 6, 1993, p. D7. Copyright © 1993 by The New York Times Company. Reprinted by permission.
31. Peter Lewis, "Of Privacy and Security: The Clipper Chip Debate," *The New York Times,* April 24, 1994, sect. 3, p. 5. Copyright © 1994 by The New York Times Company. Reprinted by permission.
32. John Markoff, "Wrestling over the Key to the Codes," *The New York Times,* May 9, 1995, sect. 3, p. 9. Copyright © 1995 by The New York Times Company. Reprinted by permission.
33. Steven Levy, "Battle of the Clipper Chip," *The New York Times Magazine,* June 12, 1994, p. 49.
34. Ibid., p. 60.
35. Dorothy E. Denning, "Clipper Controversy: Key Escrow Scheme Protects Personal, National Security," *Computerworld,* July 25, 1994, p. 106.
36. Fyodor Dostoyevsky, "The Gambler," in *The Short Stories of Dostoyevsky* ed. William Phillips. New York: The Dial Press, 1945, p. 188.
37. Lisa Newton, "Gambling: A Preliminary Inquiry," *Business Ethics Quarterly,* October 1993, p. 407.
38. Gerri Hirshey, "Gambling Nation," *The New York Times Magazine,* July 17, 1994, p. 36.
39. Joseph Maglitta, "High-Tech Wagering: Jackpot or Jeopardy," *Computerworld,* February 7, 1994, p. 29.
40. See the Code of Ethics for Engineers, *National Society for Professional Engineers.*

References

ARRANGED BY SUBJECT MATTER

GENERAL COMPUTER ETHICS

BYNUM, TERRELL W. (ed.). *Computers and Ethics.* New York: Blackwell, 1985.

DEJOIE, ROY, GEORGE FOWLER, and DAVID PARADICE. *Ethical Issues in Information Systems.* Boston: Boyd & Fraser Publishing Company, 1991.

ERMANN, DAVID M., CLAUDIO GUITIERREZ, and MARY B. WILLIAMS (eds.). *Computers, Ethics and Society.* New York: Oxford University Press, 1990.

FORRESTER, TOM, and PERRY MORRISON. *Computer Ethics: Cautionary Tales and Ethical Dilemmas in Computing.* (2nd Edition). Cambridge, MA: MIT Press, 1994.

GENTILE, MARY, and JOHN SVIOKLA. "Information Technology in Organizations: Emerging Issues in Ethics and Policy," Cambridge, MA: *Harvard Business School Publications,* 1991.

GOULD, CAROL (ed.). *The Information Web: Ethical and Social Implications of Computers.* Boulder, CO: Westview-Press, 1989.

GRILLO, JOHN P., and ERNEST KALLMAN. *Ethical Decision Making and Information Technology.* Watsonville, CA: Mitchell McGraw-Hill, 1993.

JOHNSON, DEBORAH. *Computer Ethics.* (2nd ed.) Englewood Cliffs, NJ: Prentice Hall, 1994.

JOHNSON, DEBORAH, and JOHN SNAPPER (eds.). *Ethical Issues in the Use of Computers.* Belmont, CA: Wadsworth Publishing Company, 1985.

JOHNSON, DEBORAH, and HELEN NISSENBAUM (eds.). *Computers, Ethics and Social Values.* Englewood Cliffs, NJ: Prentice Hall, 1995.

LAUDON, KENNETH. "Ethical Concepts and Information Technology," *Communications of the ACM,* (December 1995), pp. 33–39.

MASON, RICHARD. "Four Ethical Issues of the Information Age," *MIS Quarterly,* (March 1986), pp. 46–55.

OZ, EFFY. *Ethics for the Information Age.* Los Angeles: Wm C. Brown Communications, Inc., 1994.

ROSENBERG, RICHARD. *The Social Impact of Computers.* New York: Harcourt Brace Javonovich, 1992.

SPINELLO, RICHARD. *Ethical Aspects of Information Technology.* Englewood Cliffs, NJ: Prentice Hall, 1995.

Special Issue—"Communications, Computers and Networks," *Scientific American,* (September 1991).

INFORMATION ETHICS AND PRIVACY ISSUES

BRANSCOMB, ANNE. *Who Owns Information?* New York: Basic Books, 1994.

CESPEDES, FRANK, and H. JEFF SMITH. "Database Marketing: New Rules for Policy and Practice," *Sloan Management Review,* (Summer 1993), pp. 7–22.

CHALYKOFF, JOHN, and NITIN NOHIRA. "Note on Electronic Monitoring," Cambridge, MA: *Harvard Business School Publications, 1990.*

CLARKE, ROGER. "Information Technology and Dataveillance," *Communications of the ACM,* (May 1988), pp. 498–512.

CULNAN, MARY J. "How Did They Get My Name? An Exploratory Investigation of Consumer Attitudes Toward Secondary Information Use," *MIS Quarterly,* (September 1993), pp. 341–363.

CULNAN, MARY J., and PRISCILLA REGAN. "Privacy Issues and the Creation of Campaign Mailing Lists," *The Information Society,* 11 (1995), pp. 85–100.

DOSS, ERNI, and MICHAEL LOUI. "Ethics and the Privacy of Electronic Mail," *The Information Society,* 11 (1995), pp. 223–235.

MARX, GARY T., and SANFORD SHERIZEN. "Monitoring in the Job: How to Protect Privacy as Well as Property," *Technology Review,* (November–December 1986), pp. 63–72.

MASON, RICHARD, and MARY CULNAN. *Information and Responsibility: The Ethical Challenge.* Thousand Oaks, CA: Sage Publications, Inc., 1995.

PENZIAS, ARNO. *Ideas and Information.* New York: W.W. Norton & Company, 1989.

REGAN, PRISCILLA. *Legislating Privacy: Technology, Social Values and Public Policy.* Chapel Hill, North Carolina: University of North Carolina Press, 1995.

ROTHFEDER, JEFFREY. *Privacy for Sale: How Computerization Has Made Everyone's Life an Open Secret.* New York: Simon & Schuster, 1992.

SCHOEMAN, FERDINAND. *Philosophical Dimensions of Privacy: An Anthology.* Cambridge, England: Cambridge University Press, 1984.

SIPIOR, JANICE, and BURKE WARD. "The Ethical and Legal Quandary of E-Mail Privacy," *Communications of the ACM,* (December 1995), pp. 48–54.

SMITH, JEFF. *Managing Privacy: Information Technology and Corporate America.* Chapel Hill: The University of North Carolina Press, 1994.

WARE, WILLIS. "The New Faces of Privacy," *The Information Society,* 9 (1993), pp. 195–211.

WARE, WILLIS. "The Digital Persona and its Application to Data Surveillance," *The Information Society,* 10 (1994), pp. 77–92.

WEISBAUD, SUZANNE, and BRUCE REINIG. "Managing User Perceptions of E-Mail Privacy," *Communications of the ACM,* (December 1995), pp. 40–47.

WESTIN, ALAN. *Privacy and Freedom.* New York, N.Y.: Atheneum, 1967.

INTELLECTUAL PROPERTY

CLAPES, ANTHONY LAWRENCE. *Software, Copyright, and Competition.* Westport, CT: Quorum Books, 1989.

CLAPES, ANTHONY LAWRENCE. *Softwars: The Legal Battles for Control of the Global Software Industry.* Westport, CT: Quorum Books, 1993.

DAVIS, G. GERVAISE. "War of the Words: Intellectual Property Laws and Standardization," *IEEE Micro,* (December 1993), pp. 16–22.

HECKEL, P. "Debunking the Software Patent Myths," *Communications of the ACM,* (June 1992), pp. 121–140.

JOHNSON, DEBORAH G. "Should Computer Programs Be Owned?" *Metaphilosophy,* 16 (1985), pp. 276–288.

KAHIN, BRIAN. "The Software Patent Crisis," *Technology Review,* (April 1990), pp. 55–59.

SAMUELSON, PAMELA. "Why the Look and Feel of Software User Interfaces Should Not Be Protected by Copyright Law," *Communications of the ACM,* (May 1989), pp. 563–572.

SAMUELSON, PAMELA. "How to Interpret the Lotus Decision (And How Not To)," *Communications of the ACM,* (November 1990), pp. 30–33.

SAMUELSON, PAMELA. "Is Information Property?" *Communications of the ACM,* (March 1991), pp. 15–18.

SAMUELSON, PAMELA. "Software Compatibility and the Law," *Communications of the ACM,* (August 1995), pp. 15–22.

STALLMAN, RICHARD. "Why Software Should Be Free," Free Software Foundation, Inc.

STALLMAN, RICHARD, and S. GARFINKEL. "Against User Interface Copyright," *Communications of the ACM,* (November 1990), pp. 15–18.

STEIDLMEIER, PAUL. "The Moral Legitimacy of Intellectual Property Claims: American Business and Developing Country Perspectives," *Journal of Business Ethics,* (February 1993), pp. 157–164.

U.S. Congress, Office of Technology Assessment. *Finding a Balance: Computer Software, Intellectual Property, and the Challenge of Technological Change.* Washington, D.C.: U.S. Government Printing Office, 1992.

SECURITY AND COMPUTER CRIMES

BAINBRIDGE, D.I. "Hacking—The Unauthorized Access of Computer Systems: The Legal Implications," *Modern Law Review,* (March 1989), pp. 236–245.

BARKER, RICHARD. *Computer Security Handbook.* Blue Ridge Summit, PA: TAB Professional Reference Books, 1991.

BRANSCOMB, ANNE W. "Rogue Computer Programs and Computer Rogues: Tailoring the Punishment to Fit the Crime," *Rutgers Computer and Technolgy Law Journal* 16 (1991), pp. 1–61.

CHESWICK, WILLIAM, and STEVEN BELLOVIN. *Firewalls and Internet Security: Repelling the Wily Hacker.* Reading, MA: Addison-Wesley Publishing, 1994.

DENNING, DOROTHY. "The U.S. vs. Craig Neidorf," *Communications of the ACM,* (March 1991), pp. 25–43.

HANSEN, R.L. "The Computer Virus Eradication Act of 1989: The War Against Computer Crime Continues," *Software Law Journal* 3 (1990), pp. 717–747.

PARKER, DONN. "The Many Faces of Data Vulnerability," *IEEE SPECTRUM,* (May 1984), pp. 46–48.

LEVY, STEVEN. *Hackers: Heroes of the Computer Revolution.* Garden City, N.Y.: Doubleday, 1984.

SPAFFORD, EUGENE. "Are Computer Hacker Break-ins Ethical?" *Journal of Systems Software,* (January 1992), pp. 41–47.

TRAMONTANA, J. "Computer Viruses: Is There a Legal 'Antibiotic'?" *Rutgers Computer and Technology Law Journal,* (Spring 1990), pp. 253–284.

LIABILITY, SAFETY AND RELIABILITY

CHARLES, ROBERT. "Computer Bulletin Boards and Defamation: Who Should Be Liable? Under What Standard?" *Journal of Law and Technology,* 2 (1987), pp. 121–150.

COLLINS, ROBERT W. "How Good is Good Enough," *Communications of the ACM,* (January 1994), pp. 76–86.

COLLSTE, GORAN. "Expert Systems in Medicine and Moral Responsibility," *Journal of Systems Software,* 17 (1992), pp. 19–24.

DICATO, EDWARD M. "Operator Liability Associated with Maintaining a Computer Bulletin Board," *Software Law Journal,* 4 (1990), pp. 147–159.

JENSEN, ERIC C. "An Electronic Soapbox: Computer Bulletin Boards and the First Amendment," *Federal Communications Law Journal,* 39 (1987), pp. 217–258.

JOHNSON, DEBORAH, and JOHN MULVEY. "Accountability and Computer Decision Systems," *Communications of the ACM,* (December 1995), pp. 58–64.

JOYCE, ED. "Software Bugs: A Matter of Life and Liability," *Datamation,* (May 1987), pp. 15–20.

LEVESON, NANCY, and CLARK TURNER. "An Investigation of the Therac-25 Accidents," *Computer,* (July 1993), pp. 18–41.

MYKYNTN, KATHLEEN, PETER MYKYNTN, and CRAIG SLINKMAN. "Expert Systems: A Question of Liability," *MIS Quarterly,* (March 1990), pp. 30–37.

NISSENBAUM, HELEN. "Computing and Accountability." *Communications of the ACM,* (January 1994), pp. 32–43.

NYCUM, SUSAN. "Liability for Malfunction of a Computer Program," *Journal of Computers, Technology and Law,* 7 (1979), pp. 1–22.

ROSS, PHILIP E. "The Day the Software Crashed," *Forbes,* (April 25, 1994), pp. 142–156.

STERN, RICHARD. "Microsoft and Vaporware," *IEEE Micro,* (April 1995), pp. 6–7; 84–85.

SOCIAL ISSUES

Computer Professionals for Social Responsibility, "Serving the Community: A Public-Interest Vision of the National Information Infrastructure," Palo Alto, CA: CPSR National Office, 1994.

DAVIDOW, WILLIAM, and MICHAEL MALONE. *The Virtual Corporation.* New York: HarperBusiness, 1992.

DUNLOP, CHARLES, and ROB KLING. *Computerization and Controversy: Value Conflicts and Social Choices.* Orlando, FL: Academic Press, 1991.

DUNLOP, CHARLES, and ROB KLING. "Controversies about Computerization and the Character of White Collar Worklife," *The Information Society,* 9 (1993), pp. 1–29.

FOGELMAN, MARTIN. "Freedom and Censorship in the Emerging Electronic Environment," *The Information Society,* 10 (1994), pp. 295–303.

JONES, STEVEN. *CyberSociety: Computer-Mediated Communication and Community.* London: Sage Publications, Inc., 1995.

LEVY, STEVEN. "Battle of the Clipper Chip," *The New York Times Magazine,* (June 12, 1994), pp. 35–43.

MOWSHOWITZ, ABBE. "Virtual Organization: A Vision of Management in the Information Age," *The Information Society,* 10 (1994), pp. 267–288.

ROSENBERG, RICHARD S. "Free Speech, Pornography, Sexual Harassment, and Electronic Networks," *The Information Society,* 9 (1993), pp. 285–331.

SPINELLO, RICHARD. "Philosophical Reflections on Free Speech in Cyberspace," *Proceedings of the Fourth National Computer Ethics Conference.* Washington, D.C., 1995.

TOFFLER, ALVIN. *The Third Wave.* New York: William Morrow and Company, 1980.

ZUBOFF, SHOSHANA. *In the Age of the Smart Machine: The Future of Work and Power.* New York: Basic Books, 1988.

Appendix

ACM CODE OF ETHICS AND PROFESSIONAL CONDUCT*

Preamble.   Commitment to ethical conduct is expected of every member (voting members, associate members, and student members) of the Association for Computing Machinery (ACM).

This Code, consisting of 24 imperatives formulated as statements of personal responsibility, identifies the elements of such a commitment. It contains many, but not all, issues professionals are likely to face. Section 1 outlines fundamental ethical considerations, while Section 2 addresses additional, more specific considerations of professional conduct. Statements in Section 3 pertain more specifically to individuals who have a leadership role, whether in the workplace or in a volunteer capacity such as with organizations like ACM. Principles involving compliance with the Code are given in Section 4.

The Code shall be supplemented by a set of Guidelines, which provide explanation to assist members in dealing with the various is-

*Adopted by ACM Council, October 16, 1992. Reprinted by permission of the Association for Computing Machinery © 1993.

sues contained in the Code. It is expected that the Guidelines will be changed more frequently than the Code.

The Code and its supplemented Guidelines are intended to serve as a basis for ethical decision making in the conduct of professional work. Secondarily, they may serve as a basis for judging the merit of a formal complaint pertaining to violation of professional ethical standards.

It should be noted that although computing is not mentioned in the imperatives of section 1.0, the Code is concerned with how these fundamental imperatives apply to one's conduct as a computing professional. These imperatives are expressed in a general form to emphasize that ethical principles which apply to computer ethics are derived from more general ethical principles.

It is understood that some words and phrases in a code of ethics are subject to varying interpretations, and that any ethical principle may conflict with other ethical principles in specific situations. Questions related to ethical conflicts can best be answered by thoughtful consideration of fundamental principles, rather than reliance on detailed regulations.

1. **General Moral Imperatives.** As an ACM member I will . . .

1.1 Contribute to society and human well-being.
1.2 Avoid harm to others.
1.3 Be honest and trustworthy.
1.4 Be fair and take action not to discriminate.
1.5 Honor property rights including copyrights and patents.
1.6 Give proper credit for intellectual property.
1.7 Respect the privacy of others.
1.8 Honor confidentiality.

2. **More Specific Professional Responsibilities.** As an ACM computing professional I will . . .

2.1 Strive to achieve the highest quality, effectiveness and dignity in both the process and products of professional work.
2.2 Acquire and maintain professional competence.
2.3 Know and respect existing laws pertaining to professional work.
2.4 Accept and provide appropriate professional review.
2.5 Give comprehensive and thorough evaluations of computer systems and their impacts, including analysis of possible risks.
2.6 Honor contracts, agreements, and assigned responsibilities.
2.7 Improve public understanding of computing and its consequences.
2.8 Access computing and communication resources only when authorized to do so.

3. **Organizational Leadership Imperatives.** As an ACM member and an organizational leader, I will . . .

3.1 Articulate social responsibilities of members of an organizational unit and encourage full acceptance of those responsibilities.
3.2 Manage personnel and resources to design and build information systems that enhance the quality of working life.
3.3 Acknowledge and support proper and authorized uses of an organization's computing and communication resources.
3.4 Ensure that users and those who will be affected by a system have their needs clearly articulated during the assessment and design of requirements; later the system must be validated to meet requirements.
3.5 Articulate and support policies that protect the dignity of users and others affected by a computing system.
3.6 Create opportunities for members of the organization to learn the principles and limitations of computer systems.

4. **Compliance with the Code.** As an ACM member, I will . . .

4.1 Uphold and promote the principles of this Code.
4.2 Treat violations of this code as inconsistent with membership in the ACM.

GUIDELINES

1. **General Moral Imperatives.** As an ACM member I will . . .

1.1 Contribute to society and human well-being.
This principle concerning the quality of life of all people affirms an obligation to protect fundamental human rights and to respect the diversity of all cultures. An essential aim of computing professionals is to minimize negative consequences of computing systems, including threats to health and safety. When designing or implementing systems, computing professionals must attempt to ensure that the products of their efforts will be used in socially responsible ways, will meet social needs, and will avoid harmful effects to health and welfare.

In addition to a safe social environment, human well-being includes a safe natural environment. Therefore, computing professionals who design and develop systems must be alert to, and make others aware of, any potential damage to the local or global environment.

1.2 Avoid harm to others.
"Harm" means injury or negative consequences, such as undesirable loss of information, loss of property, property damage, or unwanted environmental impacts. This principle prohibits use of computing technology in ways that result in harm to any of the following: users, the general public, employees,

employers. Harmful actions include intentional destruction or modification of files and programs leading to serious loss of resources or unnecessary expenditure of human resources such as the time and effort required to purge systems of "computer viruses."

Well-intended actions, including those that accomplish assigned duties, may lead to harm unexpectedly. In such an event the responsible person or persons are obligated to undo or mitigate the negative consequences as much as possible. One way to avoid unintentional harm is to carefully consider potential impacts on all those affected by decisions made during design and implementation.

To minimize the possibility of indirectly harming others, computing professionals must minimize malfunctions by following generally accepted standards for system design and testing. Furthermore, it is often necessary to assess the social consequences of systems to project the likelihood of any serious harm to others. If system features are misrepresented to users, coworkers, or supervisors, the individual computing professional is responsible for any resulting injury.

In the work environment the computing professional has the additional obligation to report any signs of system dangers that might result in serious personal or social damage. If one's superiors do not act to curtail or mitigate such dangers, it may be necessary to "blow the whistle" to help correct the problem or reduce the risk. However, capricious or misguided reporting of violations can, itself, be harmful. Before reporting violations, all relevant aspects of the incident must be thoroughly assessed. In particular, the assessment of risk and responsibility must be credible. It is suggested that advice be sought from other computing professionals. See principle 2.5 regarding thorough evaluations.

1.3   Be honest and trustworthy.
Honesty is an essential component of trust. Without trust an organization cannot function effectively. The honest computing professional will not make deliberately false or deceptive claims about a system or system design, but will instead provide full disclosure of all pertinent system limitations and problems.

A computer professional has a duty to be honest about his or her own qualifications, and about any circumstances that might lead to conflicts of interest.

Membership in volunteer organizations such as ACM may at times place individuals in situations where their statements or actions could be interpreted as carrying the "weight" of a larger group of professionals. An ACM member will exercise care to not misrepresent ACM or positions and policies of ACM or any ACM units.

1.4   Be fair and take action not to discriminate.
The values of equality, tolerance, respect for others, and the principles of equal justice govern this imperative. Discrimination on the basis of race, sex, religion, age, disability, national origin, or other such factors is an explicit violation of ACM policy and will not be tolerated.

Inequities between different groups of people may result from the use or misuse of information and technology. In a fair society, all individuals would have equal opportunity to participate in, or benefit from, the use of computer resources regardless of race, sex, religion, age, disability, national origin, or other such similar factors. However, these ideals do not justify unauthorized use of computer resources nor do they provide an adequate basis for violation of any other ethical imperatives of this code.

1.5   Honor property rights including copyrights and patents.
Violation of copyrights, patents, trade secrets, and the terms of license agreements is prohibited by law in most circumstances. Even when software is not so protected, such violations are contrary to professional behavior. Copies of software should be made only with proper authorization. Unauthorized duplication of materials must not be condoned.

1.6   Give proper credit for intellectual property.
Computing professionals are obligated to protect the integrity of intellectual property. Specifically, one must not take credit for others' ideas or work, even in cases where the work has not been explicitly protected by copyright, patent, etc.

1.7   Respect the privacy of others.
Computing and communication technology enables the collection and exchange of personal information on a scale unprecedented in the history of civilization. Thus there is increased potential for violating the privacy of individuals and groups. It is the responsibility of professionals to maintain the privacy and integrity of data describing individuals. This includes taking precautions to ensure the accuracy of data, as well as protecting it from unauthorized access or accidental disclosure to inappropriate individuals. Furthermore, procedures must be established to allow individuals to review their records and correct inaccuracies.

This imperative implies that only the necessary amount of personal information be collected in a system, that retention and disposal periods for that information be clearly defined and enforced, and that personal information gathered for a specific purpose not be used for other purposes without consent of the individual(s). These principles apply to electronic communications, including electronic mail, and prohibit procedures that capture or monitor electronic user data, including messages, without the permission of users or bona fide authorization related to system operation and maintenance. User data observed during the normal duties of system operation and maintenance must be treated with strictest confidentiality, except in cases where it is evidence for the violation of law, organizational regulations, or this Code. In these cases, the nature or contents of that information must be disclosed only to proper authorities. (See 1.9.)

1.8 Honor confidentiality.
The principle of honesty extends to issues of confidentiality of information whenever one has made an explicit promise to honor confidentiality or, implicitly, when private information not directly related to the performance of one's duties becomes available. The ethical concern is to respect all obligations of confidentiality to employers, clients, and users unless discharged from such obligations by requirements of the law or other principles of this Code.

2. More Specific Professional Responsibilities. As an ACM computing professional I will . . .

2.1 Strive to achieve the highest quality, effectiveness, and dignity in both the process and products of professional work.
Excellence is perhaps the most important obligation of a professional. The computing professional must strive to achieve quality and to be cognizant of the serious negative consequences that may result from poor quality in a system.

2.2 Acquire and maintain professional competence.
Excellence depends on individuals who take responsibility for acquiring and maintaining professional competence. A professional must participate in setting standards for appropriate levels of competence, and strive to achieve those standards. Upgrading technical knowledge and competence can be achieved in several ways: doing independent study; attending seminars, conferences, or courses; and being involved in professional organizations.

2.3 Know and respect existing laws pertaining to professional work.
ACM members must obey existing local, state, province, national, and international laws unless there is a compelling ethical basis not to do so. Policies and procedures of the organizations in which one participates must also be obeyed. But compliance must be balanced with the recognition that sometimes existing laws and rules may be immoral or inappropriate and, therefore, must be challenged. Violation of a law or regulation may be ethical when that law or rule has inadequate moral basis or when it conflicts with another law judged to be more important. If one decides to violate a law or rule because it is viewed as unethical, or for any other reason, one must fully accept responsibility for one's actions and for the consequences.

2.4 Accept and provide appropriate professional review.
Quality professional work, especially in the computing profession, depends on professional reviewing and critiquing. Whenever appropriate, individual members should seek and utilize peer review as well as provide critical review of the work of others.

2.5 Give comprehensive and thorough evaluations of computer systems and their impacts, including analysis of possible risks.
Computer professionals must strive to be perceptive, thorough, and objective when evaluating, recommending, and presenting system descriptions and alternatives. Computer professionals are in a position of special trust, and

therefore have a special responsibility to provide objective, credible evaluations to employers, clients, users, and the public. When providing evaluations the professional must also identify any relevant conflicts of interest, as stated in imperative 1.3.

As noted in the discussion of principle 1.2 on avoiding harm, any signs of danger from systems must be reported to those who have opportunity and/or responsibility to resolve them. See the guidelines for imperative 1.2 for more details concerning harm, including the reporting of professional violations.

2.6   Honor contracts, agreements, and assigned responsibilities.
Honoring one's commitments is a matter of integrity and honesty. For the computer professional this includes ensuring that system elements perform as intended. Also, when one contracts for work with another party, one has an obligation to keep that party properly informed about progress toward completing that work.

A computing professional has a responsibility to request a change in any assignment that he or she feels cannot be completed as defined. Only after serious consideration and with full disclosure of risks and concerns to the employer or client, should one accept the assignment. The major underlying principle here is the obligation to accept personal accountability for professional work. On some occasions other ethical principles may take greater priority.

A judgment that a specific assignment should not be performed may not be accepted. Having clearly identified one's concerns and reasons for that judgment, but failing to procure a change in that assignment, one may yet be obligated, by contract or by law, to proceed as directed. The computing professional's ethical judgment should be the final guide in deciding whether or not to proceed. Regardless of the decision, one must accept the responsibility for the consequences.

However, performing assignments "against one's own judgment" does not relieve the professional of responsibility for any negative consequences.

2.7   Improve public understanding of computing and its consequences.
Computing professionals have a responsibility to share technical knowledge with the public by encouraging understanding of computing, including the impacts of computer systems and their limitations. This imperative implies an obligation to counter any false views related to computing.

2.8   Access computing and communication resources only when authorized to do so.
Theft or destruction of tangible and electronic property is prohibited by imperative 1.2—"Avoid harm to others." Trespassing and unauthorized use of a computer or communication system is addressed by this imperative. Trespassing includes accessing communication networks and computer systems,

or accounts and/or files associated with those systems, without explicit authorization to do so. Individuals and organizations have the right to restrict access to their systems so long as they do not violate the discrimination principle. (See 1.4.) No one should enter or use another's computer system, software, or data files without permission. One must always have appropriate approval before using system resources, including .rm57 communication ports, file space, other system peripherals, and computer time.

3. Organizational Leadership Imperatives. As an ACM member and an organizational leader, I will . . .

3.1 *Articulate social responsibilities of members of an organizational unit and encourage full acceptance of those responsibilities.*
Because organizations of all kinds have impacts on the public, they must accept responsibilities to society. Organizational procedures and attitudes oriented toward quality and the welfare of society will reduce harm to members of the public, thereby serving public interest and fulfilling social responsibility. Therefore, organizational leaders must encourage full participation in meeting social responsibilities as well as quality performance.

3.2 *Manage personnel and resources to design and build information systems that enhance the quality of working life.*
Organizational leaders are responsible for ensuring that computer systems enhance, not degrade, the quality of working life. When implementing a computer system, organizations must consider the personal and professional development, physical safety, and human dignity of all workers. Appropriate human-computer ergonomic standards should be considered in system design and in the workplace.

3.3 *Acknowledge and support proper and authorized uses of an organization's computing and communication resources.*
Because computer systems can become tools to harm as well as to benefit an organization, the leadership has the responsibility to clearly define appropriate and inappropriate uses of organizational computing resources. While the number and scope of such rules should be minimal, they should be fully enforced when established.

3.4 *Ensure that users and those who will be affected by a system have their needs clearly articulated during the assessment and design of requirements; later the system must be validated to meet requirements.*
Current system users, potential users, and other persons whose lives may be affected by a system must have their needs assessed and incorporated in the statement of requirements. System validation should ensure compliance with those requirements.

3.5 *Articulate and support policies that protect the dignity of users and others affected by a computing system.*
Designing or implementing systems that deliberately or inadvertently demean individuals or groups is ethically unacceptable. Computer professionals who are in decision making positions should verify that systems are designed and implemented to protect personal privacy and enhance personal dignity.

3.6 *Create opportunities for members of the organization to learn the principles and limitations of computer systems.*
This complements the imperative on public understanding (2.7). Educational opportunities are essential to facilitate optimal participation of all organiza-

tional members. Opportunities must be available to all members to help them improve their knowledge and skills in computing, including courses that familiarize them with the consequences and limitations of particular types of systems. In particular, professionals must be made aware of the dangers of building systems around oversimplified models, the improbability of anticipating and designing for every possible operating condition, and other issues related to the complexity of this profession.

4.   Compliance with the Code. As an ACM member I will . . .

4.1   Uphold and promote the principles of this Code.
The future of the computing profession depends on both technical and ethical excellence. Not only is it important for ACM computing professionals to adhere to the principles expressed in this Code, each member should encourage and support adherence by other members.
4.2   Treat violations of this code as inconsistent with membership in the ACM.
Adherence of professionals to a code of ethics is largely a voluntary matter. However, if a member does not follow this code by engaging in gross misconduct, membership in ACM may be terminated.

This Code and the supplemental Guidelines were developed by the Task Force for the Revision of the ACM Code of Ethics and Professional Conduct: Ronald E. Anderson, Chair, Gerald Engel, Donald Gotterbarn, Grace C. Hertlein, Alex Hoffman, Bruce Jawer, Deborah G. Johnson, Doris K. Lidtke, Joyce Currie Little, Dianne Martin, Donn B. Parker, Judith A. Perrolle, and Richard S. Rosenberg. The Task Force was organized by ACM/SIGCAS and funding was provided by the ACM SIG Discretionary Fund. This Code and the supplemental Guidelines were adopted by the ACM Council on October 16, 1992.

INSTITUTE OF ELECTRONIC AND ELECTRICAL ENGINEERS (IEEE)

Code of Ethics**

We, the members of the IEEE, in recognition of the importance of our technologies in affecting the quality of life throughout the world, and in accepting a personal obligation to our profession, its members, and the communities we serve, do hereby commit ourselves to the highest ethical and professional conduct and agree:

1. to accept responsibility in making engineering decisions consistent with the safety, health, and welfare of the public, and to disclose promptly factors that might endanger the public or the environment;
2. to avoid real or perceived conflicts of interest whenever possible, and to disclose them to affected parties when they do exist;
3. to be honest and realistic in stating claims or estimates based on available data;
4. to reject bribery in all its forms;
5. to improve the understanding of technology, its appropriate application, and potential consequences;
6. to maintain and improve our technical competence and to undertake technological tasks for others only if qualified by training or experience, or after full disclosure of pertinent limitations;
7. to seek, accept, and offer honest criticism of technical work, to acknowledge and correct errors, and to credit properly the contributions of others;
8. to treat fairly all persons regardless of such factors as race, religion, gender, disability, age, or national origin;
9. to avoid injuring others, their property, reputation, or employment by false or malicious action;
10. to assist colleagues and co-workers in their professional development and to support them in following this code of ethics.

**Effective January 1, 1991.

Index

A

Access (to information), 4–6, 72–100
ACCOLADE, 142–45
Accuracy (credit report), 107–8
ACM Code of Professional Conduct, xii,
    49, 262, 270–78
Acquisition (of information), 3–4; 51–71
AIMS, 59
Amdahl Corporation, 148–49
American Airlines, 52, 58–61
American Express, 76
America Online, 194, 198
Anonymity (in cyberspace), 244–46
Anonymous server, 245
Anti-Defamation League (ADL), 194–
    95
Apple Computer, 225
Apple v. Microsoft, 11, 138, 141–42
ARPANET, 243
Aristotle, 16
AT&T, 162, 235, 237, 249
AT&TGIS, 203, 205
Atari, 142–45
Atomic Energy of Canada (AECL),
    198–99

B

Being Digital, 138
Bentham, Jeremy, 27–28
Beta products, 227–28
BITNET, 243
Blameworthiness, 16, 192
Borland International, Inc., 138–42, 224
Branscomb, Anne, 73
Bulletin Board liability, 15–16, 192, 193–98

C

Capital One, 76
Casino (in cyberspace), 262
Castle, David, 114
Categorical Imperative, 33–34
Caulfield, Judge Barbara, 144
Cementos Mexicanos, 239
Censorship, 18–19, 246–48, 251–54
Chemical Bank, 15
Chicago (code name for *Windows*), 26,
    193, 224–30